An
EDUCATIONAL LEADER'S
Guide to
CURRICULUM
MAPPING

This book is dedicated to
Margaret "Ma" Hale,
my wonderful mother-in-law.
Thank you for your love and grace.
Thank you for always being there
for me, Johnny, and your granddogs.

—Janet Hale

This book is dedicated in remembrance of
Timothy Dunlap.
Because remembering him is easy,
I do it every day.
But there's an ache within my heart,
that will never go away.

—Rick Dunlap

An
EDUCATIONAL LEADER'S
Guide to
CURRICULUM MAPPING

CREATING and SUSTAINING COLLABORATIVE CULTURES

JANET A. HALE
RICHARD F. DUNLAP, Jr.

Foreword by
Heidi Hayes Jacobs

CORWIN
A SAGE Company

For information:

Corwin
A SAGE Company
2455 Teller Road
Thousand Oaks, California 91320
(800) 233-9936
Fax: (800) 417-2466
www.corwin.com

SAGE Ltd.
1 Oliver's Yard
55 City Road
London EC1Y 1SP
United Kingdom

SAGE India Pvt. Ltd.
B 1/I 1 Mohan Cooperative
    Industrial Area
Mathura Road, New Delhi 110 044
India

SAGE Asia-Pacific Pte. Ltd.
33 Pekin Street #02-01
Far East Square
Singapore 048763

Printed in the United States of America

Library of Congress Cataloging-in-Publication Data

Hale, Janet A.
An educational leader's guide to curriculum mapping: creating and sustaining collaborative cultures/Janet A. Hale, Richard F. Dunlap, Jr.
    p. cm.
Includes bibliographical references and index.
ISBN 978-1-4129-7419-6 (pbk.)

  1. Curriculum planning. 2. Teacher participation in curriculum planning. 3. Educational leadership. I. Dunlap, Richard F. II. Title.

LB2806.15.H346 2010
375'.001—dc22   2010012039

This book is printed on acid-free paper.

10   11   12   13   14   10   9   8   7   6   5   4   3   2   1

Acquisitions Editor:	Cathy Hernandez
Editorial Assistant:	Allison Scott
Production Editor:	Cassandra Margaret Seibel
Copy Editor:	Adam Dunham
Typesetter:	C&M Digitals (P) Ltd.
Proofreader:	Jenifer Kooiman
Indexer:	Gloria Tierney
Cover Designer:	Michael Dubowe

Contents

List of Figures

Foreword

You hold *An Educational Leader's Guide to Curriculum Mapping* in your hands. I believe this book represents a landmark contribution to the field of curriculum mapping. Janet Hale and Rick Dunlap have zeroed in on the role of leadership. The effectiveness of a mapping initiative rests largely in the foresight and proficiencies of leadership teams to galvanize a faculty, to engage in purposeful objectives, and to plan imaginatively to engage learners. As they write, "leadership is not management." Their chapters help coach administrators and teacher leaders into considering best practices and possibilities to systematically plan for quality curriculum design and review.

This book provides detailed examples of how to establish professional-development and administrative maps that model the very practices that teachers should be considering for their learners. This creates a cycle of communication and openness breaking from the past tendency toward separateness between leaders and staff. Most importantly, a major theme here is *sustainability*. There is a certain fickleness in education, where it is so easy to start a program and drop it for another. The authors provide leadership with the long view to help you integrate mapping into the ongoing fabric of school life. You will not only take comfort and learning from their text but Hale and Dunlap also give detailed and useful examples of administrative maps and resources to assist any school leader K–12.

Leading schools in the 21st century requires new competencies to match the needs of learners, their teachers, and their communities. Curriculum mapping is a modern approach that provides both a collaborative process and an electronic platform for educators to make strategic choices for their students. In particular, there have been a few key curriculum leaders who have contributed mightily to the work, and Janet Hale and Rick Dunlap are two of them. Hale and Dunlap have been relentless and vigilant advocates for precision in mapping.

Janet's (2008) first mapping book with Corwin, *A Guide to Curriculum Mapping*, added depth and detail to my Curriculum Mapping model, and I am so aware of and grateful for Janet's contribution. On countless occasions, I have had the opportunity to hear educators across the country and overseas refer to Janet's coaching. Janet's knowledge, humor, and warmth, which reaches the schools where she has consulted, is reflected directly in her writing. Most of all, Janet has patience. She conveys to the first-time "mapper" that this is a process and that we never "arrive" at a finished point. Knowledge keeps growing. Learners keep changing. Our mapping tools keep evolving as well. We need dynamic thinking.

I met Rick Dunlap almost 10 years ago when he was first attending the annual Curriculum Mapping Institute as principal of West Chester High School in Pennsylvania. Right from the start, it was clear that Rick was no ordinary leader. Over the years that followed, he has brought teams of his lively and committed faculty to make robust workshop presentations that consistently received stellar evaluations. This man knows how to motivate and inspire his colleagues. He creates teacher leaders, engaged learners, and quality curriculum.

When I developed the Curriculum Mapping model in 1997, I believed that open and transparent communication between colleagues in real settings was critical in making these choices and that emerging technologies would make this possible. Little did I know what would follow. Looking back, it was not possible to see how so many educators would build on the model, refine it, and make it stronger. It was also not possible to see that mapping would become a global enterprise through the energy of school personnel and programming work of multiple education-software groups. I am grateful to Hale and Dunlap for deepening that work. As professionals, Janet and Rick are concurrently pragmatic and scholarly in their writing. As people, they support their colleagues with loyalty, empathy, and respect. I recommend *An Educational Leader's Guide to Curriculum Mapping* as a critical acquisition for those desiring to navigate the mapping process.

—Heidi Hayes Jacobs

Preface

A leader is one who knows the way, goes the way, and shows the way.

—John C. Maxwell

Maxwell's (1999–2010) leadership qualities—knowing, going, and showing—are critical regardless of profession or endeavor. Gaining personal and collaborative awareness of how these qualities factor into administrators and teachers being the leaders of a curriculum mapping initiative is the foundation for *An Educational Leader's Guide to Curriculum Mapping.*

Curriculum mapping is a model for designing, refining, replacing, upgrading, and reviewing curriculum planning, resulting in a framework that provides form, focus, and function. *Mapping* is a verb, which characterizes this model's use of steps, procedures, and processes to produce various types of curriculum maps that are used by teachers as a framework for communication and questioning current and future curriculum design needs and instructional practices (Hale, 2008; Jacobs, 1997, 2004; Jacobs and Johnson, 2009; Udelhofen, 2005, 2008). Communication points and generated questions are addressed through a lens that sees all teachers committing to keeping what is in the students' best interests in the forefront of all curriculum decision making (Jacobs, 1997).

An important consideration for implementation is the realization that there needs to be adequate time for administrators, teacher leaders, and all teachers in a learning organization to comprehend curriculum mapping's complexities, especially the extensive learning and engagement teachers undergo when a curriculum mapping initiative is first put into action.

Curriculum mapping is a second-order, systemic-change and growth model. If it is perceived as a first-order change, it is difficult to succeed in curriculum mapping becoming an ongoing component of a learning organization's curriculum culture (Hale, 2008; Jacobs, 1997; Kallick, 2006; Marzano, Waters, & McNulty, 2005; Senge, Cambron-McCabe, Lucas, Smith, & Kleiner, 2000).

Jacobs and Johnson (2009) point out that curriculum mapping's systemic process serves as a catalyst to

- Develop a dynamic, focused, and articulated curriculum for all students in the school;
- Strengthen the alignment of all aspects of instruction in the system;

- Connect all school-improvement initiatives in the school;
- Create a long-term vision for change and implementation plans;
- Integrate a feedback loop that provides data and feedback used to continually sharpen the focus; and
- Rethink the support structure and resources needed to ensure lasting change. (p. 105–106)

Curriculum mapping is a valuable and worthwhile endeavor for a district and each school in the district, which collectively represent the learning system. When administrators and teacher leaders thoughtfully consider how to best convey and encourage districtwide teacher leadership, the probability for reaching systemic sustainability increases. Wee (2007) differentiates leadership and management:

Leadership is not management. Management is what we do. Leadership is who we are. Leadership is influencing people to contribute their hearts, minds, spirits, creativity, and excellence and to give their all for their team. The servant-first [leader] makes sure that other people's highest priority needs are being served. Legitimate leadership, influence, is built upon serving, sacrificing, and seeking the greatest good of those being led. (p. 1)

Sustainability matters in curriculum mapping. Curriculum maps are living, breathing documents that evolve based on the ongoing needs of students throughout a learning organization. Jacobs and Johnson (2009) reflect on the reality that our learners are constantly evolving.

Our learners are always moving into their future. The question is whether we, as educators, are doing all that we can to prepare them. It is hard to stay current on every breakthrough in every field of study. We have our hands full in schools, yet we advise periodic and regular reviews of maps to update them and to keep our work timely are a critical part of becoming an operational learning community. (p. 105)

Administrators and teacher leaders spearheading a curriculum mapping initiative often ask for insights into how to best support teachers in the ongoing mapping process. While the size of a district or school may affect specific planning and implementation decision making, the considerations shared in this book are universal in nature. Whether you are an administrator or teacher leader in a private school where kindergarten to Grade-12 students are housed in one building or campus, or you are an administrator or teacher leader in a large-scale public school district, it is recommended that you read this book in its entirety.

OVERVIEW OF THE CONTENTS

An Educational Leader's Guide to Curriculum Mapping has two focuses. Chapters 1 through 5 provide insights into a variety of systemic considerations for developing, implementing, and maintaining a curriculum mapping initiative. These chapters provide useful information for administrators and teacher leaders who are exploring the possibilities of implementing curriculum mapping or who may have begun implementation but have experienced unforeseen roadblocks or pitfalls.

Chapters 6 and 7 provide information and considerations for writing administrative maps. Since curriculum mapping provides a model for communication, many administrators are choosing to create evidence of professional development and/or administrative roles using their learning organization's online mapping system.

Chapters

Chapter 1 lays a foundation for thinking of curriculum mapping as a collaborative, systemic process.

Chapter 2 addresses the reasons for establishing a clear mission and vision, a districtwide strategic plan, and schools' action plans to support a curriculum mapping initiative. It also highlights leadership considerations administrators need to be aware of to best support teachers involved in the curriculum mapping process.

Chapter 3 informs central-office administrators of critical considerations that enable and support teacher leadership and provide insight into working collegially to establish and execute a strategic implementation plan.

Chapter 4 expresses considerations district-curriculum directors and school-site curriculum teacher leaders need to think about when supporting teachers in designing curriculum maps and using created maps.

Chapter 5 provides critical points principals need to consider to best support teachers within and among school sites. Building trust, supporting teachers as curriculum design and curriculum practice leaders, establishing a curriculum council, and using the maps are addressed.

Chapter 6 explains the differences between two kinds of administrative maps, *professional development* and *professional roles*, then focuses on the protocols for writing professional development administrative maps.

Chapter 7 addresses protocols for writing professional roles maps. This kind of map is written by an administrator to document his or her job responsibilities, actions, and evidences of completion.

Appendix A provides detailed information and considerations for developing systemic unit names and provides an example of the comprehensive nature of the mapping process.

Appendix B lists the United States Marine Corps' officer leadership traits and principles, which are applicable to leading those involved in any systemic initiative.

Chapter Questions

While some people learn and process best in isolation, more often learning becomes solidified when there are opportunities to discuss the new information with others and transfer the learning to personal application. It is recommended that you form a book study with colleagues. As your group engages in reading through the book, each chapter ends with a series of questions designed to be discussion starters for in-person or web-based group meetings.

Sample Curriculum Map Months

The last two chapters contain sample administrative-map *months.* Providing a month versus an entire school year is intended to allow for a variety of administrative-map examples. All maps—curriculum maps and administrative maps—are *live* and *interactive* when viewed in an online mapping system. The sample map months in this book are static and cannot convey the full scope of the connective-map database experienced when viewing and using maps in a mapping system.

Each sample map month is displayed in a table. As each commercial mapping system has a unique configuration, a table generically conveys the map-element information without needing to be concerned with the specifics for a particular mapping system.

Supplemental Reading

If you are just beginning your curriculum mapping journey, and this is the first professional reading you have engaged in on this subject, it is recommended you also read *A Guide to Curriculum Mapping: Planning, Implementing, and Sustaining the Process* (Hale, 2008). There are specific terminology and concepts associated with curriculum mapping. While this book explains some in detail, it may aid your understanding to also read *A Guide to Curriculum Mapping* as it provides an in-depth look at the intricacies of mapping and complements the leadership focuses highlighted throughout this book.

Acknowledgments

Challenges are stepping stones or stumbling blocks. It is a matter of how you view them.

—Unknown

Anything that is worthwhile causes us to face, and overcome, challenges. There were times during our writing journey that we faced professional and personal stepping stones. Without the continuous support of those we admire, we may have treated our stones as stumbling blocks.

Janet Hale

- *Rick Dunlap*—Thank you for setting an example of excellence, both personally and professionally. Your mirror/window leadership (when things go wrong you look in the mirror to determine what the problem is . . . when things go well you look out the window and praise those you believe earn the credit) allows your students, teachers, and administrators to shine!
- *Heidi Hayes Jacobs*—Thank you for writing the Foreword. Your wisdom and ability to think locally and globally continually challenge me. Your passions both professionally and personally are contagious. I am grateful to you as a colleague and a friend.
- *Cathy Hernandez*—It was wonderful working with you again! Your kindness, patience, and expert editorial advice are greatly appreciated.
- *Cassandra Seibel*—Your layout decisions made all of the pages and figures flow. Thank you for being an incredible editor.
- *Adam Dunham*—Thank you for your editing expertise. Your revisions and suggestions enhanced the wording and intended messages.
- *Greg Lind*—How can I adequately express my thanks for challenging each chapter's word choice, sentence fluency, and conventions? (I will miss our *a* versus *the* hour-long discussions!) You have caused me to grow as a writer and as a person. Your students, colleagues, friends, and family are fortunate to have you in their lives.
- *Kim Baumann, Brad Condra, Liz Fisher, Mike Fisher, Mary Helen Hart, Janette Newell, Eileen Riley, and Nancy Schmidt*—Thank you, thank you, thank you for all of your advice. I enjoyed getting your reviews as you

continuously brought different perspectives that collectively improved every chapter.

- *Mike Allen, Kim Baumann, Beth Beckwith, Rhonda Benz, Mark Clark, Mike Fisher, Wendy Ivey, Louie Jensen, Kyle Lanoue, Valerie Lyle, Louise Murnighan, Teresa Perkins, Victoria Tabbert*—Thank you for contributing administrative-map-month samples. I admire all of you, your work ethics, caring natures, and love for teachers and students!
- *Johnny Hale*—Special thanks to my husband for always encouraging and uplifting me. When someone believes in you, all things are possible.
- *To my friends, who love me unconditionally*—Spending days and weeks working and writing caused me to oftentimes keep in touch via phone calls and e-mails. I look forward to getting back to in-person hugs and conversations, which are worth much more than a thousand long-distance words.

Rick Dunlap

- *Janet Hale*—Thank you for giving me the opportunity to learn, collaborate, and write with you. Your expertise has enabled me to become a better educator. I value your professionalism. I am grateful for your friendship. Thank you!
- *Heidi Hayes Jacobs*—Thank you for including me in your work and giving me your support. You continue to inspire me. You are an advocate for students, a teacher among teachers, and a true educational leader.
- *Bena Kallick*—Thank you for giving me my first shot at writing. Your wisdom is infectious.
- *Eileen Riley, Scott Rafetto, and the rest of the faculty of West Chester East High School*—Thank you for your friendship, feedback, and support. I am honored to work with both you and the others at East High School. The two of you and our faculty give the term *professional learning community* a whole new definition. You are master teachers whose leadership enables all of us to accomplish our goals as a team.
- *Helen, Rick, Ali, and Pat*—I am thankful for your encouragement and support. Thank you.
- *Mom and Dad*—Thank you for your support and love. You are the best. I love you.
- *Tim*—I miss you and love you, Dad.

PUBLISHER'S ACKNOWLEDGMENTS

Corwin gratefully acknowledges the contributions of the following reviewers:

Nancy Bishop
Assistant Superintendent of Curriculum and Instruction
Octorara Area School District
Atglen, PA

Allison Brown
Secondary Curriculum Coordinator
Shawnee, OK

Christine Correa
Director of Curriculum & Instruction
Shakopee Schools
Shakopee, MN

Alice L. Learn
Assistant Superintendent
Horseheads Central School District
New York, NY

Jennifer Mahan-Deitte
Coordinator of Curriculum, Assessment, & Instruction and School
Improvement
SW/WC Service Cooperative—Marshall
Marshall, MN

Miriam Wahl
Field Advisor for Whole School Initiative
Lafayette County School District
Batesville, MS

About the Authors

Janet A. Hale is an educational consultant and trainer who specializes in curriculum mapping. She travels extensively to work with rural, urban, and inner-city learning organizations. She enjoys assisting newcomers to the curriculum mapping model, supporting implementation procedures, aiding struggling initiatives, and advising those ready for advanced mapping. Her experiences as an elementary, middle, and high school teacher combined with a master's degree in leadership and curriculum are an asset when helping teachers and administrators just starting or already engaged in the mapping process.

Since 1988, Janet has developed a variety of national educational seminars and trainings. She has written an assortment of educational supplementary materials and has presented in conferences sponsored by the Association of Supervision and Curriculum Development, the International Reading Association, the Association of Christian Schools International, and Curriculum Designers.

Her book titled *A Guide to Curriculum Mapping: Planning, Implementing, and Sustaining the Process* (2008) is published by Corwin.

Janet resides in Tucson, Arizona. At home, she enjoys working in her desert garden, which blooms beautifully in the spring. She also enjoys being with her family and friends, who bloom beautifully in her heart year round.

She can be contacted via e-mail at teachtucson@aol.com or by phone at 520-241-8797. You may like to visit her website: www.CurriculumMapping101.com.

Richard F. Dunlap, Jr., is well-known for his administrative leadership. Currently, he is principal of West Chester East High School in West Chester, Pennsylvania. During his professional career, he has been a special education teacher, assistant principal of a middle school and high school, and principal of a national award-winning middle school.

He earned a master's degree in bilingual/bicultural studies and a doctorate in educational leadership from Immaculata University.

He presents at national and international conferences on curriculum, leadership, and literacy as well as serving as a curriculum mapping consultant.

Rick's promotion of teacher leadership at his current high school is featured in a chapter in *Using Curriculum Mapping and Assessment Data to Improve Learning* (Kallick & Colosimo, 2009), published by Corwin.

Prior to pursuing a career in education, Rick served as an officer in the United States Marine Corps. He is a recipient of the Chaplain of Four Chaplains Award.

Rick resides in Garnet Valley, Pennsylvania. When he is not busy working, he enjoys bike riding and spending time with his family and friends. He can be contacted via e-mail at rfd1350@gmail.com or by phone at 484-832-3710.

What Shifts in Thinking Are Imperative for Collaborative Curriculum Mapping?

You are today where your thoughts have brought you. You will be tomorrow where your thoughts take you.

—James Allen

During a regional curriculum mapping conference, Dr. Heidi Hayes Jacobs opened with a personal story (Jacobs, 2008). She shared that in her family, an entering-the-teen-years ritual for each nephew and niece is to come to New York and explore New York City with his or her aunt.

On a large screen, she displayed a bird's-eye-view photograph she took while on the observation deck of the Empire State Building. The image of the Manhattan streets and buildings captured the hustle and bustle of the fast-paced city life. Jacobs mentioned that, as she stood on the observation deck, the city's landscape reminded her of a district's bird's-eye view of its curriculum work. Just as the city dwellers function synchronously concerning personal and collective actions, a district must do so as well.

Jacobs then pointed out that while one can appreciate a city's panoramic view, to truly know its residents, you must descend and walk through the streets and enter its buildings. She then displayed a café storefront photograph. She mentioned that this ground-level view captures the what, where, when, why, who, and how of a city's life. Educationally, this view represents the individual buildings and classrooms where administrators, teachers, and—most important—students learn and grow.

She concluded by informing the audience that curriculum mapping is similar to the two photographs. Time must be spent zooming out to get the big picture of a district's vertically aligned curriculum, and time must be spent zooming in to focus on the curriculum living in each school site and classroom.

COLLABORATIVE CURRICULUM DESIGN

If administrators and teacher leaders involved in implementing a curriculum mapping initiative are not trained initially and well-informed, their view of curriculum mapping may be that of a simple record-keeping model. If this is the thinking when planning and implementing the mapping process, the initiative will most likely fail.

Curriculum mapping is a *systemic* model. When implemented, it relates to or affects the entire learning organization. For curriculum mapping to be effective, a district and its individual schools must be willing to work together to design, apply, and modify curriculum in an ongoing manner.

An important shift in thinking is that curriculum mapping is a second-order change model (Hale, 2008). Marzano, Waters, and McNulty (2005) agree that "deep [second-order] change alters the system in fundamental ways, offering a dramatic shift in direction and requiring new ways of thinking and acting" (p. 66). Second-order change causes members of a learning organization to make personal and collective mental shifts that affect all aspects of curriculum work.

This differs from first-order change, where a product or program is purchased by a district or school, and its actual implementation can be in the short or long run individually embraced or disregarded. Because of this, the intended systemic, long-term benefits of most first-order implementations are never realized.

An Aspen Grove Mentality

Administrators and teacher leaders must embrace the reality that curriculum mapping requires a shift in thinking from *I* to *we.* It succeeds only in a collaborative environment. The entire learning organization must begin to function, or expand functioning, as one system. A tree grove analogy best expresses curriculum mapping's mutually supportive environment.

Before the onset of a curriculum mapping initiative, a school or district often functions like an oak grove. Each individual tree (teacher), or section of the grove (grade level, department, or entire school), acts *independently* from the other trees in the grove. While it is true that an oak tree's roots run deep and work diligently to gain the necessary nourishment to sustain its branches and leaves, curriculum mapping asks an oak grove to morph into an aspen grove.

Aspen trees are the largest single organism in the world (Eldredge & Wynne, 2000). All the trees in a grove are related back to a single seedling. When you view the splendor of an aspen grove, you are, in essence, viewing one tree. The grove shares—and survives—based on one *interdependent* root system. If a portion of the root system is not functioning or communicating well, the entire grove is in jeopardy.

Curriculum maps housed in a web-based mapping system mimic the connectivity of an aspen grove's root system. Courses offered in a school or throughout a district are interconnected through relational units of studies. A student may experience 40 to 65 teachers in a K–12 academic experience (Jacobs, 2004). If students' K–12 teachers function as an oak grove rather than an aspen grove, they most likely will not receive the best possible, guaranteed, and most viable education (Jacobs, 1997, 2004; Marzano, 2003).

Curriculum mapping's sustainability rate increases when administrators and teachers develop an aspen grove mentality. This is not necessarily an easy shift, but it is an important one for exercising the ongoing curriculum mapping process.

Teacher-Designed Curriculum

Curriculum mapping asks all teachers involved in student learning and instruction for individual or multiple disciplines to be intimately involved in the curriculum processes and procedures. Acting as an aspen grove, who better to determine the systemic student-learning expectations than those who are closest to and most intimate with the students (Jacobs, 2004)?

Another important mental shift in thinking for both administrators and teachers is that, within curriculum mapping, curriculum *work* can be divided into two focuses. Curriculum *design* is individually and collaboratively defining the *what, where, when, why,* and *who* of student learning. *Who* in this context is not a teacher; it is a *course.* For example, if a state has algebra course standards and a district or school offers an Algebra I and Algebra II course, defining which course (who) gets what learning based on breaking apart the standards is part of the design process. Sometimes, a standard statement or statements may span two or more years. Teachers must collegially determine the grade level or grade levels that will address the learning associated with the standard statement or statements.

Curriculum *practice* is a teacher's or teachers' choices for *how* to best deliver the instruction to ensure learning as well as measuring and evaluating the learning acquisition. While curriculum mapping views curriculum design and curriculum practice as symbiotic, when initially implemented mapping first and foremost focuses on horizontal and vertical articulation of the student-learning design and then blends in an ongoing focus on best-practice classroom instruction.

Teachers learning to become curriculum designers and writing curriculum maps often ask how lesson plans fit into the scheme or pattern of curriculum work. Lesson plans are used for planning *daily* instruction by teachers to prepare for their teaching. Approximately 90% of the information in lesson plans is instructional practice while approximately 10% of the information represents the learning focus or focuses. Curriculum maps are *monthly* records where the collective map elements represent approximately 90% learning and 10% practice (Figure 1.1).

It is natural for teachers to wrestle with the notion of focusing on curriculum design. Teachers are most often comfortable with, and well trained in, curriculum practice. Design is a *scheme or pattern that affects and controls function or development.* A significant shift in thinking is asking teachers to be in charge of defining a scheme or pattern for generating the articulated student learning throughout a school and district.

This may be a new responsibility for teachers. Many learning organizations have traditionally given this role to outside sources (e.g., companies) or administrative curriculum specialists and a few select teachers. Therefore, administrator and teacher leaders must be mindful of each map element's connection to the concept of curriculum design versus instructional practice.

Design Elements

The first seven elements listed in Figure 1.1 are design elements directly related to learning and standards-based expectations. *Standards,* whether state, national, or self-generated, are what teachers must collegially work together to break apart and articulate using design-writing protocols to determine the remaining design elements.

Figure 1.1   Curriculum Map Elements Classification

Map Elements	Curriculum Design/Learning	Curriculum Practice/Teaching
Standards		
Unit Name		
Essential Questions/Supporting Questions		
Concepts		
Content		
Skills		
Assessments/Evaluations		
Resources		
Activities/Strategies		

Unit names, when applied systemically, refer to or are based on the terms included within *standards'* expectations. Reasons for considering this element with design in mind are explained in detail in Appendix A. It is important for teachers when designing curriculum to consider not only horizontal (one academic year) learning but vertical (series of academic years) learning as well. When planning for the design process, how to best house and access the organization of the articulated curriculum within a curriculum mapping system needs to be considered, which includes developing systemic unit names.

If a school or district is using *essential questions* and *supporting questions,* the intent and purpose for using these types of questions is to drive and focus the expected learning, therefore meeting the criterion for structural design.

Content, or as some choose to include, *concept,* is defined as *what the students must know.* In a curriculum map, a concept is written as a generalized statement. Content is written as a noun or noun phrase and descriptor (Hale, 2008). When designing concepts or content, teachers most often choose to structure student learning through the use of theme or topic learning, while others may choose to design curriculum using interdisciplinary learning, or when appropriate, student-centered learning (Jacobs, 1997, 2004).

Skills are intra-aligned to the appropriate content learning within a curriculum map, often through the use of alphabet intra-alignment coding. The writing protocol when designing skill statements is a *measurable verb-target-descriptor* (Hale, 2008). When writing this element, teachers and administrators often have a difficult time separating curriculum design from instructional practice. This is due to teachers having a comfort level and familiarity with writing lesson plans and administrators with reading lesson plans.

During a quality map-writing training phase, a fifth-grade teacher, Kelli, tried to apply the new learning to writing a personal science map for one month. She and 12 other teachers were meeting for a feedback session.

Kelli volunteered to display her map month on a large screen for a public facilitator-learner dialogue. Once the map month was displayed, all the teachers scanned her map to see what she had written given the map elements' writing protocols learned during their initial map-writing training sessions.

The facilitator, Jane, asked Kelli what element she would like to have the feedback focused on. She shared that she was struggling the most with writing skill statements. Jane began by reading aloud what was written in the content field:

Content

A. Earth's Layers: Continental Crust, Oceanic Crust, Upper Mantle, Mantle, Outer Core, Inner Core

She then read aloud the first intra-aligned skill statement:

A1. Identify visually and in writing 6 layers sequentially from outer to inner layers using an apple

(Continued)

(Continued)

Jane turned to Kelli and asked her if she was pleased with how she had written this skill statement. Kelli said she was satisfied with its wording since she remembered to start with a measurable verb (*identify*) and included a target to inform map readers how the students are assessed (*visually and in writing*).

Jane asked her if she noticed anything that may be of concern in the descriptor *the six layers sequentially from outer to inner layers using an apple.*

Kelli contemplated the question for a moment and reread the descriptor a few times. She then mentioned she thought it was fine.

The facilitator informed her that the descriptor included an activity. Kelli scrunched her eyebrows while contemplating why Jane made this comment. A few teachers in the group began to whisper enthusiastically. As learners, they were excited because they knew the answer. Kelli noticed them talking and asked one of the teachers to tell her what she was not seeing. The teacher said she thought it was the word *apple.* She continued, "You can have your students use an apple. I can have my students use an orange; and someone else can use Play-Doh."

Jane nodded her head in agreement. She affirmed what the teacher mentioned and asked Kelli how she could revise her map to reflect the intent of the skill. Kelli thought for a moment and then exclaimed, "Model! Identify visually and in writing the six layers sequentially from outer to inner layers using a model."

Her face beamed as she realized what she had been doing. Kelli revised the skill statement immediately using the add/edit feature of the district mapping system while the rest of the teachers observed her revision on the large screen.

"A3 is an activity, isn't it?" Kelli inquired. The entire group read silently:

A3. Write a list in order of each layer's thickness

Jane asked Kelli why she asked this question. Kelli shared that what they just talked about for the first skill was making her wonder about this statement's opening *write a list.* "While *write a list* is measurable, is this really the skill I want from my students, or is it representing an activity?" she asked.

The teachers began to talk softly to one another while Kelli, deep in thought, began to rewrite the skill statement. The teachers and facilitator observed her revision on the screen:

A3. Identify in writing each layer's thickness using standard and metric measurement

"The word *list* really is just part of an activity, or even an assessment. What I really want the students to do is *identify* the thickness of each layer. I remember you sharing with us that when someone reads a map's aligned content and skills, if the elements are written with clear and precise descriptors, he or she should be able to design an assessment that accurately measures the aligned learning. When I reread my skill statement, I realized that when I test my students' ability they have to use both standard and metric measurements, which my map did not include. So, not only did I need to revise the measurable verb, I needed to revise the skill's descriptor," Kelli said, evaluating her revision by sharing her thoughts with Jane and the group.

Jane and Kelli proceeded to read aloud and revise, with audience inter-action, a few more skill statements. To bring closure to Kelli's feedback session, Jane asked her to share with the group what she had learned most from the session. Kelli expressed that it was not as easy as she thought it was going to be to write curriculum maps—especially skill statements. She added that she is a good teacher, but this is something that had never been asked of her before. She felt that while writing curriculum with design in mind was extremely frustrating at times, she found the analytical thought process beneficial to her, and ultimately for her students, because it forces her to question and reflect on what it is that she really wants them to know and be able to do.

She then mentioned that, when teachers begin to work together to design collaborative maps, the thought process will be the centerpiece to their conversations. Kelli concluded by sharing, "If I or we cannot articulate what students must know and be able to do when designing maps, how can we articulate it well when we are in front of them?"

Curriculum maps are not pseudo lesson plans. Administrators must be trained alongside teacher leaders and teachers in the ability to apply the design protocols and processes necessary to develop quality curriculum maps as the writing expectations differ from writing lesson plans.

For example, after initial training focused on writing skill statements, it takes teachers a significant amount of time to consistently write skill statements reflecting design. It is not as easy as administrators and teacher leaders often assume it is for teachers to learn the art of designing skill statements.

If administrators have not been trained well in the complexities and intentions of curriculum mapping, it can be detrimental to establishing an atmosphere of mutual respect. For example, a principal intends to provide design feedback focusing on writing quality skill statements. Instead of reviewing a teacher's map to make certain each skill statement does not include any reference to an activity, the principal reads through the teacher's map and shares that the skill statements need to consistently begin with a capital letter. This teacher, and others, will quickly become turned off and see no meaningful purpose for writing maps to aid in improving student learning. It is therefore crucial that adequate personal practice-application time and collegial discussion focused on how to write quality map months with *design in mind* is provided to administrators and teacher leaders.

Those responsible for leading the curriculum mapping initiative must be given adequate time to (1) personally apply their learning through writing sample map months, often referred to as *practice mapping;* (2) be provided quality feedback on the personal practice-map-writing attempts; and (3) eventually model providing quality map-writing feedback to others using a facilitator-learner forum to aid in gaining confidence using the language of mapping when articulating areas of quality and needed improvements to a map's elements. This should take place prior to administrators and teacher leaders leading and supporting all teachers in the district involvement in the mapping process.

Assessments/evaluations is the remaining design element. It is unique in that it is classified as both design and practice. The design aspect refers to the necessity that what students must know and be able to do (content and skills) needs to have an assessment designed to accurately measure the learning expectations. A teacher is not going to test students on Greek roots if they have been learning Latin roots. Likewise, a teacher is not going to ask students to test a self-generated hypothesis if they have not first learned the steps involved in the scientific process.

If two or more teachers are teaching in separate classrooms and responsible for different students, they may or may not come to agreement on assessments used to measure content and skill learning. In other words, teachers may or may not agree on *how* to test the expected learning. For example, one teacher may choose to give a multiple-choice test, another chooses to have students write an expository report, and a third teacher chooses to have students create and post a podcast on the Internet.

Practice Elements

As teachers are often allowed personal choice in creating or selecting *assessments* and *evaluations,* the assessments and evaluations element also falls into the classification of curriculum practice. For example, there may be a teacher task-force-designed rubric that must be used by all teachers when measuring a specific grade level's ability to write a memoir. If so, the use of the rubric is a practice choice. Design plays a role in the development of the rubric to ensure that it accurately evaluates the content and skill learning expectations.

Resources are considered curriculum practice. This is often a shift in thinking for teachers, teacher leaders, and administrators. Hale (2008) states,

> In curriculum mapping, textbooks, kits, and materials are not perceived as the curriculum. They are resources that enable or enhance the curriculum and the learning process. Curriculum mapping recognizes teacher determined concepts, content, skills, and assessments aligned to strategically analyzed national, state, local, or self-generated standards as the curriculum. Depending on past initiatives and professional development, this may be a small or large shift in thinking for a learning organization's teachers. . . . It is of the essence that administrators and teachers are informed up front that mapping the curriculum does not equal copying a textbook's main teaching points or listed standards connections. If this takes place, curriculum maps would need major revamping during every adoption cycle to match the new textbook's representation of learning. (p. 27)

When including resources in a map, the recorded materials are meant to convey to self and others that which is pertinent to student learning success. It does not mean list everything that is included in a lesson plan. For example, the chapter, chapters, or series of pages from a current textbook; interactive whiteboard lesson references; DVD titles; songs, poems, and other forms of literature; or websites are worthwhile entries. Most online mapping systems have features to link to lesson-plan templates that allow teachers to include daily and weekly resources and their specific usage in general and for differentiation.

Activities/strategies, self-generated by teachers or included in adopted programs, kits, or textbooks, are considered instructional-practice choices. Similar to assessment and evaluation choices, teachers may or may not come to a collective agreement on instructional methods. Because of this, collaborative maps, such as a Consensus Map, may or may not include agreed-upon activities or strategies.

Response to Intervention (RTI) tier-one, tier-two, and tier-three strategies are often included in Consensus Maps by special education teachers to give classroom teachers options for students who are not meeting learning represented by the content and skills included in the map.

It is important to remember that a curriculum map is a monthly record of learning—not a daily one. Therefore, activities and strategies included in a map are written in an abbreviated version and use intra-alignment coding to the skill or skills they are supporting. If desired, more detailed explanations and information pertaining to an activity or activities can be attached to the map using the selected mapping system's attachment procedure.

A Beginning Frustration

When beginning the map design process, teachers are sometimes frustrated by the fact that, at the onset, the main focus is on curriculum design rather than instructional practice. Teachers love nothing more than to be provided opportunities to get together and share activities and strategies that help their students be successful learners. It is an important shift in thinking that, for a time, curriculum mapping will ask teachers to first focus on design to ensure a horizontally and vertically articulated curriculum.

Once the maps have been reviewed by teachers through the grade levels and they are satisfied with their teacher-designed learning expectations, the ongoing mapping process focuses primarily on curriculum practice, the activities and strategies that ensure all students are successful in reaching independency of the agreed-upon learning expectations (Jacobs, 1997, 2004).

Curriculum Mapping System Library Analogy

Another important shift in thinking coupled with the necessity for all teachers in the district to function as an aspen grove is the systemic nature of an online curriculum mapping system.

At a mapping system training, a teacher expressed her thoughts that a mapping system serves as the soil for all the roots in the aspen grove. This teacher realized what research has proven. Analogies aid learners in conceptually understanding complex concepts (Alvermann & Phelps, 1998).

An analogy that works well to explain how maps and map data are housed within a mapping system is to compare its organization to a public library.

When you walk into a library, you already have an idea of where you want to go based on how a library is traditionally set up. If you want a nonfiction title, you will walk to that section of the library. If you want to find a cookbook, a specific genre of nonfiction, you would refine your search and go to the

(Continued)

(Continued)

specific area within the nonfiction section. In a curriculum mapping system, teachers or administrators wanting to locate maps can do so based on a particular *school, discipline,* or *grade level.*

A library is filled with bookcases. In a mapping system, each *course* (e.g., Grade 1 Mathematics; Grade 7 Music Appreciation; Calculus) equals a bookcase. When looking at a particular bookcase in a library, one's eyes scan the titles on the shelves. In a mapping system, each course's *shelves* are the *months* in an academic year.

When scanning a specific shelf in a library, you begin to slow down to read the specific titles on the spines of the books on that shelf. In a mapping system, there are no books. Instead, there are pseudo *binders* wherein a *unit name* has been, figuratively speaking, slipped into the spine's clear sheath. This allows map readers to know in a broad sense what is contained within a map's particular binder. For example, a social studies map may include a unit name titled WESTWARD MOVEMENT: ACROSS THE PLAINS.

The mapping-system binder concept is a way of thinking about managing *units of study.* In most curriculum mapping systems, the map elements cannot be recorded unless there first is a unit name entered to create a shell for containing a unit of study's information. Because of this, it is wise to be proactive and consider developing or at least discussing unit names systemically across the district to ensure the electronic database functions as one system (see Appendix A). When teachers begin to review horizontally, and most importantly, vertically designed curriculum for potential learning gaps, repetitions, and absences, as well as relevancy and vigor, the ability to locate areas of concern and issues becomes easier.

Just as a library has systemic order, a mapping system, to function at its best, needs to be thought of as having a similar systemic order. Early on in the mapping process, it is important that administrators and teacher leaders recognize the selected mapping system as the soil for the aspen grove regardless of the type of curriculum maps housed within the mapping system:

- Essential Maps (a district-level map wherein there are two or more like schools; for example, five elementary schools; three middle schools; two high schools);
- Consensus Maps (a particular school site's collaborative maps); or
- Projected/Diary Maps (operational curriculum evidence in a teacher's personal maps).

Which Map Type Should We Begin Designing?

Districts involved in curriculum mapping for multiple years will have both collaborative maps (Essential Maps and/or Consensus Maps) and personal Projected/Diary Maps. At the onset of many mapping initiatives, strategic planners often deliberate over which type of map to begin with: collaborative or personal. There is no right or wrong answer. Rather, studying a district's culture, history of curriculum work, and its current or potential meeting structures reveals what is best for a district.

Curriculum mapping is a field of study that grows and adapts as educators apply the model and create frameworks addressing ongoing curricular needs. Regardless of direction, from collaborative to personal or personal to collaborative, the critical consideration is that teachers must be actively involved in the curriculum maps' designing process.

When choosing to begin with projected/diary mapping, Jacobs (1997) states,

> I suggest the faculty meeting time be provided for teachers to work on maps privately in their classrooms. . . . Once the maps are completed, each teacher becomes an editor for the map for the entire building. First, each faculty member should become familiar with his or her colleagues' curriculum as well as the scope of all the maps. (p. 10–11)

Once map evidence for a full academic year is recorded for a specific discipline, teachers meet to horizontally articulate what they collectively value concerning student learning based on state standards and other forms of data analysis. This process is followed by a collaborative vertical review to articulate the learning over a series of academic years. The results of the collegial curriculum conversations and decision making are evident in the school's Consensus Maps. The process thus far for a given discipline, such as science, may take two to three years.

If a district consists of multiple like schools (e.g., a district with *five* elementary schools; *two* middle schools; and *one* high school), selected teachers are asked to serve on a task force to design systemic Essential Maps based on the like schools' Consensus Maps' learning expectations to serve as the cornerstone for student learning expectations in all of the similar schools. A newly designed Essential Map may affect the current learning included in Consensus Maps and Projected/Diary Maps. Revisions to the maps would take place as needed.

Due to the onset of increased accountability for student performance that often requires teacher-designed curriculum, some districts are choosing to begin the long-term mapping process by having teachers first collegially design collaborative maps (Essential Maps and/or Consensus Maps) before asking teachers to annually document the operational curriculum through Projected/Diary Maps (Tribuzzi, 2009). Jacobs and Johnson (2009) comment,

> Some schools elect to start with consensus mapping first and then move to individual maps. Unfortunately, outside pressures can be a contributing factor to rushing the process. Sometimes because of schools' performances on mandated assessments, they feel compelled to start with consensus maps to address major gaps or inconsistencies in what is taught across the grades and subjects. In schools with little or no curriculum anchors, starting with consensus maps can be very effective. (p. 67)

The term *consensus* is often used to generically indicate *coming to agreement*. As mentioned previously, throughout this book, specific map terminology is used for those involved in the collaborative agreement decision-making process: districtwide agreement (Essential Maps) and school-site agreement (Consensus Maps).

A second reason for starting with collaborative mapping is that teachers often become frustrated with the mapping process when asked to first work diligently to independently generate Projected/Diary Maps and then are asked to work interdependently to create collaborative maps that often include a new collegially agreed-upon organizational design. Habits formed when writing personal maps that are changed when collaboratively mapping cause unwanted frustration. When the mapping process flows from Projected/Diary Map to Consensus Map to Essential Map, teachers often voice the question, "Why didn't we start with collaborative mapping, so we could agree on the organization instead of beginning with us personally mapping?"

When designing collaborative maps first, the process often affects the systemic order for mapping various disciplines. For example, elementary schools often prefer to work collaboratively on one discipline at a time, especially for the first one or two K–12 discipline focuses. Because of this, middle school and high school departments that are not a part of the current K–12 discipline focus can still work collegially concerning their disciplines and design Consensus Maps within their school sites and, if appropriate, Essential Maps for the district. During this time, Grades 6–12 collaborative maps would not be considered teacher-approved systemically until there are articulated and aligned K–12.

Disciplines such as art, music, physical education, and technology can begin to work collegially districtwide early on as there are not as many teachers districtwide as there are in disciplines such as language arts and social studies.

Regardless of whether a district chooses to start with teachers collegially designing collaborative curriculum maps or individually designing Projected/Diary Maps, all teachers must be first provided adequate time to understand the purposes of mapping and become quality curriculum designers and gain confidence in writing maps using the learned design protocols. This practice mapping time often lasts half a school year for teachers to reach a comfort level to begin the official design process.

CONCLUSION

Albert Einstein insightfully conveyed, "Teaching should be such that what is offered is perceived as a valuable gift and not as a hard duty" (ThinkExist.com, 1999–2010). Curriculum mapping can seem a hard duty if administrators and teacher leaders have not given thoughtful planning and support to the systemic nature of this model and strategically premeditated how to shift the thinking of all members districtwide.

Curriculum mapping is meant to affect the entire system and how it functions (Hale, 2008; Jacobs, 1997, 2004; Kallick & Colosimo, 2009; Udelhofen, 2005, 2008). Districts with the greatest success rate have highly visible, engaged leadership at all levels. Administrators and teachers must work together, mobilized by a common mission, vision, goals, and mutual trust and respect during all phases and aspects of a mapping initiative (Udelhofen, 2005).

The remaining chapters focus on providing administrators and teacher leaders with insights into the necessary personal and collaborative considerations when implementing and supporting a curriculum mapping initiative to ensure it reaches sustainability.

REVIEW QUESTIONS

After responding to the following questions and exercise, meet with a colleague or small group to reflect on one another's responses.

1. How has reading this chapter helped you gain insight into the systemic nature of curriculum mapping?

2. Create an analogy to represent and explain curriculum mapping's systemic environment. Share it with your study partner or partners.

3. Does your district function as an oak grove or an aspen grove? (Provide examples to support your response.) How will this affect the systemic implementation and requisite to function interdependently?

4. All those involved in the ongoing curriculum mapping process need to be able to articulate the difference between, as well as synergy of, curriculum design and curriculum practice. What curriculum work examples in your school or district can be used to help define and articulate the two focuses? *(Example: A book study or workshop series on instructional delivery is focusing on curriculum practice; a rubric-creation training series is focused on both curriculum design and curriculum practice; and an in-depth study of newly released state standards is focusing on curriculum design.)*

2

What Are Critical Considerations for Curriculum Mapping Leadership?

I start with the premise that the function of leadership is to produce more leaders, not more followers.

—Ralph Nader

While curriculum mapping may be implemented in a single school, it is most often a districtwide initiative. For curriculum mapping to be systemically sustainable, district and school-site administrators must work harmoniously. If not in sync, there will be a disconnect concerning the initiative's implementation. Likewise, to reach sustainability, administrators at all levels must work proactively to recognize and support teachers as the true leaders of a mapping initiative.

DEFINING LEADERSHIP

Administrative leaders guide the culture and cultural changes within their institutions. Given that responsibilities and roles of administrative leaders have increased over the years, it is important to reflect on quality characteristics in an administrative leader. Heightened curriculum design and instructional-practice responsibilities affect all levels of educational leaders: superintendents, assistant superintendents, principals, assistant principals, curriculum supervisors, curriculum directors, and classroom teachers. All levels must work collegially like never before. Hoerr (2005) states,

> Good leaders change organizations, great leaders change people. People are at the heart of any organization, particularly a school, and it is only through changing people—nurturing and challenging them, helping them grow and develop, creating a culture in which they all learn—that an organization can flourish. Leadership is about relationships. (p. 7)

Leadership is characterized as *the capacity or ability to lead.* In reality, leadership is a combination of the characteristics, traits, principles, and skills necessary to influence others to take ownership in accomplishing a task, mission, or goal, regardless of the organization. For example, the United States Marine Corps defines leadership traits and principles to serve as a tool to judge personal and collective leadership characteristics (see Appendix B).

Leadership Characteristics

Some leadership characteristics are more important than others when considering a systemic model such as curriculum mapping. One of the most important is *integrity,* which enables effective communication, a central component of curriculum mapping. Integrity builds trust and honesty as information is shared back and forth between a superintendent and district administrators, a curriculum director and curriculum coaches, or a principal and his or her faculty.

In curriculum mapping, educational leaders, both administrators and teachers, are asked to make leadership judgments related to planning, implementing, and sustaining the process (Hale, 2008). *Judgment* is a leadership characteristic that aids in the collaborative decisions needing to be made. This is especially true of building leaders who must ensure that necessary change can happen via creating or modifying current resources and structures to enable teacher leadership and curriculum work (Jacobs, 2004). The consistency in applying sound judgment increases the level of trust and loyalty constituents have for an educational leader. Having a positive and affirming allegiance is important as it helps build trust and support, which enables teamwork to be accomplished easily and more effectively.

Knowledge is another significant characteristic because educational leaders in the 21st century encounter large amounts of need-to-know-now information that affects communication and decision making. When a curriculum mapping initiative begins, administrative leaders must be willing to become active learners because supporting teachers as design leaders may be a new paradigm.

Teacher leadership plays a critical role in mapping sustainability. Empowering teachers to assume leadership roles builds their self-worth. When teachers make informed decisions using knowledge of instructional theories and practices, curriculum design protocols, and ongoing student data, *working as a team* is essential. Leaders who promote teaming enable and encourage teachers to work wholeheartedly with a cooperative, collegial demeanor. As administrative leaders promote and support teacher leadership, they solidify success and sustainability due to the shared leadership. This form of leadership means that everyone involved in the initiative must be willing to accept justified and constructive criticism. For some administrators, this may prove personally difficult. When an administrator is willing to admit he or she has made a poor decision or was misinformed, teachers are most often forgiving and willing to forget. Tenacity coupled with transparency is a cornerstone to successful educational leadership.

Transformational Leadership

Glanz (2006a, 2006b, 2006c, 2006d, 2006e, 2006f, 2006g) wrote a seven-series collection of leadership skills specifically for principals. His skill sets are categorized into seven leadership types: operational, instructional, cultural, ethical, spiritual, school-community, collaborative, and strategic. When combined, they embrace a term known as *transformational leadership*. Many define transformational leadership as *a leader or leaders enabling a group to develop into a learning community through a shared learning experience*.

Marzano, Waters, and McNulty (2005) examine transformational leadership and the work of Bass (1985) and Burns (1978) by comparing the work of theories and theorists on leadership. A transformational leader encourages individual members of the group to participate in collaborative learning experiences and ongoing application and allows each member of the group to have an equal voice, whether a member is sharing information or providing thoughts and opinions on the current status or future direction of an initiative. This encouragement is central to curriculum mapping. Transformational leadership embraces teaching, coaching, mentoring, facilitating, inspiring, influencing, and bringing about effective change. Through the incorporation of teacher leadership via curriculum mapping cabinets and councils (Hale, 2008; Jacobs, 1997, 2004; Udelhofen, 2005, 2008), the mapping process embraces the necessity for teachers and administrators to work together side by side to transform the learning environment for administrators, educators, and students.

The past and present cultures of a school and district need to be understood and recognized in order to promote true change; implement an initiative; and develop an active, participatory learning community. Administrative leaders must have a realistic perception of the history of their learning environments. They must recognize which teachers and administrators have covert or overt and positive or negative influences in a school or district.

Likewise, it is wise to be up front about subcultures and their influence in the district and in each building. Many schools have a culture or cultures that reflect the policies and norms of the district on the surface, yet a subculture or subcultures have a strong influence on whether things are accomplished or not. It is difficult for administrators, especially principals, to promote and improve student achievement without addressing these concerns forthright. When administrators ask influential leaders to play a key role in promoting collegial schoolwide or districtwide learning communities, it can prove to be one of the strongest and most effective resources when implementing change.

Collaborative Leadership

James Humes (quoted in Leon, 2005) says that *"the art of communication is the language of leadership"* (para. 1). Past and present school cultures and climates impact the nature and form of communication and collaboration within each school in a district (Glanz, 2006a). Curriculum mapping asks teachers to be collegial curriculum designers and curriculum practitioners both horizontally (one grade level or course) and vertically (series of grade levels or courses), a task they may not have undertaken before. Therefore, to promote sustained cultural and collaborative leadership, administrators must be willing to be personal risk takers as learners and leaders. They must also be open to asking teachers to be learners and leaders through the requisites and professional development involved in a mapping initiative.

To increase students' academic and social achievements, teachers are asked to analyze, discuss, and implement instructional delivery and assessment practices for the teacher-designed curriculum. Collaborative leadership assists in sustaining curriculum mapping based on the premise that all members desire to improve one's personal professional abilities due to the collective beliefs and efforts. A curriculum mapping initiative is considered sustainable when the model's components have become a natural way of doing business, a part of the district and each school's everyday educational life (Jacobs, 2004).

ADMINISTRATIVE LEADERSHIP CONSIDERATIONS

Organizing district- and school-level leadership to support and sustain curriculum mapping work is accomplished by establishing various working groups. The curriculum mapping cabinet, a districtwide implementation and sustainability leadership team, is responsible for enabling and ensuring all teachers identify with and participate in the mapping process. This team consists of teacher leaders from all school sites: principals, and when appropriate, assistant principals; and curriculum oriented district administrators (Hale, 2008; Jacobs, 1997).

The term *cabinet* may already be established in a district to represent a team other than curriculum mapping. If this is the case, an alternative reference name can be used to refer to the curriculum mapping cabinet as well other designated curriculum mapping leadership teams (Figure 2.1). Since these leadership terms are commonly used in the curriculum mapping model, they will be used throughout this book.

Supporting a Curriculum Mapping Initiative

Utilizing the curriculum mapping process as a tool to improve student learning and achievement requires systemic leadership focused on a second-order change. An important shift in thinking to ensure this change occurs is consistently and continuously recognizing publicly that curriculum mapping is about a *process*, not a product. The collegial discussions and decision-making processes

Figure 2.1   Curriculum Mapping Leadership Teams

Term	Definition
Curriculum Mapping Coordinator(s)	Person or persons responsible for the overall management of a curriculum mapping initiative who serves as a liaison and key communicator between Curriculum Mapping Cadre, Curriculum Mapping Cabinet, and Curriculum Mapping Councils; administrators at all levels, board members, and the community.
Curriculum Mapping Cadre	A team of approximately five to seven people, including the Curriculum Mapping Coordinator(s), who share the responsibilities of strategic planning and implementation. They also serve as the learning organization's curriculum mapping resident experts.
Curriculum Mapping Cabinet	A districtwide team consisting of teachers, administrators, and the Curriculum Mapping Cadre who represent the diversity of all grades, all disciplines, and support services. Cabinet members become proficient in the mapping process and serve as districtwide experts. The members participate in making ongoing districtwide mapping decisions as well as approving, developing, modifying, and expanding the large-scale learning organization's curriculum mapping action plans. Cabinet members serve a dual role by also being members of a school-site Curriculum Mapping Council.
Curriculum Mapping Council	A school-site-specific team of teachers and administrators who represent all grade levels, disciplines, and support services. Council members become proficient in the mapping process and serve as in-house experts. The council members support the districtwide action plans as well as collaboratively develop and implement school-site curriculum mapping action plans.

are the heart of curriculum mapping. Curriculum maps are *by-products* of teachers working collaboratively and individually to design and review curriculum.

The components of the mapping process need to be embedded in professional development centered on teachers learning how to design and review curriculum as well as learning, analyzing, and engaging in curriculum practices that ensure all students meet or exceed the agreed-upon learning expectations. Jacobs (2004) affirms,

> We know that our efforts for professional development are successful when we see targeted gains in student performance. When there is a systemic focus with a common place to share findings the conditions for success grow. Mapping becomes the arena. (p. 125)

Jacobs (2010) mentions that, to have an effective environment in the 21st century, a learning organization must consider interconnected structures that influence curriculum design, instructional practice, and related professional development: "the schedule (both short and long term); the way we group our learners; personnel configurations; and the use of space (both physical and virtual)" (p. 13).

For this collegial environment to become a reality, administrators, regardless of position in the district, must express loyalty to the initiative both in talk and action.

Each school-site administrator plays an important role in expressing loyalty. Principals are recognized as the catalyst for second-order change within schools (Glanz, 2006d; Glatthorn & Jailall, 2009; Robbins & Alvy, 1995). If one or more principals are not willing to buy into curriculum mapping and covertly or overtly display discontent, the systemic intention of mapping will not be achieved. A side effect of this will be teachers who are discontented or disengaged based on the displayed attitude of the administrative leadership.

Another districtwide and school-site consideration that must be addressed is the issue of mistrust. If there is mistrust between (1) teachers and a principal, (2) principals in two or more schools, or (3) the schools and the district administration, it may appear at first as if curriculum mapping is being implemented and established. However, a culture of mistrust will affect chances of reaching sustainability. Mutual trust and respect expressed by administrators, teacher leaders, faculties, and staffs play a critical role in establishing an interdependent, collegial environment.

When a school's teachers are not provided adequate time or support in gaining the knowledge base necessary to fully participate in the mapping process, their abilities to move mapping forward are difficult. The more systemic mapping becomes (e.g., developing Essential Maps, conducting across-district like or mixed discipline collaborations), the more obvious a lack of support becomes. Lack of administrative solidarity can cause a crack, and potentially a chasm, in the mapping process.

Leading Educational Initiatives

Too often, educational leaders make the mistake of starting an initiative in districts, schools, and departments without developing a buy-in level that eventually leads to a high percentage of commitment, accomplishment, and reaching sustainability. While it is said that total buy-in may not be possible, majority buy-in is possible if proper preplanning—including a prologue and step-by-step implementation—takes place (Hale, 2008; Jacobs, 1997, 2004).

After multiple years of trying to reach curriculum mapping sustainability, one of the greatest lessons learned in a midsized district was the negative effects that a lack of commitment from the district's administrative leadership can have from the onset.

The lack of genuine commitment for the mapping initiative was fueled by misunderstanding and frustration due to the district embarking improperly without a cohesive professional development model. Unfortunately, the district tried to embrace mapping using a top-down model rather than a teacher-led leadership model. Buildings were left on their own to individually train teachers and develop curriculum maps. Because there was no recognized teacher-led, districtwide leadership in place, the curriculum mapping process was marginalized by some schools and totally ignored by

(Continued)

(Continued)

others. There were a few schools, however, that were able to internally develop powerful professional learning communities and meaningful curriculum experiences due to the collegial culture and climate already in place within their buildings.

After six years of mapping, this district finally started to look at vertically aligning curriculum between the middle schools and high schools. The actual work and accountability of the developed maps became the responsibility of the three assistant principals and one high school principal—with no true teacher representation and involvement. The elementary schools who started the mapping process years before the secondary schools finally decided in frustration to go in a different direction and use another model of curriculum repository that did not link fluidly with the curriculum in the secondary schools.

A *get it done* mentality permeated this district. No districtwide professional development or curriculum design time was allocated for teachers in or among the schools. The only professional development related to the curriculum mapping process was achieved by an individual building's principal and faculty who believed in the worth of curriculum mapping. This particular building has developed curriculum maps that truly reflect the collegial nature of the mapping process and evolved into an outstanding learning community that embraced both curriculum design and curriculum practice.

It is important to note that this school district has since revamped its entire curriculum mapping process under new administrative leadership and teacher leadership. At the time of this writing, it is starting to systemically mirror the work of the individual buildings where the process was successful. The school district is beginning to understand the value and worth of combining the leadership of administrators and teachers districtwide.

It is essential—before any systemic initiative is started—that a district creates teams of teacher leaders and administrators. These teams must be willing to learn, and in turn, train and support each school's initiative-focused learning process. Awareness of the systemic nature of curriculum mapping and the implementation necessities includes informing school board members, superintendents, central-office staff, building principals, and teacher leaders in each school. This is accomplished best by establishing a districtwide curriculum mapping cabinet and school-site curriculum mapping councils (Hale, 2008; Jacobs, 1997, 2004). Once a systemic initiative has begun, the appropriate amount of time for adequate training and application makes a difference in its success.

In order to properly support teachers, administrators need to address potential structure changes to ensure professional development and curriculum work time that is strategically coordinated not only within a building but throughout a district—both horizontally and vertically. According to Darling-Hammond and Richardson (2009), "research shows professional development lasting 14 or fewer hours showed no effects on learning. The largest effects were for programs offering 30–100 hours spread out over 6–12 months" (p. 49). This translates to approximately 8.25 hours per month in a calendar year.

A suburban high school that was heavily involved in the curriculum mapping process was introduced to a literacy program that was being considered as a schoolwide initiative based on the literacy professional development that had been going on for five years across the curriculum.

Reading and writing were not only learned and reinforced by reading specialists and English teachers but also by teachers in science, social studies, and math classrooms. Student reading and writing scores on the state assessment rose over time. Now that the faculty was considering a new program, the first call to action was to see if the program was a good fit given the map evidence of the required student learning. After small- and large-group mixed-discipline review meetings, the program was unanimously accepted as a resource to enhance student-learning requisites. The teachers are now developing cross-curricular numerical literacy through the curriculum mapping review process.

This high school has enjoyed systemic success because of the combined leadership of teachers and administrators. The principal, a transformational leader, supported the implementation of professional learning communities.

Initially, a team of three teachers and the principal attended the annual national curriculum mapping conference where they learned about the ongoing components of the mapping process. At the end of each conference day, the team completed team-building activities to develop trust.

The cadre's desire to work as a team grew after returning from the conference. Their knowledge of mapping increased by participating in conferences, workshops, and professional development sessions. The team worked hard to develop a sound understanding of curriculum mapping. Because the team collegially trained together, they were able to help one other grow professionally. Donaldson (2009) shares, "The best professional learning experiences help aspiring leaders integrate skills, knowledge, and personal meaning as they perform" (p. 14). As their knowledge of curriculum mapping grew, each team member in turn learned more about teacher leadership. The level of trust increased and permitted them to function in positive ways to enlist and train others in the curriculum mapping process.

Each year, the team added new members and sustained the team for seven years. The original 15 members were still a part of the team. They were invited to present their personal curriculum mapping journey and learning experiences with others through national and regional conference sessions. The full team continues to go to an annual conference for training and networking.

Many of the team members fill key leadership positions in the structure of the high school's levels of organization, serving as department chairs or curricular liaisons. The integrity of this team maintains an ever-stronger level of integrity as the years go by, even as team members come and go. The trust developed with one another and throughout the campus has endured the test of time and the team has taken ownership of new district, building, and departmental initiatives that enter into the building's ongoing curriculum work.

Initiative Considerations

Administrators and teacher leaders are often plagued with the task of leading faculties in the *flavor of the month* initiative. This manner of professional development often leads to angry teachers and wasted time. It also turns teachers off, which makes becoming effective curriculum leaders and learning communities difficult. Reeves (2009) notes, "Educators are drowning under the weight of initiative fatigue, attempting to use the same amount of time, money, and emotional energy to accomplish more and more objectives" (p. 14). Administrators who focus on initiatives strategically and incorporate initiatives with a systems perspective are more likely to be successful (Glanz, 2006g). Likewise, they include teachers in a leadership capacity.

Effective administrators find ways to synthesize new and ongoing initiatives. They do not introduce new initiatives until outdated or ineffective ones are concluded. Administrators and teacher leaders need to look for gaps and overlaps in ongoing and new initiatives. If there is a link between two initiatives wherein they can become one, connecting them gives the initiatives more sustainability and strengthens the ability to improve student achievement. Administrators, with teacher leaders' input, periodically need to, figuratively speaking, pull the weeds before planting new flowers (Reeves, 2009).

It is recommended that building administrators and teachers are held accountable for a *small number* of districtwide and school-site initiatives during any given school year (Ramsey, 2003; Reeves, 2009). One hundred percent of a teacher's and administrator's teaching day should be devoted to student learning and achievement based on clear understanding of the curriculum being delivered. Therefore, when teachers are provided ongoing preplanned built-in contractual time away from students to engage in horizontal, vertical, like-group, and mixed-group collegial curriculum work, the chances of the initiative failing diminishes. To reach systemic sustainability, curriculum mapping must become the lens through which all curriculum initiatives are viewed. Curriculum mapping is meant to be the hub of both curriculum design and instructional practice (Jacobs, 1997, 2004).

ESTABLISHING VISION, MISSION, AND ACTION PLANS

Strategic planning involves establishing, or possibly revisioning, a learning organization's vision, mission, and series of goals to be accomplished through action plans.

Vision and Mission Statements

Establishing and revisiting a districtwide vision statement and mission statement are important to clarify the reason for pursuing *any* initiative. Some districts dedicate many days to developing such statements. Robert Dufour (2005) says it best: *keep it simple.* He recommends the vision statements be clear and to the point. Most complex statements can be boiled down to a straightforward sentence, such as:

To ensure student achievement, both curricular and social, in and beyond the school years.

Many learning organizations are revisiting and reversioning their vision and mission statements to accentuate the necessity for ensuring the success of 21st-century learners. Most revisions include an obligation to foster and support global competencies involving critical thinking, problem solving, worldwide cultural engagement, and technology involvement related to both curriculum design and instructional practice (Jacobs, 2010).

A vision statement is what a district desires its learners (students, teachers, and administrators) to become. A vision statement is then translated into a mission statement or statements to further aid in the vision's attainability and sustainability (Glanz, 2006g). A mission statement or statements represent the reason or reasons why a district is moving forward to reach its vision at both a district and school-site level. An attainable statement includes concretely knowing what each school and the district needs to do to achieve the desired outcome and work collegially and constantly to reach that desired mental picture (Ramsey, 2003). For example, Tyson's (2010) Mabry Middle School faculty worked diligently to capture in words their vision statement's desire to empower and engage students and make "learning irresistible" (p.115). Tyson shared,

> The school moved from a long and somewhat lofty mission statement that could not be easily evaluated to one that would serve as the yardstick against which every action at the school would be measured: "Maximize student achievement in a culture of caring" . . . One of the most significant standards that emerged for measuring classroom practice was this: To what extent were students authentically engaged in their own learning? (p. 120)

Goals and Action Plans

Along with generating or reversioning vision and mission statements, strategic planning involves creating goals specific to its initiatives that can be accomplished through district and school-site action plans. The goals and action plans need to be thoughtful, purposeful, systemic, and systematic (Glanz, 2006g). The number of goals for districtwide improvement must be realistic and attainable (Reeves, 2009). They must characterize expectations in short-term increments that eventually lead to long-term sustainability (Ramsey, 2003; Reeves, 2009).

A district's curriculum mapping goals and strategic action plans are developed, monitored, and periodically revisited by the curriculum mapping cadre and cabinet. They are initially written or refined based on previous curriculum work during a period of time known as the *prologue* (Hale, 2008; Jacobs, 1997, 2004). The prologue often lasts one-half to a full year before full-scale implementation.

During the prologue, the curriculum mapping cabinet and councils learn (1) the purpose for each type of curriculum map; (2) how to write a map, including the curriculum design and instructional practice map elements with systemic quality in mind using a selected mapping system; (3) how to prioritize standards and break apart standards to scaffold learning expectations; and (4) how to conduct formal and informal curriculum reviews (Hale, 2008). This fourfold learning process enables the administrators and teacher leaders responsible for the initiative to address implementation questions and concerns and formulate strategic action plans and incremental goals.

During the prologue, and beyond, it is vital that administrators and teacher leaders remind themselves and others that curriculum mapping begins with a focus on curriculum design. Once the teachers have collaboratively and systemically articulated the design, curriculum practice conversations and instructional reviews become an integral component of the ongoing mapping process.

Action Plan Considerations

As mentioned previously, action plans are written to express the small steps or stages to accomplish an initiative's implementation phases and respective goals. When examining the prospective strategic districtwide and school-site curriculum mapping action plans, the leadership may choose to apply a mapping review strategy to gain insights and viewpoints from various perspectives. Jacobs (1997) established the *Seven-Step Review Process* as an effective way to review curriculum data:

1. Collecting the Data

2. The First Read Through

3. Small-Group Review

4. Large-Group Comparison

5. Immediate Revision

6. Research and Development

7. New Review Considerations

Just as there may be gaps, repetitions, and absences in the curriculum (Jacobs, 1997, 2004), there may be some in the drafted action plans. The beauty of this model is that any review, curriculum specific or otherwise, can be conducted using its five sequential meeting principles (Figure 2.2).

An outgrowth of using this model for noncurriculum reviews is that administrators and teacher leaders, once they have experienced the review process firsthand, often become advocates of the process being used for conducting curriculum specific reviews.

The strategic planning process becomes transformational when the leadership is working collegially to improve student achievement and ensure teacher growth through professional learning communities and the use of reviews. Johnson and Johnson (2004) reflected on this when studying the long-term journey that transformed their district:

> After starting our school improvement journey using curriculum mapping as a tool, we have, indeed, transformed. Our students have made marked improvement in performance, we have enhanced our leadership capacity on every level, and we have refined our focus and consistency in instruction. (p. 36)

Figure 2.2   Five Meeting Review Principles

1. Based on a predetermined review focus (e.g., problem, issue, concern, bright spot), a large group is formed with small groups predefined within the large group.

2. Appropriate curriculum maps and/or other forms of data are first studied individually by each review team member. Personal notes are taken and brought to a small-group meeting.

3. Individual findings are collaboratively shared and discussed during the small-group meeting. Key discussion points, comments, and suggestions are recorded. Each small-group's meeting summary is given or made available to each large-group member. Each member individually reads the collective commentaries before the large-group meeting commences.

4. The large group collaboratively discusses the data, findings, and commentaries. Decisions made are either immediately implemented or designated as needing further exploration. If exploration is necessary, the focus is revisited until decisions can be effectively made.

5. Once decisions have been made and actions taken, the large group is disbanded. The review team may someday meet again if a new or previous focus warrants participation from the same large-group members.

Cultural and Historical Realities

Before districtwide or school-site curriculum mapping action plans can be planned, reviewed, and solidified, administrators and teacher leaders must address the overt and covert districtwide and school-site-specific cultures and historical initiative implementation realities. If this is not discussed upfront and openly, it can greatly impact the implementation and eventual success or failure of the initiative.

A large school district had established a nine-member curriculum mapping cadre consisting of five district administrators and four teacher leaders. Before establishing the curriculum mapping cabinet, the cadre decided to first learn as much as possible about curriculum mapping. They attended the national curriculum mapping institute as well as regional curriculum mapping conferences. The members talked with districts that had been successful and districts where the initiative had failed. The cadre also hired a curriculum mapping consultant to aid them in their strategic planning and initial implementation phases.

During their initial meeting with the consultant, the curriculum mapping cadre members emphasized issues concerning past and present cultural history related to the district as a whole as well as individual school sites. The issue of greatest concern was a districtwide *hill and valley* mentality.

(Continued)

(Continued)

Topographically and figuratively, this problem creates a great divide. The income of the hill families is greater than that of the valley families. The hill schools considered themselves better academically than the valley schools. Because of this, the teachers in the two groups did not work collegially. This culture was detrimental in so many ways, not only for the students but for the teachers and the community as well.

Changing the culture to functioning as one system was imperative for strategically planning long-term goals. From the onset, the curriculum mapping cadre acknowledged that it would be vital to properly establish and train the curriculum mapping cabinet and councils to ensure this new mentality.

The assistant superintendent of curriculum made curriculum mapping *the* initiative for the first two years of implementation. Based on the strategic action plans, all professional development focused on learning the complexities of mapping as well as moving toward an *even plains* mentality.

Equally important were all of the building principals who embraced the action plans and were active participants in the curriculum mapping cabinet. Likewise, when the curriculum mapping councils were established, they allowed the teachers to become the leaders of the mapping initiative within their respective school sites.

While there were bumps in the road and changes made to the strategic action plans based on input from the curriculum mapping cabinet and council members, the cultural change goal was reached within the first two years of implementation.

The teachers and administrators still mention the freshness with which teachers now approach professionalism systemically and truly work collegially not only within a school site but also throughout the district. The curriculum mapping cadre often comments that the district has truly become an aspen grove.

Sometimes, a district or school may want to take a pulse check of the current behavioral culture. Administrators and teacher leaders may choose to acquire the desired information through focus groups. These groups may contain representatives from different schools and central-office staff who can provide leadership with valuable information pertaining to the initiative. Discussions with focus groups can also foster ideas on how to best implement and accomplish the initiative to reach sustainability. Nings, e-mail exchanges, or personal interviews are other ways to gather data on culture and history. If the current culture is not healthy, it may be best to gather the data through anonymous online surveys.

Embedded Within Strategic Planning

An important shift in thinking is that curriculum mapping best serves students and teachers when it is perceived as an overarching umbrella for all curricular initiatives. Through the lens of curriculum mapping, what once may have been a series of seemingly unrelated initiatives become interconnected.

Curriculum mapping must be embedded in the districtwide strategic planning process from the onset of the initiative to achieve the best implementation results. If a district starts the mapping initiative without first placing it in the strategic plans, stakeholders will realize early on that it needs to be included. It is important to remember that there will most likely be annual new-to-the-district administrators and teachers who need to be trained in the complexities of curriculum mapping. They will also need to know what has happened in the past related to the mapping initiative as well as the current district and respective school-site strategic action plans.

As part of the strategic planning, it is recommended that administrators and teacher leaders attend regional and national curriculum mapping conferences during the first three to five years of establishing curriculum mapping. This creates opportunities to network with other schools and districts to expand the possibilities for using curriculum mapping to improve student learning as well as nurturing teachers as leaders (Jacobs, 2004; Kallick & Colosimo, 2009). While this can somewhat be accomplished through online forums, both synchronous and asynchronous, there is something engaging and electrifying when meeting in person that cannot be as easily achieved virtually.

Building Site Considerations

When writing strategic action plans, it is important to be aware that curriculum mapping as a model for conducting ongoing curriculum work cannot be established quickly if it is meant to reach sustainability (Hale, 2008). As shared previously, a prologue may take up to a full year before reaching all teachers in the district. Once the curriculum mapping cabinet has gone through the process of learning the complexities of mapping, these administrators and teacher leaders representing each school site work together to establish a curriculum mapping council within their respective school sites. They aid in training the council members who in turn train the remaining teachers within each school site. This *train-the-trainer model* allows the systemic process of mapping to be established and nurtured by the teacher leaders and supported by administrators (Jacobs, 1997, 2004). The teacher leaders also provide insight and leadership in the direction and advancement of the mapping initiative. These teachers play a key role in influencing others to see the value in mapping and aid in ensuring the initiative becomes integrated into the way the school and district conduct the ongoing curriculum work.

Imperative to the success of a curriculum mapping council is the role of the principal. While he or she is involved in the initiative in a leadership capacity, a principal must do so in a supportive leadership role rather than a controlling one. Teachers may not have been given such a level of power and the ability to make decisions before this initiative. Therefore, they may not feel confident in a leadership role. A principal must create a delicate balance between nurturing and supporting without taking over the leadership responsibilities.

A school district had a great deal of success with its strategic action plan. The plan was phased in over three years. The curriculum mapping cadre created a curriculum mapping cabinet that in turn trained school-site councils regarding curriculum mapping basics. The curriculum mapping council members worked extensively to train their building departmental teams or grade levels in the seven-step review process.

Key to the review process being useful was the principal at each school site reversioning the structure of available time to ensure teachers have time to regularly meet both horizontally and vertically. Through creative planning and readjusting scheduling, the teachers found opportunities to meet, and they found these times invaluable.

At one high school, during a second phase of using the seven-step review process, each departmental team determined what was a departmental curriculum concern or issue to be analyzed using the newly established review process and team-generated protocols. One department's concern was the need for graduate credits to better overlap with state testing requirements. The teachers decided that the review-process data to address their concern would include (1) the Projected/Diary Maps of the teachers currently teaching these courses, (2) graduate credit requirements, and (3) state testing guidelines. Based on a master schedule plan devised by the principal and council members, the teachers had adequate time to review the data before meeting in small groups. When ready, the small groups met in a large group to articulate the vertical course concerns. The ongoing collegial process eventually led to not only designing school-site Consensus Maps, but improved alignment of course work to graduation requirements.

Since the district consists of three high schools, after each high school's departments went through the articulation process internally, during a series of districtwide professional development days, the cross-school department teachers worked to design Essential Maps within the district's mapping system. The high school departmental teams continue to work together in the cyclical process of mapping reviews both internally and districtwide. When the teachers meet, sometimes the focus is on curriculum design; other times, it is on curriculum practice. The focus is always based on the ongoing commitment to attaining the district's mission and vision statements.

The goal of creating systemic agreement for student learning would have never been achieved if each school's principal had not committed adequate time, a servant-leader mindset, and a shared effort to support curriculum mapping and the processes it involves. In the long run, it took the collaborative teamwork of district administrators, building principals, curriculum supervisors, and departmental teams to accomplish the administrators' collaborative goal to reach mapping sustainability.

Professional Learning Communities

The above-mentioned district is an example of teachers working collegially as *professional learning communities*. Many schools and districts have established professional learning communities (PLCs) to support their curriculum work, both for design and practice. While PLCs have become commonplace, this term can have various definitions depending on the person or persons promoting its use. Regardless, there is a leadership theme that transcends any definition. Hord (1997) states,

> The school change and educational leadership literatures clearly recognize the role and influence of the campus administrator (principal, and sometimes assistant principal) on whether change will occur in the school. It seems clear that transforming a school organization into a learning community can be done only with the sanction of the leaders and the active nurturing of the entire staff's development as a community. . . . [This is] a good starting point for describing what these learning communities look like and how the principal "accepts a collegial relationship with teachers" (Rainey, personal communication, March 13, 1997) to share leadership, power, and decision making. (p. 1)

The systemic nature of establishing well-functioning professional learning communities, both at each school site and districtwide, does not happen overnight. Ideally, all principals function as a cohesive team and stay rooted in the desire to develop and nurture the district as an aspen grove. For some, this is a shift in thinking and behavior. Effective leaders, both administrators and teachers, exert a powerful influence on student achievement and the effectiveness of schools (Davies, 2005).

CONCLUSION

Critical considerations mentioned in this chapter affect the likelihood that curriculum mapping reaches sustainability. Teachers need to become the leaders of the initiative through (1) establishing, training, and supporting a curriculum mapping cabinet and each school's council; (2) building or expanding leadership trust in teachers being curriculum designers; and (3) conducting curriculum design and instructional practice reviews. Curriculum mapping is an ongoing, systemic process. It is not a method for creating quickly generated map products. Mapping is an active, mentally engaging environment that asks all teachers to work collaboratively as well as individually to improve student learning through designing and reviewing curriculum both horizontally (in one grade level or course) and vertically (in a series of grade levels or courses). Aligning curriculum mapping with the district's vision and mission and developing strategic action plans and step-by-step goals aids in ensuring implementation success. As administrators and teachers work together as visionaries, students reap the benefits through curriculum mapping's emphasis on ongoing improvement of teacher-designed (and, when appropriate, student-designed) articulated curriculum and instructional best practices.

REVIEW QUESTIONS

Based on your district's past and present curriculum-related initiatives, both failed and flourishing, discuss your responses with a colleague or in a small group to reflect on one another's responses.

1. When you think of a great educational leader, considering both teachers and administrators, who is the person and what outstanding leadership characteristics come to mind?

2. What types of formal educational-leadership training have you experienced that can benefit you and others while establishing and sustaining a curriculum mapping initiative?

3. How would you summarize the critical leadership considerations that stood out as being the most important to you when reading this chapter?

4. Does your district or school currently have a mission and vision statement? If yes, do you perceive curriculum mapping aligning with the current vision and mission? If yes, explain how it does align. If not, what needs to be considered for reversioning to meet the needs of 21st-century learners?

5. All levels of administrators must work together to support the planning and implementation of a curriculum mapping initiative. The principal is a vital player in ensuring sustainability. Will buy-in and true support from all principals, as well as district administrators, be an issue? If yes, how will this be proactively addressed, monitored, and resolved?

6. Does your school or district use a *flavor-of-the-year* approach to implementing initiatives and professional development focuses? If yes, how has this affected the past and current cultures? How do you perceive this changing when implementing curriculum mapping?

7. What current initiative or initiatives can be combined with or filtered through curriculum mapping as the curriculum work hub? Are there any initiatives that can be officially cut, suspended, or reframed as the district implements curriculum mapping?

3

What Should District Administrators Consider to Support Teacher Leadership?

The secret of getting ahead is getting started.
The secret of getting started is breaking your complex overwhelming
tasks into small manageable tasks, and then starting on the first one.

—Mark Twain

During a break at a national curriculum mapping conference, a small group of administrators were talking in a foyer. One administrator shared that he was relatively new to curriculum mapping. He asked, "What should I do as an assistant superintendent to best support our curriculum mapping initiative?" Three of the administrators mentioned they had been involved in mapping for five, three, and two years, respectively. As they expressed their thoughts, two themes emerged: *restructuring time* and *supporting teacher leadership.* One administrator pointed out that implementing curriculum mapping asks administrators, teacher leaders, and ultimately all teachers to rethink why, how, and when to meet.

Another expressed that there are complexities involved in the systemic nature of curriculum mapping. He discovered that those at a district level sometimes do not realize the complexities of this model and assume it is a simple *go-do-and-succeed* initiative.

They agreed that administrators at all levels must understand that mapping is a multifaceted initiative that must be well planned and executed in phases until eventually all teachers are involved. If it is not carried out in this manner, there is a good chance curriculum mapping will ultimately fail or have to be reformed and restarted.

One administrator said that restarting is exactly what happened in her district:

It was a mess. After we realized that mapping is more than just asking teachers to create a map for each course they teach, we had to relearn what curriculum mapping is really all about. We then started over from just about square one. It was rough going. Teachers were not happy with the fact that we "put the cart before the horse." We publicly admitted that we had started too quickly. After a few meetings with administrators, teachers, and union reps, we were able to move forward with our new collective understanding. That was three years ago, and we are finally feeling confident and seeing clearly that curriculum mapping is the venue for conducting all of our curriculum work.

The administrators finished their conversation by sharing contact information and headed to attend various breakout sessions. As he walked into a session with one of the administrators, the assistant superintendent shared that he brought two curriculum directors and five principals with him to the conference and was looking forward to sharing what he had learned from their break-time conversation with his team.

What Mark Twain expressed about *getting ahead* is true. A complex task such as implementing curriculum mapping must be broken down into small, manageable tasks. When too much is done too soon, it does not support sustainability and promotes failure or false starts that frustrate rather than inspire.

District administrators must be aware of all that is involved in curriculum mapping's systemic model and begin shared planning and learning with other district administrators, school-site administrators, and teacher leaders. Collectively, these leaders must determine how best to initiate and support curriculum mapping so it is successful during each phase of implementation and reaches sustainability.

All administrators must become intimately aware of all aspects and components of curriculum mapping to truly understand how to ensure mapping's success. As previously mentioned, if this is the first book you have read on curriculum mapping, it is recommended that you also read *A Guide to Curriculum Mapping: Planning, Implementing, and Sustaining the Process* (Hale, 2008). It provides in-depth information related to fundamental learning and the step-by-step tasks necessary for preparation and implementation, such as who specifically should be included in a curriculum mapping cabinet or a curriculum mapping council.

Restructuring meeting time and supporting teachers as leaders are both vital to building leadership capacity. This aspiration begins best by creating a network of leaders through the establishment of the various curriculum mapping leadership teams as well as eventual inclusion of all teachers in the mapping process. While a district administrator must be visible, accessible, approachable, and engaged to ensure any initiative's success, as Lao Tzu (1999–2010), a sixth-century philosopher, wisely noted, "a leader is best when people barely know he exists, when his work is done, his aim fulfilled, they will say: we did it ourselves."

DISTRICT ADMINISTRATOR POSITIONS

Districts vary greatly in size, organization, responsibilities, and job titles. The job titles in this book may be different from those in your district, but the implementation and sustainability considerations remain the same.

The term *district administrator* refers to anyone in charge of areas or departments directly or indirectly related to curriculum design and curriculum practice, such as a superintendent or assistant superintendent of curriculum. District administrators most often reside at a central-office location. They are responsible for organizing, maintaining, and supporting each school site's integrity related to one or more curriculum focuses. Sometimes, an administrator has a combined district-level position and school-site-level position. For example, in a small district, the assistant superintendent may also be the principal of the high school. This chapter focuses on district-level support whereas Chapter 5 focuses on what a principal or assistant principal needs to consider to support teachers and ensure leadership capacity.

District administrators often oversee colleagues in support-team positions. For example, an assistant superintendent of curriculum may supervise a 10-member team of discipline- specific and category-specific directors. Chapter 4 specifically addresses directors' support considerations while this chapter focuses on the collegial team efforts of all administrators as they consider various support structures while involved in the preplanning and implementation phases.

Some district administrators are directly responsible for maintaining accountability for curriculum consistency throughout the district as well as within each school site. They are also held accountable for providing curriculum information to a school board and the community. Curriculum maps designed, reviewed, revised, and maintained by teachers should be a component of a district and school sites' desired vision, mission, and goals. District administrators need to support this desire by communicating that curriculum mapping synthesizes all ongoing and new curriculum oriented initiatives.

DISTRICTWIDE ADMINISTRATIVE SUPPORT

Superintendent Valerie Truesdale noticed her district had undergone demographic changes that were affecting student achievement. She and those in leadership roles began exploring the potential benefits of curriculum mapping. Truesdale (Truesdale, Thompson, & Lucas, 2004) commented,

> Such changes challenged district leaders to address new curricular and instructional issues to ensure high expectations and student achievement remained strong. District leaders searched for solutions and found

curriculum mapping provided useful tools to help build a strong, cohesive learning community. (p. 11)

She worked alongside district administrators, teacher leaders, and teacher teams to rethink how to best focus on student learning. Regarding challenges for providing adequate support, she observed,

Educators needed to connect with colleagues as they struggled to change teaching practices so they could meet comprehensive standards. Teams of teachers were challenged to think through the mind of a child rather than with the child in mind. In other words, they were asked to envision learning opportunities as if they were individual children moving from kindergarten to 12th grade in the district. What experiences would students have? What would connect learning for them? The resulting plan had to include specifics so that educators could examine the total structure and establish a strong community of learning. (p. 13)

Part of examining the *total structure* included addressing the existing time structures that allowed, or did not allow, teachers to meet horizontally and vertically within school sites as well as districtwide (Jacobs, 2010). Truesdale (Truesdale, Thompson, & Lucas, 2004) worked diligently to alter time structures and add professional work days that included summer-work opportunities. The time-structure alterations and additions did not happen in one year. It took a period of years, which on occasion needed approval by the school board and community.

Because she (1) worked on the complex task of implementing curriculum mapping by breaking the task down into manageable tasks, and (2) asked administrators and teachers to work as an interdependent learning community, the sustainability of curriculum mapping has lasted beyond her years in the district. One reason curriculum mapping continues to flourish in this district is Truesdale (Truesdale, Thompson, & Lucas, 2004) realized early this initiative's recommended leadership structure needed to be put into place. She made certain each leadership team was actively involved in the decision-making process and strategic planning from the curriculum mapping cadre to the cabinet to the councils. She made teacher leadership a priority. Throughout the implementation phases, she made certain the initiative belonged to the teachers and was supported by all the administrators.

Superintendent or Assistant-Superintendent Support

The superintendent needs to provide the initial support for establishing and maintaining a curriculum mapping initiative. He or she must support the process by articulating a clear mission, vision, and message that curriculum mapping initially focuses on systemic curriculum design, then transitions to a focus on instructional practice related to the teacher-designed curriculum. The superintendent must continuously communicate to all administrators and teachers that the district will *stay the course* with the curriculum mapping initiative. A superintendent may be directly responsible for the curriculum mapping initiative or assign the responsibility to an assistant superintendent. If the latter, it is important that the superintendent remains involved in the strategic planning process and implementation, including providing the necessary time for professional learning by the leadership involved in the prologue. Jacobs (2004) comments, "As I have observed schools and districts develop their mapping projects, ample preparation time has characterized the most effective attempts" (p. 1). It is important for a superintendent who has delegated the planning and implementation of curriculum mapping to others to attend meetings and trainings, even if only periodically for an hour or so, to extend the message that the initiative is important to all stakeholders.

Active participation also includes informing the school board regularly on the curriculum mapping planning stages and implementation phases. Ongoing communication is important for ensuring continued support, as board members can only make supportive decisions when well-informed. If there is a struggle between district administrators and the school board, it may be difficult to begin or sustain the ongoing mapping process.

The average life expectancy of a superintendent across the nation is approximately five-and-a-half years (Kowalski, 2006). If upper-level management has been a revolving door, it will affect any large-scale initiative implementation. Teachers will have difficultly buying in to curriculum mapping because initiatives will have come and gone along with district administrators' arrivals and departures. Even in districts with low turnover, there still needs to be discussion about curriculum mapping's sustainability and the necessity for ongoing district and school-site-level administrative support. It is therefore critical to establish consistency and continuity in the leadership teams involved in curriculum mapping. The curriculum mapping cadre, cabinet, and councils become the stabilizing agents that carry the torch when there are changes in district or school-site administration.

Just as superintendents and assistant superintendents retire or move on, so do curriculum directors, principals, and teacher leaders. Ongoing support for training and mentoring those new to any educational position is critical for maintaining long-term curriculum mapping sustainability. It is important to allow new administrators and teachers ample opportunities to be learners, including participating in book studies; receiving in-district training; and time to attend local, regional, or national curriculum mapping trainings or conferences.

Assistant Superintendent of Curriculum

In many districts, the assistant superintendent of curriculum is recognized as the curriculum mapping coordinator and is responsible for implementing and monitoring a curriculum mapping initiative. It is important that the curriculum mapping coordinator and curriculum directors clearly and repeatedly impress upon administrators and teachers that the curriculum design process is systemic and ongoing. It may take a few years to shift to this kind of thinking.

Supporting a systemic-thinking mindset is important for two reasons. First, it sets a tone for creating an aspen grove mentality, as the entire district will be asked to function interdependently when designing articulated curriculum. Second, because each discipline's articulated curriculum will eventually be housed and managed in an online mapping system, there will be the necessity to conduct early systemic curriculum task-force work that will bring teachers together that will have varying degrees of understanding concerning the complexities of curriculum mapping. For example, designing systemic unit names (see Appendix A) or creating systemic common vocabulary may involve teachers who are not currently members of the curriculum mapping cabinet and councils.

District administrators must contemplate how the district will support an initiative that is dependent on sufficient time, technology, professional development, and facility structures that permit teachers to meet regularly horizontally and vertically within each school and across the district. What appears to be currently sufficient most often is not once curriculum mapping becomes the way all curriculum work is conducted.

As there are many disciplines offered in a school district, the curriculum mapping coordinator, cadre, cabinet, and councils will need to strategically plan how to manage the order in which various disciplines will systemically design collaborative maps. Hale (2008) points out,

> If curriculum mapping is a districtwide initiative it is recommended that *one* discipline be selected as the first districtwide *focus*. . . . The selection of a districtwide discipline focus does *not* mean that only those teaching the discipline participate in the mapping process. *Everyone maps.* All disciplines will eventually have a turn at being *the* focus. Every teacher needs to personally internalize (a) the mapping process; (b) how to write a quality map; (c) recording the map elements within a mapping system; and (d) using a mapping system's data retrieval features to drive curriculum decision making. (p. 21)

Hale continues,

> Selecting an initial districtwide discipline to begin the process of ensuring a spiraled curriculum void of gaps, repetitions, and absences will have design implications. For example, while elementary teachers are only mapping mathematics, middle school and high school teachers will have some teachers mapping mathematics and others mapping various disciplines. Therefore, it may take four to five years to vertically map and align the collective disciplines of mathematics, science, social studies, and language arts since the elementary teachers are at a slight disadvantage. To expedite the vertical-articulation process once teachers have internalized how to design and write maps, some learning organizations have elementary teachers divide up the yet-to-be-mapped disciplines and each grade level designs. (p. 21)

Everyone maps means everyone is involved and engaged in collegial curriculum work that eventually results in curriculum maps as the by-products of collaborative and individual work. For example, one district's special services director, based on input from his special education teachers, chose to have special education teachers add modifications and accommodations for specific students (using students' initials) to the appropriate general education Projected/Diary Maps. The special education teachers were mapping even though they did not have individual maps. They were a part of each school site's by-products by working closely with the general education teachers to document the agreed-upon modifications and accommodation, which served as an ongoing and accumulative database for this student population and was easily accessible using their district's mapping-system search feature.

On occasion, usually in smaller school districts, the curriculum mapping coordinator may be a teacher placed on special assignment. If this is the case, the teacher must be (1) cognizant of central-office protocols and procedures; (2) recognized as a respected leader by both district and school-site administrators as well as teachers in all school sites; (3) strong in one's ability to coordinate and manage the various curriculum mapping leadership teams and developed strategic plans; and (4) able to communicate effectively the components and complexities of mapping to district and school-site administrators, teachers, school board members, and the community. Regardless of who is designated as the curriculum mapping coordinator, establishing and supporting teacher leadership is imperative. This begins by establishing the curriculum mapping cadre to gain insight and initial understanding of the process and begin to outline the large and small tasks necessary for implementing the initiative. The curriculum mapping cadre will then participate in the prologue alongside the curriculum mapping cabinet members and, eventually, the curriculum mapping councils.

Wiles (2009), reflecting on why curriculum initiatives break down, mentions that "one of the major errors of many curriculum improvement efforts is to plan without involving others . . . Curriculum leadership is to promote such collaboration for success" (p. 16).

In a medium-sized district the central-office administrators were not aware of the systemic nature of mapping. They decided to first implement curriculum mapping only at the elementary level. They did so without first establishing and training a curriculum mapping cabinet. The next academic year, curriculum mapping was introduced to the administrators and teachers in the middle schools. Because there was no systemic administrative and teacher-leadership accountability, the curriculum mapping process began to fade quickly in the elementary schools.

When the initiative was introduced to the high school at the onset of the third implementation year, the initiative had lost its footing at both the elementary schools and middle schools. While there were a few administrators and teachers who found curriculum mapping valuable, there was not enough buy-in to build systemic capacity. The initiative ultimately failed because there had been no initial district strategic planning or establishing systemic leadership and teacher ownership before the initiative was formally introduced.

Empowering Teacher Leadership

While the curriculum mapping cabinet should include a curriculum mapping coordinator, cadre members, curriculum directors, a technology director, all principals, and teacher leaders from each school site, the majority of the cabinet members need to be classroom teachers (Hale, 2008; Jacobs, 1997). The selection process for choosing teachers requires thoughtful planning because personalities and collegial abilities greatly affect how a leadership team operates (Wiles, 2009). It is wise to balance the members' strengths. A mix of inquisitive, logical, analytical, and reflective thinkers is recommended.

Collectively, this combination represents a realistic balance of the teachers in all the schools in a district. It is recommended that one or more union or teacher-association representatives be cabinet members as questions may come up concerning official requisites regarding time management, empowering teachers, and legalities as the district strategic plan is developed. As the curriculum mapping cabinet begins its prologue, numerous questions will be posed as members draft the strategic plan. All questions should be filtered through the district's created or reversioned vision and mission statements.

The following questions are intended to stimulate thinking and generate decision-making conversations. When answering these or any questions posed, it is important to address them through the lens of providing administrative-support structures that allow and encourage teachers to become the leaders and caretakers of the initiative.

How Is This Initiative Going to Lead to Improving Learning and Teaching?

The central part of this question is *going to lead to.* Curriculum mapping is not a quick fix (Hale, 2008). It is a systemic model that continuously addresses curriculum design and instructional practice. While these two educational facets can be viewed independently, there ultimately is synergy between them. When the two are triangulated with assessment data, the ability for teachers to make informed, collegial curriculum decisions increases and positively impacts student learning.

Because curriculum mapping is based on establishing a continuous curriculum work process, it improves student learning gradually and steadily over a number of years. The ultimate purpose of implementing and sustaining curriculum mapping is to improve each student as a learner and one's self as a learner-educator. Jacobs (2004) notes,

> Success in a mapping program is defined by two specific outcomes: measurable improvement in student performance in the targeted areas, and the institutionalization of mapping as a process for ongoing curriculum and assessment reviews. (p. 2)

Necessary shifts in thinking and actions will not happen overnight. All administrators, directors, and teacher leaders must constantly support and promote the initiative in a positive light. All stakeholders must not have an *"end product"* mindset or a *"let's get this done by tomorrow"* mentality. When teachers realize that professional learning time focused on strategic curriculum and instruction questions that lead to deep, introspective conversations *is* mapping, having curriculum maps in a mapping system accessible by all simply provides the evidence of those conversations and collegial decision making.

How Will Curriculum Mapping Become the Overarching Process for How We Conduct Our Curriculum Work Districtwide and in Each School Site?

Jacobs (2004) uses the term *hub* rather than *overarching process* when taking into consideration the systemic nature of mapping. She shares, "Curriculum mapping not only provides us with a hub for focusing our current efforts, but also provides us with a tool to launch curriculum plans for our students' futures" (p. 137). The center of a wagon wheel is called the hub. Curriculum mapping needs to become the center point from which all curriculum-related initiatives extend. The related-initiative spokes branching off the hub connect to the outer rim, which represents the teachers and students continuously engaged in the learning process (see Figure 3.1).

Figure 3.1   Curriculum Mapping: The Curriculum Work Hub

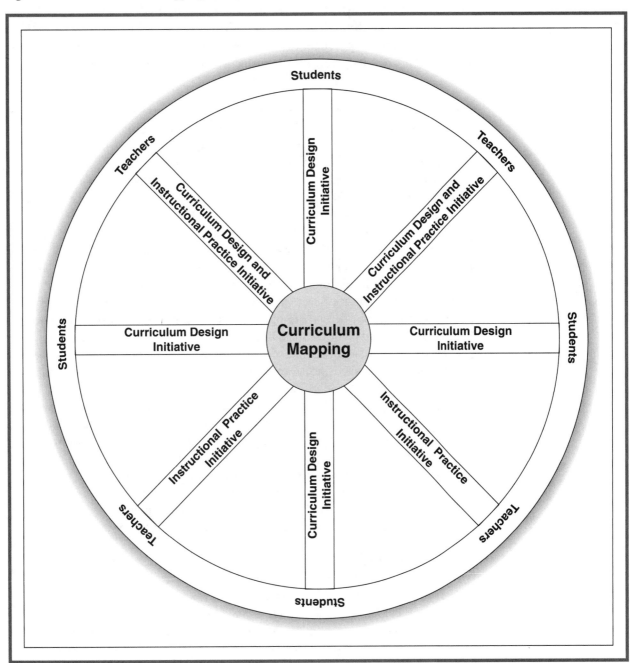

It is not uncommon for administrators and teachers to view any new curriculum-related initiative with caution. To commit to any initiative means buy-in both personally and professionally, and emotionally and academically. When districts or schools try to simultaneously implement too many initiatives without allowing any one initiative to become embedded into the culture before starting a new initiative, sustainability is unlikely. Adding curriculum mapping to this type of initiative scenario affects its potential for improving student learning and achievement.

The curriculum mapping coordinator and cadre members need to spend time up front analyzing the effectiveness of the district and school sites' current initiatives. With input from teachers and administrators, there may be found one or more ineffective initiatives that can be terminated. It is also important to determine and clarify whether each existing initiative is focused on curriculum design, curriculum practice, or a combination of both. While brainstorming, some find it helpful to record the results on a wagon-wheel graphic organizer.

To encourage buy-in, an elementary school curriculum mapping council decided to conduct a three-dimensional wagon-wheel activity. The faculty met in the library and sat at each table in mixed-grade-level groups. The council members began the meeting by asking teachers to share review points from their last meeting. The council members then reminded them of the current meeting's focus, which was to continue to shift their thinking and view curriculum mapping as the center of all curriculum work. They began the wagon-wheel activity by handing out a sentence strip with a current initiative's name written on it in black lettering to a group of three to four teachers. In all, they handed out nine curriculum focused initiative strips. In the center of each table were two colored markers. Red represented curriculum design and blue represented instructional practice. Each group was asked to discuss the initiative on their strip and decide if the initiative's focus was curriculum design, curriculum practice, or both. When the teachers in each group came to agreement, they wrote the group's response on their strip using the appropriate color.

When everyone had their initiative strip labeled, the groups were asked to walk around the room and share their findings with other groups. After a few minutes, the council members asked everyone to gather in front of a bulletin board that was covered with butcher paper and had an outer wide rim labeled *teachers—students—teachers—students* in a repeated pattern. Each group was asked to staple their initiative strip from the outer rim to the center so that all the inner ends of the initiative strips met in the center. The large group backed up a few steps to take in the entire visual representation. A council member held up a large paper plate with the words *curriculum mapping* written on it in bold letters. She asked for a volunteer teacher to stand near the bulletin board with her. She handed the plate and a stapler to the teacher and asked him to hold on to both, and the large group would let him know what he needed to do in a moment.

She posed the question, "If curriculum mapping is meant to be the hub of all the curriculum work that takes place in this school and throughout the district, where does the curriculum mapping plate need to be stapled?" The response was voiced simultaneously, "In the center." The volunteer teacher stapled the plate in the center where all the initiatives converged. The teachers stood back and contemplated what was now displayed on the bulletin board. After a few moments, the council members asked everyone to return to the tables. To close the activity, the teachers were directed to share their personal and collaborative thoughts related to the wagon-wheel display and how the display created or expanded the understanding that curriculum mapping is not one more curriculum thing; instead, it is the hub of all their curriculum work.

Visuals and analogies aid in supporting learning and understanding. Nonetheless, even when these types of learning aids are incorporated into trainings and meetings, it will take time before all teachers will truly perceive curriculum mapping as the hub. It may feel like it is *something more we have to do* for the first few years until mapping becomes the natural manner in which a district and each school conducts its curriculum work.

Sometimes in medium-sized to larger districts, district-level support is provided by placing teachers on special assignment as full-time curriculum mapping facilitators. If one or more teachers are designated curriculum mapping facilitators, they are often considered central-office personnel even if housed at a school site or sites. Curriculum mapping facilitators work closely with the curriculum mapping coordinator, cadre, and cabinet members to aid in planning, implementing, and monitoring the district strategic plan. They are often assigned to specific schools to work alongside the principal and, when in place, the curriculum mapping council members help to carry forward the initiative when introduced to all teachers.

If the support for designating teachers as districtwide curriculum mapping facilitators is not feasible due to budgetary limitations, each school site will need to depend on its curriculum mapping cabinet and council members to serve as school-site facilitators. Regardless of whether facilitators are full time, part time, or if facilitation is carried out by school-site cabinet or council members, the district and school-level administrators must support these teachers as leaders with ample personal-learning opportunities, so they can, in turn, provide the necessary training and support to other teachers as learners, curriculum designers, and fellow curriculum leaders (Hale, 2008; Jacobs, 2004; Jacobs & Johnson, 2009).

From the onset of a curriculum mapping initiative and each year thereafter, connections between and among multiple curriculum work initiatives need to be embedded into the district strategic plans and each school site's action plan.

How Can Curriculum Mapping Aid in Meeting Requisites for Our Students With Special Needs, Gifted Students, and English Language Learners?

Many districts have a director of special services, or pupil services, who manages and supports the needs of students requiring special services. He or she must interpret and comply with federal and state regulations pertaining to these students.

It is recommended that this person be an active part of the curriculum mapping cadre or cabinet in the beginning stages of collective learning. This enables him or her to work alongside the cadre and cabinet members to determine how to best blend various curriculum mapping components and processes with the curriculum work engaged in by the special services and with the general education teachers.

It is recommended that special services teachers become members of the curriculum mapping cabinet and councils as well. As they learn about curriculum mapping, they can aid the director in determining how being involved in the curriculum mapping process will aid their students. This allows them to work alongside general education teachers instead of feeling like mapping is merely another documentation requisite, as their students already have individual educational plans and other accountability documentation.

Regardless of a student's special services adaptations, his or her learning needs are initially diagnosed through an extensive comparative analysis with the general education curriculum. Because of this, both general education teachers and special services teachers need to work collegially to design the vertically articulated general education curriculum. When a special services teacher needs to analyze the academic or related needs of a particular student, having instant access to the planned and operational curriculum database available within the curriculum maps in the selected mapping system proves beneficial.

Soon after the passage of Response to Intervention (RTI) legislation, a district's curriculum mapping cabinet chose to add the imminent implications to the next cabinet meeting's agenda. The district had been mapping for six years and had Essential Maps, Consensus Maps, and Projected/Diary Maps in most disciplines. The cadre's director of special services pointed out that her staff and teachers had begun conversations focused on the implications of RTI, knowing it would need to be implemented and embedded within the district and each school site's curriculum work.

As the meeting progressed, the director and special education teacher cabinet members presented highlights of the legislation and shared their collaboratively brainstormed ideas for how the curriculum maps may be useful as a form of data collection and analysis when focusing on students struggling with their learning based on RTI definitions.

One special education teacher said that the district's Essential Maps and each school site's Consensus Maps are technically where all learners, including Tier 1 learners, should be successful students with little or no intervention assistance. Tier 2 and Tier 3 learners, who need more specific intervention strategies and activities, are ultimately expected to be transformed into Tier 1 independent students. She said that one idea the special education teachers thought of was using the activities/strategies element field in the Essential Maps and Consensus Maps to collegially determine and record a variety of tiered activities and strategies to provide aid for the general education teachers who are also accountable for servicing these students.

The director and the special education teachers orally synthesized the thoughts discussed by the cabinet members in small-group and large-group discussions. The cabinet members agreed that the ramifications of RTI needed to be explored in more detail before any systemic decisions could be made. They decided to present what had been expressed in the meeting at their respective schools during curriculum mapping council meetings and follow up with a faculty meeting and an online survey. Based on the feedback from teachers and administrators during the meetings and from those participating in the survey, a districtwide special education meeting took place. Their recommendations were presented to the curriculum mapping cabinet and were unanimously accepted.

The special education teachers worked closely with the general education teachers in their respective school sites to determine the tier-level activities and strategies best suited for specific content and skills included in the Consensus Maps. The general education and special education teachers then began to utilize the activities and strategies in the classrooms and discuss their effectiveness for individual students during RTI meetings.

How Will Technology Services Be Involved in Our Curriculum Mapping Initiative?

Technology has become embedded in a district's operational functions and instructional functions. For a curriculum mapping initiative, teachers will eventually be involved in conducting curriculum work using a selected online mapping system. All teachers and administrators will need a user account. Commercial mapping systems have an annual subscription cost per user. Hale (2008) mentions that "the communication device—a 21st-century tool—is a specific-to-mapping system, an interactive, integrated database of maps" (p. 217). Continual advances in curriculum mapping systems and compatible software programs have accelerated the ability of teachers to focus on the triangulation of curriculum data, assessment data, and classroom practices to improve student learning (Kallick & Colosimo, 2009). Therefore, the value of a mapping system as a worthwhile curriculum tool far outweighs the cost of annual subscriptions.

School board approval may be necessary for the initial and ongoing funding. Likewise, to support the use of an online mapping system, purchasing relational technology may be necessary, such as replacing older computers, purchasing more computers to enable ease of computer access, or increasing adequate districtwide or school-site-specific bandwidth.

If a district's technology director or supervisor is not officially a member of the curriculum mapping cadre or cabinet, he or she should be a part of the mapping-system selection process as technical questions will need to be addressed. Since this person may not be familiar with the big picture of mapping, it may be wise to ask him or her to sit in on some of the initial curriculum mapping cadre or cabinet training to gain a basic understanding and familiarity with mapping terminology.

While the days of paper-and-pencil curriculum maps are obsolete, if a mapping system cannot yet be purchased due to budgetary constraints, teachers can begin the process of writing practice map units using a word-processing document until subscriptions can be purchased. If the time becomes longer than desired and teachers begin the design process using word-processing software, the maps need to be frequently accessed and used to aid in curriculum work collegial conversations and decision-making meetings. With the eventual purchase of an online mapping system, some mapping software companies will aid in transferring the word-processed maps to the selected mapping system.

All mapping systems have the ability to embed sites, streaming videos, documents, and images into curriculum maps. If teachers are not yet comfortable with the ongoing advancements in technology and tools, there may be a need for supporting teachers in this area through inservices, workshops, or mentoring.

A technology director diligently worked to promote the use of 21st-century technology in all classrooms in her district. She was able to procure a *Classrooms for the Future* grant that placed a substantial amount of software and hardware into the hands of teachers and students in all three of the district's high schools. The grant provided web-based training designed by the State Department of Education.

As teachers moved through the training modules, they began to utilize the various hardware components, such as whiteboards and clickers, for instructional purposes. The instructional hardware enabled teachers to use video, slides, and manipulatives during instructional and assessment phases of student learning. Student active participation benefits were immediate due to the formative-assessment feedback capabilities that the software and hardware provided.

The teachers involved in the grant met not only to discuss ways in which the software and hardware generated a powerful, engaging learning environment, but to determine the best placement of the instructional technology information within their curriculum maps. After collegial dialogue and some experimentation, they found it beneficial to include the most successful use of the available instruction technology in the practice-related elements including assessments/evaluations, activities/strategies, and resources.

At a subsequent curriculum mapping cabinet meeting, the technology director shared that due to the accessibility of all teachers' maps in the mapping system, many of the middle schools' and elementary schools' teachers were showing great interest in learning more about the use of instructional technology and tools. They had seen and viewed the attached technology and tools included in the high school teachers' maps.

What Are the Budgetary Implications Related to a Curriculum Mapping Initiative?

Budgetary-support considerations will extend beyond providing annual mapping-system subscriptions and ancillary support, such as computer availability, bandwidth, and ongoing professional development and assistance. As the director of financial services or business manager is often not a member of the curriculum mapping cadre, he or she needs to be well informed of the short- and long-term budgetary needs related to a curriculum mapping initiative.

While the budgetary needs will be greater in the first one to five years, there will always be financial-support considerations. At the onset of a curriculum mapping initiative, administrators and teacher leaders, and eventually all teachers, will need support that may include (1) consulting fees; (2) in-district training fees; (3) support materials or services, including book or media purchases, substitute teachers, and summer work days; and (4) out-of-district curriculum mapping or curriculum-related conferences or workshops. It is important to consider all potential operational costs when developing the district strategic plan and each school site's action plan.

While some may consider *time* an indirect budgetary consideration, time will eventually affect ongoing planning and sustaining of the initiative. After curriculum mapping has reached all teachers, and all teachers are asked to be actively engaged in curriculum design, the most common request is more time for working collegially and dialoguing horizontally and vertically within school sites and throughout the district.

The caveat to this is that teachers do not want to lose student-contact time to meet. Many school districts reconsider the master calendar and discuss time-support options, such as adding days to the academic year set aside for full-day, curriculum work professional development opportunities for teachers to work on aspects of mapping, such as designing or revising maps; triangulating assessment data, maps, and instructional practice; or learning new or extending understanding of curriculum-related initiatives. While this may not be a necessity when mapping is first introduced, it is a consideration that needs to be proactively considered, explored, and discussed by district administrators.

Strategic Planning Considerations

District administrators need to ensure district and school-site administrators and teacher leaders are knowledgeable and confident in being able to strategically plan the implementation phases as well as serve as catalysts, trainers, and supporters for each school site's teachers and support staff. If the district strategic plan includes bringing the entire district together for a professional development day, it is important that teachers and administrators are adequately prepared for the speaker or speakers presenting the keynote address and, if included, breakout sessions. Feedback from these sessions is crucial for informing the curriculum mapping cadre and cabinet if the strategic plan can move forward as outlined or if modifications to any phase needs to take place.

During the prologue and first year of full implementation, it is recommended that the curriculum mapping cabinet meet monthly or bimonthly (Hale, 2008). During the prologue, the cabinet members will be learners and strategic planners. During the first year of full implementation when all teachers are involved in the learning process, the cabinet meeting focuses shift to supporting; troubleshooting; and, when appropriate, modifying the strategic plans. As the years progress the curriculum cabinet members will meet less regularly and each school-site council will meet monthly or bimonthly to build teacher-leadership capacity.

A large district conducted a two-year prologue involving the assistant superintendent of curriculum and an eight-member cadre. The cadre included district-level administrators and respected teacher leaders. They worked diligently to draft a manageable systemic strategic plan, including step-by-step implementation phases. At the end of the second year, the cadre conducted a three-day basic mapping training for the newly formed curriculum mapping cabinet that consisted of 45 teacher leaders and 15 school-site principals.

During the next school year, the cadre continued training the curriculum mapping cabinet members while simultaneously starting to share information districtwide so that all teachers could begin laying a foundation of common terminology and mapping language. By the beginning of the second half of the school year, each school site's curriculum mapping council was formed. Training of the next level of leadership took place during monthly school-site meetings led by a cabinet member. There were also bimonthly, half-day districtwide trainings that brought together the collective councils' 175 teacher and school-site-administrator members. The strategic plans were monitored and adjusted somewhat during the first two years of implementation. The adjustments did not strongly affect the next implementation phase, which began at the end of the second year.

The curriculum mapping council members were to take on a stronger leadership role at their school sites. They would be responsible for directly training and supporting all teachers as they learned (1) the basic concepts of curriculum mapping, (2) the ability to independently use the selected mapping system, and (3) the ability to articulate the short- and long-term goals and purposes of implementing and sustaining curriculum mapping. A full-day transition training, known as the *"pass the leadership baton day"* by the curriculum mapping cadre and cabinet, was planned in detail. During the meeting day, each cadre member would be responsible for sharing specific information related to the new level of responsibility the council members would have during the next school year and beyond.

On the actual training day, one of the cadre members held up a large leadership-capacity flowchart that was originally presented during their initial trainings. The top of the flowchart listed the curriculum mapping coordinator followed underneath by the cadre members, the cabinet members, the council members, and lastly the remaining teachers throughout the district.

He mentioned that, for the past two years, the chart flowed in a downward fashion considering learning and leading. He then turned the chart sideways and conveyed that for the next school year, the leadership teams would transition toward each school site's council members being equally responsible for continuing implementation to reach sustainability.

He turned the chart one more time so the bottom of the chart was now at the top. He concluded by sharing, "When the leadership fully flips and all our teachers are at the top, we know we have arrived because we in this room will have become servant-leaders. Our role will be to support and ensure teachers are confident and able to continually lead the necessary improvements in our students' learning and our teaching through the lens that curriculum mapping is our hub for conducting all our curriculum work."

CONCLUSION

Curriculum mapping is a multifaceted initiative. It is intended to become the hub of a district and its schools' curriculum and curriculum-related initiatives. All stakeholders must therefore have a clear understanding and perspective of how various initiatives fit together. Implementation is not only a multiyear process, it is a multilayered process. District-level administrators must be cognizant of this initiative's need for strategic preplanning as well as an operational roll-out in step-by-step phases that ask teachers to be leaders from the onset.

Critical considerations include defining administrative and teacher-leadership roles and responsibilities, creating a well-thought-out strategic plan with the ability to be flexible and responsive to teachers as learners and curriculum designers, ensuring the structure and process can be sustained beyond any one administrative leader or academic year, and proactively concerning communication with and among all stakeholders.

While a curriculum mapping initiative may at first appear to be top down, when studied closely it is a bottom up and teacher-led initiative regarding building leadership capacity. Reaching sustainability requires administrative servant-leadership that empowers and supports teachers to be the curriculum designers and practitioners who collectively improve student achievement through ongoing large- and small-scale curriculum work refinement. Jacobs (2004) notes, "Making mapping work requires patience, persistence, and knowledge" (p. 8). When a curriculum mapping initiative is started with a thorough prologue and followed by manageable implementation phases and tasks, there will be no epilogue (Jacobs, 2004).

REVIEW QUESTIONS

While you may not be in a district-level administrator position, the information shared in this chapter is important to all who are responsible for planning and implementing a curriculum mapping initiative. Personally reflect on each question or exercise in preparation to share your thoughts with a colleague or small group.

1. Who is or will be the curriculum mapping coordinator? Is this person a district-level administrator or a teacher on special assignment? If you think your district needs two curriculum mapping coordinators, who would the second coordinator be? Would these two people both be responsible for the same focuses or tasks, or will they subdivide the responsibilities?

2. Who will be on the curriculum mapping cadre? Since it is recommended that this leadership team be composed of a mixture of administrators and teacher leaders, who do you suggest be involved from district-level administration? Who do you recommend for teacher leaders? Will these teachers be placed on special assignment or be expected to teach full

time? Will there be a monetary or other type of compensation offered to these teachers if they are expected to be teaching full time and taking on added responsibilities?

3. How long do you plan on allowing the curriculum mapping cadre to be learners before asking them to draft a strategic plan? Will the curriculum mapping cabinet also be involved in the strategic planning decision-making process?

4. How will the curriculum mapping coordinators and/or curriculum mapping cadre plan to initially inform school-site administrators, board members, and any other pertinent stakeholders of the intent of starting a curriculum mapping initiative? When do you perceive principals will need to initiate or aid in the selection process for selecting curriculum mapping cabinet members from their school sites? How long do you think the curriculum mapping cabinet will need to meet before they are confident to take their learning and planned implementation to the school-site level?

5. When do you perceive curriculum mapping councils will be established when considering the timeline necessary for conducting the prologue involving the curriculum mapping cadre and cabinet members? When and how will these leadership teams share the initial strategic plan to each school site and all teachers?

6. How do you perceive yourself supporting teachers as leaders, both districtwide and school-site leadership, to build capacity in the teachers taking ownership of the curriculum mapping initiative?

7. As components of a curriculum mapping initiative may need approval of noncurriculum mapping leadership members (e.g., school board, financial officer), how will district-level administrators inform the board members of the strategic-plan supports needed initially and in an ongoing manner?

8. How will technology needs (e.g., annual subscriptions to mapping system, bandwidth) affect implementation and sustainability? What role do you see technology services (e.g., information technology; instructional 21st-century tools coaches) playing in the preplanning and implementation phases?

9. Create a wagon-wheel graphic organizer by recording the name of each current or upcoming district curriculum-related initiative on a separate spoke. Label each initiative with a focus on curriculum design, instructional practice, or both. Exchange graphic organizers with your colleague or colleagues. Did you label each initiative with the same focus? If different, explore why your collective perceptions are not the same.

10. How will the number of current initiatives affect the implementation of your curriculum mapping initiative? Are there any ineffective initiatives that could be terminated?

What Should Curriculum Directors Consider to Support Teacher Leadership?

A good director creates an environment, which gives the actor the encouragement to fly.

—Kevin Bacon

When creating a film, all those involved must work harmoniously to ensure the final production conveys the intended message. Directors aid the cast and crew in visualizing the script and guide them to reach a shared vision. Directors are often known for their ability or inability to establish a collaborative atmosphere on the set. As Kevin Bacon shares, a good director encourages the actors to fly. Alan Parker (2009), a founding member of the Director's Guild of Great Britain, notes, "A great movie evolves when everybody has the same vision in their heads."

Just as a movie director plays a significant role in supporting the success of the intended production, curriculum directors play a significant role in supporting the implementation and sustainability of a curriculum mapping initiative.

CURRICULUM POSITIONS

The considerations in Chapter 3 focused on district administrators' support and encouragement, which includes a curriculum director if a district recognizes this position as central-office employment. It is recommended that curriculum directors are members of the curriculum mapping cadre or cabinet and are directly involved in the preplanning and prologue phases. Their unique perspectives regarding curriculum design and instructional practice at both the district and school-site levels make their input valuable in establishing curriculum mapping as an ongoing curriculum process (Figure 4.1).

The titles included in the first column of Figure 4.1 are used throughout this chapter. While curriculum position titles may vary by district, the responsibilities for each position are often similar. The responsibilities included in the last column of Figure 4.1 are not meant to be exhaustive. They represent the necessity for connectivity and continuity between administrators and teacher leaders who will need to work alongside teachers to establish, support, and sustain the curriculum mapping initiative. All school-site curriculum positions need to be members of either the curriculum mapping cabinet or respective school's curriculum mapping council, which may extend beyond those featured in Figure 4.1.

Figure 4.1   Curriculum Positions and Responsibilities

Curriculum Position	Alternative Titles	Responsibilities
District Level		
Assistant Superintendent of Curriculum	• Curriculum Director	• Oversees *all* curriculum-related design and practice, including support services and assessment or measurement accountability throughout the district • Reports to *superintendent* and *board members* • Organizes meeting focuses regarding design and practice based on administrative and teacher input as well as *district* strategic plan and *school-site* action plans • Conducts or secures training to support best practices in instructional delivery • Ensures resources are available to deliver or enhance learning expectations
Curriculum Director	• Curriculum Supervisor • Curriculum Coordinator • Program Director • Director of _____ (e.g., Special Education, English Language Learners)	• Oversees *one or more* disciplines' design and practice, support services, and assessment or measurement throughout entire district • Reports to *Assistant Superintendent of Curriculum* (Note: If there is no Assistant Superintendent of Curriculum, curriculum director reports to Superintendent and Board members) • Organizes meeting focuses regarding design and practice based on administrative and teacher input as well as *district* strategic plan and *school-site* action plans • Conducts or secures training to support best practices in instructional delivery • Ensures resources are available to deliver or enhance learning expectations

Curriculum Position	Alternative Titles	Responsibilities
		School-Site Level
Curriculum Coach	• Instructional Leader • Curriculum Liaison • Content-Area Lead Educator	• *School-site* expert in design and practice for *one* or *more* disciplines • Reports to *Principal* and *Curriculum Director* • Organizes meeting focuses regarding design and practice based on teacher input as well as *school-site* action plan and *district* strategic plan • Conducts training to support best practices in instructional delivery • Ensures resources are available to deliver or enhance learning expectations
Department Chair	• Team Leader	• *Discipline-specific* expert • Reports to *Principal* and *Curriculum Director* • Organizes meeting focuses regarding design and practice based on teacher input as well as *school-site* action plan and *district* strategic plan • Serves as liaison between teachers and principal • May plan budgetary allotment to ensure resources are available to deliver or enhance learning expectations
Grade-Level Representative	• Team Leader	• Expert in *one* or *more* disciplines • Reports to *Principal* and *Curriculum Director* • Organizes meeting focuses regarding design and practice based on teacher input as well as *school-site* action plan and *district* strategic plan • Serves as liaison between teachers and principal • May plan budgetary allotment to ensure resources are available to deliver or enhance learning expectations

Curriculum Directors

A curriculum director may be responsible for one or more disciplines or oversee a specialized area such as special services, assessments and testing, or technology integration. Curriculum directors need to work alongside district administrators and principals to ensure a consistent message is conveyed for the vision, mission, and annual goals of the district's curriculum mapping strategic plans as well as each school site's action plan. When curriculum mapping has been fully implemented and is moving toward or has reached sustainability, curriculum directors' abilities to continue to support curriculum mapping as the hub for curriculum work aids in supporting teachers as curriculum leaders.

Five years ago, a district implemented a curriculum mapping initiative. While some schools embraced mapping more strongly than others, all schools were involved in collegially designing curriculum and using curriculum maps to review and analyze ongoing learning and instructional needs. During the second year of implementation, the counselors districtwide began the

(Continued)

(Continued)

process of collaboratively designing a K–12 social-behavior curriculum based on state standards, ancillary standards, and previous work accomplished independently in several school sites.

From the onset, the director of special services was present at the counselors' work sessions to support and encourage their collegial work. She was periodically asked questions, gave advice, and shared her thoughts when appropriate. Besides being asked to help coordinate meeting dates and locations, the counselors asked her to arrange a presentation time for the school board to inform them and the community of how the collegial process was going to produce a curriculum that would better serve students as citizens in school and beyond.

During their design process, the counselors conducted a series of seven-step review cycles involving teachers from all grade levels to aid in analyzing the drafted Essential Maps. After a series of additions and modifications based on teacher feedback, the social behavior Essential Maps were put into practice to guide learning and instruction. Approximately two years later, a resources task force consisting of the director of special services, teachers, and counselors was created to reflect on selecting local, regional, and national guest speakers to support the social-behavior curriculum.

One national speaker who was approved to visit was scheduled to conduct one-hour presentations at each school site over a two-day period. The speaker was Darrell Scott, father of Rachel Scott, the first victim of the shooting rampage at Columbine High School. Mr. Scott explained to students, teachers, administrators, and caregivers that from the tragedy of that day hope and renewal were born. He mentioned that many were taking on *Rachel's Challenge,* which inspires people of all ages to start a chain reaction of doing good for a few, which will turn into doing good for many. He and his family hope to inspire students to bring positive change to their schools in the way they treat others.

Two weeks after Mr. Scott's presentations, the director of special services received an e-mail from one of the elementary schools asking if she could meet with a group of teachers and the school counselor. The e-mail did not give specifics for the meeting except to say they were excited about a mapping idea. When she first arrived at the school, she went to the front office to speak with the principal. She asked if he knew what the meeting was about. He smiled, paused, and said, "I think our teachers are finally getting what we have wanted curriculum mapping to become all along."

She pondered his comment as she walked to the conference room where the teachers and counselor were waiting. They expressed that they were inspired by Mr. Scott's presentation and had been exploring the idea of designing a K–5 curriculum based on the program materials they had ordered through the Rachel's Challenge foundation. They explained their thoughts for how to design the learning using their map format and mapping system. They expressed excitement about the potential of integrating this curriculum work with the students' social behavior learning expectations.

The director acknowledged their ownership and leadership while asking what she could do to best support them in their efforts. They wanted to know if other teachers and counselors in the district may be interested in collaboratively working on this curriculum project. She said that she would speak with the principals and assistant superintendent of curriculum about planning an open-forum, after-school meeting for those who may be interested in participating districtwide. She thanked them for contacting her and promised to send all of them an e-mail in a few days, after the next administrators' meeting. As she left the building, she reflected on what the principal had said to her. She now understood why he smiled as he expressed his thoughts.

Back at the district office, she stopped to talk to the assistant superintendent of curriculum. She told him how pleased she was with what occurred during her meeting at the elementary school. She commented that for the first time in the five years of implementing curriculum mapping she had experienced teachers and a counselor who were proactively responding to a curriculum need with *mapping in mind*. She informed him of the details of the meeting and the promise she had made them.

She left the office feeling encouraged. Her role in continuing to support all teachers and support staff in grass-roots curriculum efforts was just the beginning of the district's advanced mapping experiences that would aid in ensuring and expanding the best learning environments for all students.

A student experiences his or her K–12 learning journey one grade and one building at a time. Jacobs (1997) states, "if there are gaps [in learning] among teachers within buildings, there are virtual Grand Canyons among buildings in a district" (p. 3). When supporting teachers as design leaders in the collegial, systemic process of eliminating curriculum gaps or canyons, curriculum directors must contemplate how to best merge multifaceted group dynamics that include

- a range of discipline-specific expertise within and among school levels (e.g., elementary school, middle school, high school);
- mixed generations of teachers (e.g., Baby Boomers, Generation X, Millennials);
- potential variations of standard statements' interpretations (e.g., what a standard statement represents to one teacher may be something entirely different for another teacher teaching the same grade level); and
- when appropriate, multiple like schools coming to agreement on the essential curriculum regardless of what school a student attends (e.g., six elementary schools that feed into two middle schools, which feed into one high school).

Contemplating group dynamics is no small task. It is recommended that curriculum directors work with principals and teacher leaders to address this concern during the prologue as well as throughout the implementation phases. Considerations related to group dynamics affect the formation of the curriculum mapping cabinet, school-site councils, and when appropriate, school-site or districtwide task forces.

Because curriculum directors are not present daily in every building, they need to communicate frequently with each principal and teacher leaders during each phase of implementation. Working alongside teacher leaders to establish or expand each school's collaborative curriculum work while maintaining an aspen grove mentality and focus is vital for sustaining a curriculum mapping initiative.

When implementing a mapping initiative, curriculum directors and teacher leaders must constantly remind all teachers that, in creating collaborative curriculum maps, to first focus on curriculum design; second, on instructional practices to support the articulated design; and third, on the synergy between the two.

School-Site Teacher Leadership

School-site *curriculum teacher leaders* include curriculum coaches, department chairs, and grade-level representatives. They are often responsible for ensuring the fulfillment of one or more initiatives' annual goals or expectations due to their expertise, influence, and leverage with the teachers in their charge. Curriculum teacher leaders need to be members of the curriculum mapping cabinet or curriculum mapping councils. Their input when developing the district strategic plan as well as their respective school site's action plan is invaluable. These teachers also play a significant role in the train-the-trainer model by aiding all teachers in their school sites to comprehend the complexities of the curriculum mapping process (Jacobs, 1997, 2004).

When the curriculum mapping cadre begins to select potential members for the curriculum mapping cabinet, the assistant superintendent of curriculum and the curriculum director or directors need to consult with each school's principal concerning potential cabinet teacher leaders, including but not limited to curriculum coaches, department chairs, and grade-level representatives to create the following districtwide leadership representation:

- Balance of disciplines and special services representation;
- Group dynamics related to thinking styles and personalities;
- Mix of young and mature teachers' curriculum and cultural perspectives; and
- Political considerations, such as union representation.

Similar teacher-leader representation conversations will need to take place when the curriculum mapping cabinet members begin to form their respective school site's curriculum mapping council. If any curriculum teacher leaders were not included in the curriculum mapping cabinet, they will be members of the curriculum mapping council.

All teacher leaders involved in the curriculum mapping cabinet and councils must be willing to take risks as there is much to learn at the onset of a curriculum mapping initiative. This is not to say that everyone on the curriculum leadership teams must have bought in 100% from the onset. Often, when one or two cautious teacher leaders are purposefully included in the initial learning and planning process, they evolve into the strongest advocates. This is important as these teachers are often leaders at their school sites.

When a curriculum director holds districtwide discipline-specific meetings (e.g., all the elementary mathematics coaches) to discuss ongoing or upcoming initiatives' implications, he or she sets the tone for infusing the use of curriculum maps, the mapping system, and the review process into studying or solving curriculum concerns or problems. The sooner curriculum teacher leaders can envision, explain, and provide examples for curriculum mapping being the hub of all curriculum work, the better for all teachers since they work closely with them on an ongoing basis.

Curriculum teacher leaders may currently report to the principal and curriculum directors with a stronger emphasis on curriculum practice than on curriculum design. When implementing curriculum mapping, curriculum directors need to foster a strong focus on teacher-created curriculum design followed by a focus on instructional practice. Curriculum directors need to nurture a shift in each curriculum teacher leader's thinking from a focus specifically on his or her school's concerns to include an equal focus on K–12 systemic curriculum design.

When all teachers begin to participate in the mapping process, the curriculum mapping council meetings provide opportunities for the school-site teacher leaders to address concerns or issues that may arise during the implementation phases. While each school will attempt to collaboratively solve their own issues and concerns, if they desire input or suggestions from other school sites, council members who are cabinet members can network during an upcoming curriculum cabinet meeting.

CURRICULUM CONSIDERATIONS

As mentioned previously, curriculum directors and curriculum teacher leaders need to work together to support teachers' use of the ongoing curriculum mapping process, which includes using the maps and the mapping system to make collegial curriculum design and instructional practice decisions.

Mapping the Disciplines

"What should we first map collaboratively?" is a question that is often more complex to answer than initially imagined. Collaborative curriculum design is hard work and takes much more time than is often originally planned. During the collaborative design process, teachers are asked to focus on a three-fold procedure where they

- become extremely analytical and reflective regarding what individual standards are explicitly and implicitly asking of students and dialogue about their varied interpretations until they can reach agreement (i.e., breaking apart the standards);
- determine big ideas and transferable learning as a means to gain understanding; and
- accurately translate the agreed-upon learning expectations into quality-aligned content listings and skill statements in the curriculum maps.

Large quantities of time are needed to draft a discipline's units of study for each grade level or course and to have the units thoroughly reviewed, revised, and reviewed once again horizontally and vertically by the task-force teachers to ensure articulation. It is not uncommon for a districtwide task force to take one or two full-day work weeks to design a discipline's vertically articulated curriculum, such as K–12 Mathematics Essential Maps.

A medium-sized district included dates in the district strategic plan for designing Essential Maps during the summer break. The strategic plan's timeline had 3 separate three-day sessions scheduled to design districtwide maps in mathematics, science, and writing, respectively. The day after Memorial Day, the mathematics Essential Map task force assembled in one of the district's high school's multimedia center to begin their work. The teachers were informed and directed in the procedural steps to complete the design task. They were reminded of the school year work that included K–12 teachers districtwide participating in prioritizing the mathematic standards' strands' indicators first within each school site and then tabulating, analyzing, and reviewing the results among the collective school sites.

The mathematics curriculum director asked with which strand they wanted to begin the process of breaking apart the prioritized standard's indicators based on the predetermined big ideas. The K–8 teachers collectively decided to start with the geometry strand. The high school teachers would begin the process of working on their Essential Maps but not necessarily through units focused specifically on *geometry* based on the standards for high school learning. It took the remainder of day one and the first hour of day two for each grade-level or course team to finish translating the explicit and implicit learning for the broken apart indicators into units within the mapping system. The teachers then began a seven-step review focused on two concerns:

- Are there *gaps, repetitions,* or *absences* in the content or skills aligned to the prioritized standards horizontally or vertically in any of the *geometry* units?
- Does anyone reading any of the drafted units of study have difficulty *accurately interpreting* what is expected of students to know and be able to do based on the content listings or skill statements?

By the time the teachers had completed steps one through five of the review process (collect the data, first read-though, small-group review, large-group comparison, and immediate revision), day two was almost two-thirds over. The teachers acknowledged how beneficial the review process had been and agreed that working through the design process for the next chosen strand, *number and operations,* while there were more standard statements would most likely make the collaborative process go a bit smoother.

They went back to their grade-level or course teams to revise the geometry units as needed based on the review-process collaborative feedback. They then began to work on breaking apart the number-sense strand indicators. Toward the end of day two, the curriculum director asked the teachers to gather together at 3:00 for a debriefing session.

The assistant superintendent of curriculum arrived to listen to the debriefing sessions. After focusing on specifics they felt would make the process more efficient during day three, many teachers said they were glad they had asked to be a part of the task force because they were learning so much more than they thought they would have about their own grade's learning expectations as well as the vertical continuum of their students' learning. One teacher shared that, even though she had been teaching for 21 years, she was learning an entirely new way of thinking about the math curriculum and was looking forward to sharing what she had been learning with her colleagues back at her school site.

The curriculum director lightheartedly inquired, "Well, do you think you all can get the rest of the math strands mapped, reviewed, and revised by tomorrow afternoon?" "No!" the teachers responded in unison. They did not want to rush the process because the process was what was making all their learning agreement so valuable. The director concurred. She reminded the teachers that this was the first time the district had formed a task force to design Essential Maps. She pointed out, "As you know, we only planned three days to accomplish this task. The cadre and cabinet figured that, as we already had accomplished the districtwide prioritizing standards process, it would be easy for you to design the maps. Having now experienced firsthand the intensity and value of the design process, three days is not enough time!"

She continued, "Observing the incredible dialogue and professionalism I have seen you engage in while breaking apart the standards' indicators, translating them into the units of study, and conducting the review process has been amazing. Listening to you ask each other hard questions that cause everyone to really have to think deeply about how to best articulate what it is we want our students to know and be able to do has been remarkable. I now know this is a much slower process than I imagined it would be."

She turned toward the assistant superintendent and commented, "I would not want it to be any other way than what has taken place in this room the past two days." The teachers nodded their heads in agreement. She acknowledged their efforts and said to the assistant superintendent, "I know these teachers need two or three more full days to accomplish the excellent curriculum they are collaboratively designing. When the cadre meets next week, I will be letting everyone know that for our next two planned Essential Map disciplines we have to adjust the strategic plan and make each working session five days long."

She turned back to the teachers and continued, "And, now we have to figure out how to bring you all back together for the extra days. It is not going to be easy, as we did not plan for it. But we will find a way even if it means getting very creative to make it happen."

Attempting to conduct an intensive collaborative design process during the school year, in bits and pieces, makes it difficult to maintain a desired continuity of mental engagement. When teachers are provided an uninterrupted week of working full days, the day-to-day interactions allow teachers to keep the flow going much better than one day per quarter or several days scattered throughout the school year. Therefore, it is wise to strategically plan (1) professional development days during the school year for teachers to initially learn the mapping process and later, for meeting as learning communities, to use maps and the mapping process for their ongoing curriculum work; and (2) week-long summer sessions as long as necessary for districtwide collaborative design work.

Another factor that may influence systemic map design order is elementary teachers' participation in the collaborative design process for each discipline. Take care, given the intensity of designing just one discipline, that they are not overloaded by having to simultaneously design multiple disciplines. If a district is large enough to have elementary teachers who trust one another to agree to work on different disciplines' task forces, there is the possibility that the process of getting all the disciplines initially mapped, K–12, can go a bit faster. This must be a district-by-district decision, and many variables will affect the decision, including culture, structure, meeting capabilities, and monetary expenses that may occur due to stipends for work outside of contracted time.

If a district is large enough to need Essential Maps, and there has not been previous collaborative work in articulating learning horizontally and vertically with input from all teachers, incorporating a districtwide prioritizing standards process to gain insight and input from all teachers for how they individually and collectively value each standard statement in a particular discipline is beneficial (Hale, 2008). After each school has gone through the steps to collaboratively agree on a like-coding mark for each standard statement in each grade or course for a particular discipline, each school site's codes are recorded on a master list and given to the discipline-specific task force responsible for designing the Essential Maps. The task force first addresses the necessity for coming to districtwide agreement on the coding based on each school site's represented agreement. Once this has been determined, the task force follows the procedure for breaking apart the prioritized standard statements to design the collaborative maps (Hale, 2008).

Another consideration is that some disciplines in a district do not have a large number of teachers teaching a specific discipline's courses. For example, a district may have 230 English language arts (ELA) teachers, but only 10 art teachers and 3 family and consumer science (FACS) teachers. It is easier to gather together all of the art or FACS teachers than all of the ELA teachers. When drafting the strategic plan, there may be opportunities for more than one discipline working on Essential Maps per year. For example, if the art teachers and the physical education teachers already meet districtwide once a month, they can begin to design their respective Essential Maps during the school year while an ELA task force of 60 K–12 teachers may need to wait to meet immediately after the academic year to begin designing reading Essential Maps.

Even when the curriculum mapping cadre and cabinet are extremely diligent when considering the potential *what ifs* or *what abouts* when planning a timeline for collaborative mapping, it is highly likely that something will happen or arise that was not planned for. Therefore, always be prepared to make needed adjustments to any plans once the initiative is implemented.

Oftentimes, when it is realized that implementation of agreed-upon learning is easier to document in Projected/Diary Maps based on the designed Essential Maps and/or Consensus Maps, all disciplines want to be first in using the collaborative design process. If a district chooses to initially develop

Essential Maps and/or Consensus Maps prior to Projected/Diary Maps, there will need to be detailed discussions and decisions made concerning

- how all teachers within the discipline will provide their input regarding critical learning requisites (e.g., districtwide evidence of all teachers prioritizing unpacked standard statements results, big ideas);
- how to best support the teachers directly involved in the collaborative design process, including meeting-time structures and facilitation of the process;
- use of the mapping system for initially drafting the collaborative maps and for horizontal and vertical design reviews as well as asking for all teachers' input on the drafted maps' included elements;
- the process and expectations for providing ongoing operational evidence of the agreed-upon learning through the Projected/Diary Maps; and
- establishing protocols and procedures for feedback cycles related to the collaborative maps as they are annually reviewed or upgraded.

Systemic Unit Names

In Chapter 1, a library analogy was given in reference to the necessity of using an online mapping system. It is wise to begin the design of systematic unit names early in the implementation process in order to facilitate systematic collaborative design and to guide teachers of all disciplines toward quality maps. As mentioned previously, most mapping systems require a unit name be entered before any content or skills can be entered. Curriculum directors, curriculum teacher leaders, principals, curriculum mapping cabinet members, and if in place, council members need to understand the reason for designing systemic unit names to support the design process. Because there is a complexity to the unit name design process, Appendix A is dedicated to explaining considerations and procedures in detail. This focus provides a slice of the overall complexity involved in the interdependency of the mapping process and conveys the message that curriculum mapping is not a first-order change. When districts do not treat curriculum mapping as a second-order change, sustainability is rarely reached (Hale, 2008).

Using the Maps

Another factor that contributes to the potential of a curriculum mapping initiative dying a slow or quick death is the *nonuse* of the created maps. Udelhofen (2005) comments,

A shift in thinking is that the curriculum is a dynamic, ever-changing, continuous process—not a finished product. The best teachers have always updated their curriculum; the schools need to do the same. Just as our students, our society, and our world change on a continual basis, so must the content of the curriculum. The traditional "finished" curriculum binders that remain dormant for years at a time make it nearly impossible to modify or change any portion of these documents in a timely efficient manner. (p. 10)

Teachers who have not fully made this shift in thinking when designing collaborative maps often ask when the created curriculum maps' content and skills will be updated. Because the use of traditional hardcover binders is being replaced with real-time electronic maps housed in a mapping system that allows teachers access to the data continuously, therefore the answer is *whenever necessary.*

Having teachers conduct searches and reports within the mapping system aids their ongoing curriculum design and their instructional practice decision making. Every teacher must feel comfortable using each search and report feature. Equally important is brainstorming how each of the mapping search and report features can be used when focusing on specific aspects of student learning. Curriculum directors, along with curriculum teacher leaders and principals, need to encourage teachers to be professional learning communities and target specific learning concerns based on the combination of (1) assessment data, (2) appropriate map evidence; and (3) instructional practice evidence to conduct reviews (Kallick & Colosimo, 2009).

After being involved in a curriculum mapping initiative for two years, teachers in the high school were not seeing the benefits of recording Projected/Diary Maps or developing Consensus Maps. They thought mapping was supposed to aid them in being better teachers and producing better students, but they said it felt more like a laborious data-entry exercise.

A new principal arrived at the onset of the third year of mapping. He came from a neighboring district where his former high school had been engaged in curriculum mapping. He began to investigate why his new high school's teachers were not engaged in the process and what might be involved in their disengagement. He soon realized the teachers were making maps but not using the maps.

He decided a good way to get them actively engaged in using the maps was to first teach the teachers how to analyze released state-assessment items and compare their findings to the state-assessment results. He chose this as a beginning focus after he discovered the teachers had never been exposed to this process. He and the curriculum mapping council worked together to form professional learning communities by like and mixed departments. Each learning community was trained by the appropriate curriculum director or directors in how to analyze assessment items for single and multiple content and skills expectations.

The teachers in each learning community were then given their students' test scores and released state-assessment items from the most recent state-testing window. After the teachers completed the item-analysis process they were asked to cross-reference what was asked of the students in the state-assessment items to their curriculum maps. The teachers used the mapping system's report features to collect the necessary data. They began to notice gaps and absences in some areas of the students' learning expectations in relation to what they analyzed as necessary to be successful when taking the state assessment. The teachers immediately began to discuss how to best revise or add big ideas, content, and skills to the Consensus Maps as well as their Projected/Diary Maps for the appropriate courses. They also began to discuss resources, activities, and assessments they could use to support the revisions and additions made to the learning expectations.

At a districtwide administrators' meeting, the principal conveyed his teachers' epiphany, "It was like someone turned on the light switch. The teachers got it. They have not looked back. They are aggressively asking themselves questions related to the curriculum maps and meeting students' learning needs. They are specifically asking for more time to map. They are also having rich, collegial discussions about how they can best deliver their instruction to actively engage students and ensure the level of learning they want to see taking place. Just recently, two learning communities requested coverage for their classrooms, so they can go and observe one another teaching and provide constructive feedback on their instructional delivery styles."

Building teacher leadership capacity is at the root of curriculum mapping. Until this becomes a natural way for teachers to respond to their curriculum work, they will need support, encouragement, and direction from administrators, including curriculum directors and school-site teacher leaders.

Transitional Years

Educators can use maps to monitor learning expectations during the curriculum's transitional years. *Transitional years* are between-schools promotion years, such as elementary school to middle school or middle school to high school. There are three viewpoints in which to consider addressing this focus. The first is within a *single-feeder pattern* of schools where a particular elementary school feeds into a particular middle school, which feeds into a particular high school. The teachers involved use the learning expectations in each school's Consensus Maps to conduct their review. The second perspective is among a *multi-single-feeder pattern* of schools where two or more elementary schools feed into a particular middle school, which feeds into a particular high school. The teachers involved use the learning expectations included in the districtwide Essential Maps and/or each school site's Consensus Maps to conduct their review. The third perspective is among *multiple-feeder patterns*, which often occurs in a medium or large-sized district. For example, if a district consists of three specific elementary-to-high-school feeder patterns, the three middle schools and three high schools would meet to address learning expectations in the Essential Maps that affect students regardless of feeder pattern.

A transitional-years focus can begin asynchronously by asking the appropriate teachers in the two schools to begin the review process by analyzing the in-focus courses' content, skills, or other learning or practice expectations using the mapping system's compare-courses feature. Printouts of the reports (or saved reports in some mapping systems) can be made with personal notes written on them in preparation for an in-person meeting. When the teachers meet, they continue the review process by collegially discussing the concerns or problems they discover that may lead to necessary additions or modifications to the curriculum. If revisions are agreed upon, changes can be made immediately in the mapping system. If any changes affect instruction, conversations back at the respective school sites can address necessary materials, technology, or professional development needs.

While the above example focuses on transitional years, curriculum reviews and conversations should be happening within each school site, both between and among grade levels. Elementary and middle school teachers have a tendency to regularly conduct horizontal learning conversations, so they may need to be challenged to focus on more-vertical review conversations. In high school, the opposite is often true. High school teachers have a tendency to focus on discipline-specific vertical curriculum articulation rather than the totality of their students' horizontal learning experience. Asking all teachers in all disciplines who teach 11th grade to get together to discuss the cumulative learning or specific practices, such as assessment methods experienced by junior-year students, is not the norm, but should be as it is the students' reality (Jacobs, 2008).

Map Implementation Accountability

When considering ways to encourage the use of maps, it is important to address who will be responsible for the accountability for the implementation of the designed Essential Maps and/or Consensus Maps. There needs to be the expectation set that learning housed in Essential Maps is mandatory and needs to appear in Consensus Maps and Projected/Diary Maps. If a district only needs Consensus Maps, the learning in these collaborative maps is also considered mandatory learning, unless otherwise indicated, and needs to appear in each teacher's Projected/Diary Maps. Simply copying and pasting one type of map to become another type of map in the mapping system with no accountability for the learning implementation makes the intent of the mapping process ineffective. Likewise, the mapping process becomes stagnant if ongoing collegial dialogues focused on all levels of maps' curriculum design and instructional-practice evidence are not coupled with assessment-results conversations (Hale, 2008; Jacobs, 1997, 2004; Jacobs & Johnson, 2009; Kallick & Colosimo, 2009; Udelhofen, 2005, 2008).

It will take time to design maps at both the collaborative and personal levels. In the interim, teachers can still be encouraged and shown how to use the maps in conjunction with the mapping system's search and report features. Teachers can also be working collegially on standards conversations or related curriculum work in preparation for generating the district's and each school site's learning evidence.

While this book focuses heavily on the need for supporting the systemic, interdependent nature of mapping, it is important to note that teachers eventually keep records of the ongoing planned curriculum (Essential Maps and/or Consensus Maps), and each teacher keeps annual, accurate records of his or her operational curriculum in Projected/Diary Maps (Jacobs, 1997, 2004). Jacobs (1997) comments,

Curriculum mapping is a procedure for collecting data about the *actual* curriculum in a school district using the school calendar as an organizer. Data are gathered in a format that allows *each* teacher to present an overview of his or her students' actual learning experiences. The fundamental purpose of mapping is communication. (p. 61, emphasis added)

The *communication* Jacobs refers to can become tainted if one or more teachers do not maintain their personal Projected/Diary Maps monthly to ensure the mapping system's database accurately reflects the here-and-now learning of the current academic year. If the map data are not accurate, the search and report features' results will be invalid or skewed and can cause inappropriate decision making when conducting reviews.

Many districts' curriculum mapping leadership teams are choosing to have teachers initially design collaborative maps to use as the foundation for personal mapping. If a district is large enough to require Essential Maps, the tendency is to start at this collaborative level by forming K–12 task forces to design the maps based on districtwide input. This leads to each school site using the Essential Maps as the base for each school's Consensus Maps before official projected/diary mapping begins.

After a task force or school's teacher team has worked diligently and painstakingly to design a quality curriculum evident by Essential Maps or Consensus Maps, the question always arises, "Where is the accountability for what we have decided students will learn in each teacher's classroom?" When a teacher is expected to use any type of collaborative map to guide his or her students' learning expectations, curriculum directors need to work closely with principals, curriculum teacher leaders, and all teachers to determine how best to create an accountability environment that is teachers to teachers rather than administrators to teachers or teachers to administrators. Teacher-to-teacher accountability opportunities may include, but are not limited to

- Considering students who may end up with one or more *learning-gap* years because the new teacher-designed learning expectations do not match up with the old learning expectations in a particular school year. (e.g., second grade used to be when students learned about the planets. Based on analyzing the standard statements, the second-grade science Consensus Map does not include planets. Instead, it includes learning about the night sky's stars. This means that until the incoming kindergarteners are second graders, there will be gaps of learning that need to be addressed outside of the agreed-upon collaborative curriculum.).
- Discussing personal or collaborative instructional practices that best address students' learning expectations that may be affected by the new or revised teacher-designed curriculum.
- Designing and implementing common assessments for key learning and working in small-group teams or professional learning communities to monitor their students' results and determining intervention or extension needs to ensure students' success.

- Meeting quarterly to focus on the implementation of a newly designed collaborative map's learning expectations in relation to the reality of the operational curriculum evidence (e.g., a social studies K–12 Essential Map task force sends out an electronic survey asking for feedback from all teachers).
- Analyzing districtwide or school-site-specific learning and/or instructional practices surveys and sharing the gained information with the appropriate group or groups.

Designing and Implementing New Courses

Middle schools and high schools sometimes design new courses based on graduation requirements or elective requests. Having the ability to access the current and archived academic years of learning in curriculum maps in the mapping system can aid teachers in new-course design. When a new course has been drafted in a mapping system, like- or mixed-discipline teachers can participate in a curriculum review process in preparation for the course's approval by the appropriate group or groups, such as a department, a grade level, a school, the district curriculum administration, community partners, or the school board.

The new course can instantly be integrated into mapping reviews and collegial discussions and decision making through the search and report features in a mapping system. Adjustments to the new curriculum can take place in real time as each month passes during the first few years of implementation. Evidence of any agreed-upon modifications to the curriculum can be documented in the map through attachments or a notes feature. With access to archived academic years' maps, comparisons of the course's evolution can be tracked and analyzed. If a newly designed elective course is offered for a few years and then becomes dormant, the course's maps are retrievable from any archived years to use again at any time.

Rethinking Textbook Adoptions

Curriculum directors are often responsible for overseeing textbook-adoption cycles. With the implementation of curriculum mapping, a shift occurs in thinking that asks administrators and teachers to move away from a *textbook* frame of mind to a *resources* frame of mind (Hale, 2008). Traditionally, a curriculum director selects a team of teachers to preview and narrow potential textbooks or programs to one or more companies for a given discipline. During the selection process, the curriculum teacher leaders at each school site may be asked to discuss the pros and cons of the finalists with all the teachers and display the finalists' materials for teachers to preview and provide input. Eventually, selection decisions are made, and the company or companies are awarded.

Twenty-first-century students need to have curriculum design focused on technology learning enhanced by online tools being developed daily as well as teachers using the latest technology and tools in their curriculum practices. Jacobs (2010) acknowledges,

> As educators, our challenge is to match the needs of our learners to a world that is changing with great rapidity. To meet the challenge, we

need to become strategic learners ourselves by deliberately expanding our perspectives and updating our approaches. (p. 7)

This is not implying that there should no longer be any textbooks or programs in schools; it simply conveys the message that curriculum mapping asks administrators and teachers to reconsider learning and instructional practices in response to students' 21st-century needs rather than considering only the *way it has always been done.*

After the school year ended, a 40-member task force was brought together for one week to design K–12 reading Essential Maps. During the school year, preliminary curriculum work was conducted, including designing systemic unit names and asking teachers districtwide to participate in prioritizing the reading standards. The results of the collected data were given to the teachers as they entered the meeting room.

The meeting began with the facilitators, the English language arts curriculum director, a curriculum mapping coach, and five curriculum mapping cabinet members taking turns sharing background information relative to the design task. The curriculum mapping coach reminded the teachers that the Essential Maps would be the foundation for each school's Consensus Maps. She explained that besides including additional learning, which will be added by teachers to this school-site-specific map, it will be a school's decision whether teachers collaboratively include resources in the Consensus Maps or wait to include resources in each teacher's Projected/Diary Map.

One of the task-force members raised his hand and asked, "Why aren't we including the district-adopted reading-series resources in the Essential Maps?" The curriculum director stood up and said that while the reading series was adopted for districtwide use, the choice of how it is used has always been a school-site decision. The curriculum mapping coach added that once the task force designs the reading Essential Maps, and each school's teachers design the Consensus Maps, the district can begin to think differently about adopting a future reading series or program. She mentioned that the district may choose not to purchase a series or program at all. She added that many administrators believe the best choice will be to empower teachers as the decision makers and allow each school site to purchase what is truly needed, such as leveled readers, more nonfiction materials, Internet access, or electronic whiteboards, as the teacher-designed curriculum will be in place.

Many of the teachers raised their eyebrows at her comments. One teacher inquired, "I thought we had to adopt a company's reading series or program because the state mandates we do so. Is that not the case?"

The curriculum director addressed the question by sharing that the state does not mandate a reading series or program must be purchased. She explained that the state requires a district to purchase a series or program if the district cannot prove it has a district-created curriculum. Monies allotted for materials must then be used to secure a series or program.

She concluded by saying, "Once our district provides evidence of our curriculum, which will be our curriculum maps, the allotted funds will be

(Continued)

(Continued)

divided among our schools. Then, teachers and administrators can collaboratively select and purchase instructional materials, both hard copy and technology, that best supports the students' learning expectations."

The teachers immediately began talking to one another with a gleam in their eyes. One teacher exclaimed, "If this is true, that's great. Let's get started mapping our Essential Maps!"

Curriculum mapping directors and curriculum teacher leaders need to begin referring to adoption cycles/selections as resources cycles/selections. This mindset instantly allows teachers to be the professional curriculum leaders they deserve and desire to be.

TEACHERS AS LEARNERS

Curriculum directors often meet with curriculum teacher leaders monthly. The issues raised and addressed during these meetings often influence school-site and districtwide professional development needs. When curriculum mapping is first implemented, the initial learning curve is intense. It takes more than once (often 7 to 10 initial trainings) to truly begin to grasp the complexities involved in curriculum mapping, including the basic and advanced uses of the selected mapping system. It is wise to strategically plan for all possible professional development days to be used for teachers' curriculum mapping–oriented learning during the first one to two years of full implementation.

During the first year, teachers must be recognized and supported as *new learners* of *new information.* Strategically planning large-group trainings followed by small-group workshops, hands-on sessions, one-on-one mentoring, or other forms of differentiated support structures is important (Jacobs & Johnson, 2009). Trainings should be broken into small learning tasks and should initially be the same throughout the district. Based on ongoing input from the curriculum mapping cabinet and councils' members, the second year and on of curriculum mapping's professional development (i.e., curriculum design and/or instructional practice related to curriculum) can be personalized for each school based on its particular needs.

Professional development for implementing a successful initiative needs to incorporate a *systems approach.* This approach includes strategically planning and articulating the step-by-step process for what teachers need to learn, when it will be learned and practiced, and who will be responsible for ensuring and supporting the learning is taking place. This approach also asks those responsible for planning the professional development to consider initiatives already in place and how they are directly or indirectly connected to curriculum mapping, as this may affect professional development needs or desires.

Those responsible refers to both teacher leaders and administrators, including curriculum directors. They need to work together not only to coordinate the initial phases professional development needs but during the advanced mapping phase as well (Jacobs & Johnson, 2009). After mapping has become a natural component of a district's culture, professional development should stem from each school's teachers stating what it is that they want their learning to be focused on, which may differ by grades, departments, or disciplines.

CONCLUSION

Curriculum mapping asks teachers to be the leaders in designing a district's cohesive curriculum. Curriculum directors and teacher leaders need to be able to articulate how the components of curriculum mapping and using a mapping system will continue to support the current curriculum work as well as bring new insights and opportunities to improve curriculum and instruction. Clarity for how to support a teacher-led process to build leadership capacity and sustainability is also important. Communication for how to best support the teacher's curriculum work in using the maps and the mapping system needs to be discussed by district administrators, curriculum directors, principals, and teacher leaders involved in the curriculum mapping cabinet during the prologue and once implementation begins. Additionally, teacher-to-teacher accountability involving teachers ensuring the agreed-upon learning is taking place, supporting the learning with differentiated instruction, and evaluating student achievement using the maps is critical for teachers to see value in the mapping process. Asking teachers to continually question student learning and teacher practice by analyzing collaborative maps (i.e., Essential Maps, Consensus Maps) and the operational evidence (Projected/Diary Maps) will cause a shift in thinking from *being done* to *being renewed.*

Comprehensive prologue planning by a strong leadership team that establishes the desired curriculum vision, mission, and goals leads to a curriculum mapping initiative that is articulated and attainable. Tom Skerritt (2009), a film director, comments, "If a director doesn't communicate a clear, relevant vision of the material, it will not succeed no matter how good the material." When curriculum directors support and nurture the vision, teachers fly and students soar.

REVIEW QUESTIONS

While you may not be a curriculum director, consider this perspective when answering the following questions. Discuss your responses with a colleague or in a small group.

1. As curriculum directors and curriculum teacher leaders will be members of the curriculum mapping cabinet and/or councils, to what extent will these curriculum leaders be responsible for planning and/or facilitating teachers when designing Essential Maps and Consensus Maps?

2. Considering all the disciplines offered in your district, create a prospective timeline for the linear and/or parallel order that could be used to

systemically design the various disciplines' collaborative maps. Share your timeline and reasoning.

3. How will district and school-site curriculum leaders aid in supporting teachers in their understanding of curriculum design and instructional practice in relationship to curriculum maps, curriculum specific initiatives, and curriculum-related initiatives? Provide examples of support methods (e.g., electronic newsletters, miniworkshops, small-group or one-on-one conversations, textual and visual information accessibility via the district website's curriculum mapping home page).

4. Who will be responsible for map-implementation accountability for each discipline's vertically articulated planned learning maps (i.e., Essential Maps and/or Consensus Maps) to ensure agreed-upon student-learning expectations truly become the operational learning (Projected/Diary Maps)? Will the *who* be more than one person per discipline? If no, why? If yes, will the accountability be a mixture of administrators and teacher leaders or teacher leaders and teachers? Support your reasoning.

5. Based on what you have read in the chapters thus far, what do you envision will be key considerations when establishing both the collaborative and individual mapping process for all disciplines offered in the district? How do you perceive the various components of the mapping process will be embedded in the district strategic plan and each school site's action plans on an annual basis?

5

What Should Principals Consider to Support Teacher Leadership?

The ultimate leader is one who is willing to develop people to the point that they eventually surpass him or her in knowledge and ability.

—Fred A. Manske, Jr.

A high school principal had the responsibility of revising his school's curriculum in light of the district's new mandate to strengthen standards-based learning. Although the district consisted of three high schools, two middle schools, and seven elementary schools, Mr. Johnson was singled out to attend a national curriculum mapping conference to learn more about better linking standards to the curriculum and how curriculum mapping's decision-making process could enhance teachers' curriculum work.

He attended the conference with six department chairs. The team was both challenged and concerned by what they heard from scholars and practitioners. The message they heard was to start slow, steady, and systemically. They were trying to decide how to incorporate curriculum mapping in their school given the rapidness in which the district wanted curriculum mapping to begin.

When he returned to the district, Mr. Johnson shared the team's insights during an administrative meeting attended by the superintendent and other central-office curriculum stakeholders. Unfortunately, the district leadership did not grasp the systemic nature of curriculum mapping and mandated that each school develop its own mapping solution. When it was suggested that the district form a curriculum mapping cabinet to create districtwide teacher leadership, the superintendent said it was not necessary.

When he realized he would not get the district support he hoped for, Mr. Johnson decided to embrace the systemic nature of curriculum mapping within his school. He asked the six department chairs to select and invite additional faculty to form the high school's curriculum mapping council. The newly formed leadership team began a half-year prologue to learn as much as possible about mapping. They conducted two book studies and attended a regional curriculum mapping conference. They created vision and mission statements that embraced a standards-based curriculum and continual student learning challenges for their students' participation in local and global communities.

The council's first goal was to ensure that all teachers became actively engaged in the revision of the school's curriculum. To do so, Mr. Johnson knew that he would have to be willing to make revisions as well. He began by changing how he used weekly faculty meeting time. Mr. Johnson sent an e-mail to inform the teachers that housekeeping information would now be sent via e-mail. Faculty meetings would be dedicated to furthering the school's curriculum work. The e-mail also asked each faculty member to read two attached articles—one on standards-based curriculum reform, the second on global competencies—prior to the meeting.

At the onset of the meeting, the teachers were initially put in small mixed-discipline groups. They answered questions based on the articles' main points related to (1) revising the school's vision and mission statements; (2) instructional and assessment practices; and (3) the state's standards-reform efforts in light of state, national, and international economic, social expectations as well as information and media literacy. After mixed-group discussion time, each teacher met with his or her discipline or grade level to share each group's discussion points and address the questions based on like-discipline concerns.

Based on the challenges posed in the articles, the discussion points, and Mr. Johnson's encouragement to rethink students' learning expectations both horizontally and vertically, each discipline and department, such as counseling, planned follow-up meetings. First on the meeting agenda would be analyzing state standards with new thoughts of curriculum design to ensure students graduate as independent and interdependent local and global thinkers.

When concluding the meeting, Mr. Johnson asked teachers to share their thoughts about how the faculty meeting had been conducted. Many commented they were pleased that the focus was on student learning and teaching. Mr. Johnson acknowledged that he appreciated that the majority of teachers came to the meeting having read the articles and were deeply engaged in conversation. He ended by restating his commitment to supporting them in becoming an engaged curriculum mapping professional learning community that included his willingness to be a fellow learner and risk taker.

While Mr. Johnson's experience is hopefully the exception and not the rule, his story conveys how the principal's belief in an initiative can affect its success.

The role a principal has as an influential change agent is a key factor in facilitating school improvement. In a high-stakes accountability environment, a principal's ability to be a curriculum leader and an instructional leader is essential to school improvement (Glatthorn & Jailall, 2009).

A principal who builds leadership capacity enables teachers to foster improvement in all areas of student achievement. Based on Manske's insightful quote, the ultimate administrator is one who is willing to develop teachers to the point that they eventually surpass him or her in knowledge and ability while working interdependently as curriculum designers and curriculum practitioners. To do so, a principal must be able to balance being a manager and a leader. This is difficult, as there is a vast amount of responsibility and accountability placed on someone in this administrative position. Many principals are moving to a *shared-leadership mindset* with designated teacher leaders taking on roles and responsibilities that were once solely the principal's. A principal who is successful at striking a balance is astute, knowing when and how to question, support, and trust his or her teachers.

BUILDING TRUST AND TEACHER LEADERSHIP

Trust is *firm reliance on the integrity, ability, or character of a person or thing.* A principal's ability or inability to foster and sustain a firm interdependent reliance between him or herself and the faculty as well as among the faculty is vital to working collegially.

The Importance of Trust

Brewster and Railsback (2003) synthesized a large body of research on building trust between principals and teachers and teachers to teachers. Their findings were compiled into two series of general suggestions (Figure 5.1).

Figure 5.1   Building Trust Between Principals and Teachers and Among Teachers

Building Trust Between Principals and Teachers	Building Trust Among Teachers
• Demonstrate personal integrity • Show that you care • Be accessible • Facilitate and model effective communication • Involve staff in decision making • Celebrate experimentation and support risk taking • Express value for dissenting views • Reduce teachers' sense of vulnerability • Ensure that teachers have basic resources • Be prepared to replace ineffective teachers as a last resort	• Engage the full faculty in activities and discussions related to the school's mission, vision, and core values • Make new teachers feel welcome • Create—and support—meaningful opportunities for teachers to work collaboratively • Identify ways to increase and/or improve faculty communication • Make relationship building a priority • Choose a professional development model that promotes relationship building

Source: Brewster and Railsback (2003, pp. 12–17).

A principal exhibiting quality leadership regularly models all 10 research-based trust-between-principals-and-teachers suggestions. To build trust between a principal and his or her faculty when establishing, nurturing, and sustaining a curriculum mapping initiative, the five most important attributes are

- involving staff in decision making;
- celebrating experimentation and supporting risk taking;
- expressing value for dissenting views;
- reducing teachers' sense of vulnerability; and
- ensuring that teachers have basic resources

The following information provides thoughts related to these five attributes.

Involving Staff in Decision Making

As stated in previous chapters, curriculum mapping at both the district and school-site level is teacher led. This translates into teachers being directly involved in the decision-making process for developing annual curriculum mapping action plans; implementing and facilitating curriculum mapping professional development; and focusing on the needs of teachers when they begin to use the maps as a natural component of the ongoing curriculum work in a school, between schools, and among schools.

Celebrating Experimentation and Supporting Risk Taking

Because curriculum mapping asks teachers to be key decision makers, a principal not only needs to celebrate the risks curriculum mapping council members are willing to take but also celebrate and support the entire faculty's willingness to be risk takers. A shift in thinking that focuses on being curriculum designers as well as instructional leaders may be a challenge for some teachers. Whether a teacher is new to the profession or a veteran, having to learn new ways of operating and making decisions can be emotionally challenging. They may not feel comfortable with the necessary changes being asked of them and will need reassurance that the principal will honor their concerns regarding taking such risks. A principal must discern whether a teacher's complaints are warranted or if the teacher is simply moving through the stages of grief (denial, anger, bargaining, depression, upward turn, work through, and acceptance) that often occur with large-scale change (Chenoweth & Everhart, 2002).

There will also be teachers who enjoy a challenge and will embrace curriculum mapping the moment it is introduced. Depending on the culture and climate, these teachers may be chastised by their peers for being innovative risk takers. A principal needs to create a collegial environment where these teachers can be celebrated alongside those who are apprehensive about changes in thinking and new ways that curriculum work will be conducted.

Expressing Value for Dissenting Views

Resistance to change is an organizational reality. While it may not appear so on the surface, in actuality, the noise volume of those who are resistant is minor when compared to those who are willing to change and grow (Reeves, 2005). There will likely be some teachers who voice their unenthusiastic opinions loud and clear during the early stages of a curriculum mapping initiative. As Reeves points out, it is important for a principal to remember that this level of irritation is voiced by a few, not the majority. A delicate balance of willingness to listen to the voices of dissension while keeping the climate positive, maintaining the initiative's integrity, and continuing to move forward are crucial to supporting the majority of teachers in their efforts to be learners and risk takers. It is also important that a principal, along with the curriculum mapping council members, recognizes and addresses the faculty's potential tension based on initiative fatigue. For example, the principal highlighted in Chapter 4 addressed this concern by asking her teachers to participate in a paper-plate activity to collectively identify what they could remove from their current responsibilities.

A complex initiative such as curriculum mapping may fall by the wayside if there are

- too many new initiatives started over too short a time;
- lack of connectedness between or among multiple initiatives; and
- personnel changes that cause the support structure or structures to falter, become inconsistent, or be stopped.

If this has happened in the past, it is not unwarranted for teachers to be apprehensive when another time-intensive initiative is introduced. A school district may have multiple administrators incorporating different initiatives. If there is not clear communication among these administrators, the teachers will begin to experience initiative fatigue (Reeves, 2009). A principal must be an advocate for his or her staff to ensure they are not being overwhelmed.

When a principal can successfully link multiple initiatives and create relevance for how various learning, teaching, assessing, and evaluating focuses relate to improving students' achievements, the likelihood that curriculum mapping will reach sustainability increases.

Reducing Teachers' Sense of Vulnerability

When teachers are asked to be curriculum designers, there will most likely be some teachers who feel vulnerable, as this expectation may be an area that was not emphasized in their college or post-college courses. Most teachers feel confident in their abilities to be instructional leaders. Some may feel as if the wind has been knocked out of their sails when asked to switch their instructional gears to focus on designing curriculum.

A principal's ability to accurately recognize how systemic change and thinking differently will affect each teacher as well as his or her colleagues' efforts is significant. Vulnerability must be recognized, acknowledged, honored, and supported through differentiation in a manner that allows each teacher to move forward. This consideration is important in each school and districtwide. Teachers often have friends or family members who teach in various schools within a district. Inaccurate stories and inconsistent communiqués can negatively impact and damage school-site and districtwide trust-building efforts. It is imperative that all principals work collegially to address this concern, so that teachers hear common messages and expectations. Some districts provide monthly online or e-mail newsletters to not only convey clear expectations but also to correct information that may have been misconstrued.

Ensuring That Teachers Have Basic Resources

Equally important for supporting teachers' sense of vulnerability is ensuring the teachers have the resources necessary for implementing and sustaining mapping success. The term *basic* resources does not mean *minimal* resources. A principal needs to plan ways to provide time and meeting supports that encourage and allow teachers to be actively involved in curriculum work weekly or biweekly rather than once every month or grading period. This includes horizontal and vertical meetings focused on curriculum design and curriculum practice. Many times, the focus of the meetings will be within a school, but there will be times when focuses will necessitate meeting with teachers outside of a single school site. For example:

- In like schools (e.g., three elementary schools);
- Specific feeder pattern (e.g., one of three feeder patterns within a large district); and
- Districtwide (e.g., embedding global competencies in all disciplines).

Ongoing curriculum work takes strategic planning that involves all administrators, at all levels, and in all disciplines communicating in advance and in real time about teachers' need to meet in person or virtually. Principals are often the best at knowing multiple meeting demands for the disciplines living within their schools. This is another reason why it is important for principals to be a part of the curriculum mapping cabinet and participate in the prologue's strategic planning.

When a district begins a curriculum mapping initiative, the teachers' work times and meeting structures may not currently match the short- or long-term goals for the teachers becoming curriculum leaders. Providing adequate time to (1) meet in person, (2) make collegial decisions, (3) try out the decisions, (4) review the results, and (5) revise curriculum design or instructional practices cannot happen successfully with an inservice day or half-day one, two, or three times a year. While technology advancements afford teachers the ability to meet asynchronously, many teachers express that they gain the most personally and professionally when they have adequate time to meet in person. They comment that the dialogue and collegiality is stimulating and the results are richer and more productive.

During the prologue, central-office administrators, principals, and teacher leaders need to think creatively on how to expand or reshape the time and structure of meetings. Likewise, each curriculum mapping council, which includes the principal, needs to collegially prepare for meeting-time flexibility when developing a school's action plans. Discussions focused on simple and radical changes to the district calendar year and daily schedules should take place early on because they often must be approved by a school board well in advance of the next school year and may affect the public community if start and end times of the school day or a particular day of the week are adjusted in small or great ways. For example, a school district adjusted the school days' end times to add a weekly non-student-contact meeting time on Wednesdays. Wednesday's student day now ended one hour earlier, which, when combined with the teachers' contractual half-hour after-student day, provided teachers with one-and-one-half hours of collegial curriculum work time. The hour that was removed from Wednesday's student schedule was shifted to create an additional 15 minutes on Monday, Tuesday, Thursday, and Friday. While this change slightly affected internal bus schedules, the greatest concern was voiced by parents and guardians concerned about childcare. By working with the local after-school programs to provide earlier care on Wednesdays, this issue was resolved without great difficulty. It is important to remember that, while most teachers are willing to be collegial and are ready to do whatever is in the students' best interests, they do not like to be pulled out of their class-rooms to meet with other teachers during instructional time. It may take a few years to shift meeting structures to allow all teachers to collaborate more often and for longer periods without students being in school. Therefore, substitutes for teachers involved in professional development training or collegial work are best secured using a recognized substitute pool consisting of respected, retired teachers or substitutes whom the teachers personally select. The teachers should be confident in and comfortable with leaving their students with substi-tutes who have consistently demonstrated excellence.

Another multifaceted resource a principal needs to address involves technology:

- Computer access
- Internet access
- Personal comfort with technology
- Professional use and comfort using the selected curriculum mapping system

Hale (2008) asked practitioners to share roadblocks and successes when implementing curriculum mapping. One elementary principal shared how her school's curriculum mapping council selected some of the members to become the *tech cadre*. These teachers develop technology training for the faculty based on the teachers' differentiated learning needs:

Your teachers will represent a range of technology savvy when you introduce the selected mapping system. I found that most young teachers took to using the mapping system without hesitation. My more experienced staff, especially those with little technology training, found curriculum mapping to be a double challenge—dealing with learning the mapping elements as well as learning new technology skills. I met this concern head on by developing training sessions based on Jacobs's (2004) Differentiated Staff Development Model—Low Tech/High Curriculum, High Tech/High Curriculum, Low Tech/Low Curriculum, and High Tech/Low Curriculum. Teachers who met a quadrant criteria were given specific times to map in our computer lab.

The initial sessions were facilitated by our tech cadre, peer teachers with strong backgrounds in technology, the mapping system, curriculum, and curriculum mapping. With support from the tech cadre, district technology staff, and our curriculum mapping consultant, we were able to get everyone comfortable with mapping online within the first half year of implementation. (p. 257)

Access to outdated computers, limited computers, and slow Internet service will hurt a curriculum mapping initiative. It is difficult for some teachers to differentiate between the mapping-system software and the informational technology infrastructure. Teachers translate such frustrations into thinking that mapping is a waste of time, which is not beneficial individually or collectively. A principal's ensuring the availability of the necessary technology for all the teachers is imperative. It is recommended that an infrastructure needs survey be taken during the prologue to assess the needs per school. Budgetary requests can be identified and planned into the districtwide strategic plan.

Because teachers will be using an online mapping system constantly to not only develop maps but also use them to make, challenge, review, revise, and grow curriculum design and curriculum practices, a principal needs to budget via school or district funds to ensure that all teachers have (1) easy access to computers that have up-to-date systems and are available without spending time traveling far from a classroom to use the computers; and (2) Internet access using high-speed lines that have adequate bandwidth, not just for a particular school, but for the entire district, as there will be times when many teachers will be accessing the curriculum mapping system simultaneously.

Principals who proactively model the aforementioned five *building trust between principals and teachers* attributes will find implementing a curriculum mapping initiative more successful and less stressful. In Figure 5.1, the attributes for *building trust among teachers* is based on leadership skills and behaviors that are eventually displayed by teachers:

- Engage the full faculty in activities and discussions related to the school's mission, vision, and core values.
- Make new teachers feel welcome.
- Create—and support—meaningful opportunities for teachers to work collaboratively.
- Identify ways to increase and/or improve faculty communication.
- Make relationship building a priority.
- Choose a professional development model that promotes relationship building.

A principal's role is to encourage and support his or her faculty when considering which teachers already exhibit these attributes and which teachers are capable of exhibiting the attributes when nurtured. When forming the curriculum mapping cabinet and a school's curriculum mapping council, these teachers should be considered for selection, as they will be working alongside one another and with the principal to establish or extend a culture of teacher leadership.

Curriculum Design Leader and Instructional Leader

Administrative leaders guide the culture and cultural changes within their institutions. The responsibilities and roles of principals have increased over the years. While principals continue to be ultimately responsible for making on-site or virtual schools safe places to receive an education; enforcing district policies; developing schedules; and ordering materials, books, and supplies, the necessity to lead and encourage teacher leadership has increased. Principals are expected to be strong educational leaders. Responsibilities demand knowledge and facilitation of both best-teaching practices and curriculum design. Curriculum mapping brings this dual need to the forefront.

Encouraging the collegial nature of curriculum mapping is important to the implementation process. Curriculum mapping asks teachers to be transparent about curriculum design and instructional practice (Hale, 2008; Jacobs, 1997, 2004, 2006; Udelhofen, 2005, 2008). If teachers do not trust one another to openly share school-based and systemic curriculum design and curriculum practice concerns, thoughts, and reasoning, a curriculum mapping initiative may be difficult to implement and sustain.

Many books have been written about the necessity for a principal to be an instructional leader. While it is important for a principal to expect and encourage teachers to be engaged in best instructional practices, a principal must also be conscious of the complexities of engaging in curriculum design work. If a principal has devoted himself or herself to being an instructional leader, a personal shift in thinking to focus on curriculum design may be challenging during the prologue and implementation phases of curriculum mapping. A principal's willingness to publically address his or her desire to *know yourself and seek self-improvement* regarding the intricacies of the disciplines offered in his or her school represents a willingness to be vulnerable as a learner. This attribute is powerful. It encourages teachers and administrators to be equal, professional colleagues and lifelong learners.

A principal may not feel comfortable with the nuances of multiple disciplines or learning expectations outside of his or her field of expertise. For example, a middle school principal may have been a middle school social studies teacher before earning a degree in administration. If it has been some time since being in the classroom, he may not be familiar with the current middle school social studies learning expectations or comfortable with the elementary or high school students' learning expectations. Through a caring, trusting relationship with his faculty and teachers districtwide, his faith in his teachers' expertise and their willingness to help him gain understanding serves dually as encouragement and empowerment.

A principal's level of awareness with various disciplines design expectations should be addressed in tandem with the school's collegial trust culture based on past history and present reality.

An elementary principal, Mr. Cayman, e-mailed his faculty approximately two weeks before the school year began. He informed them that the location for the first-day faculty inservice would not be held at school and asked everyone to dress casually. He told them the day would have two focuses, collegial awareness and curriculum mapping. Within a few days, he received e-mail responses that ranged from mild enthusiasm to considerable questioning. He was not surprised by the teachers' reactions because they had recently experienced four consecutive years of difficult administrative leadership. During the past three years, 3 different principals implemented changes that proved counterproductive for the faculty and students.

Mr. Cayman initially came to the school as an interim principal when the last principal was released from his contract midyear. He spent the remainder of the school year learning as much as he could about the school's recent and past cultural and academic history, the teachers as individuals, their abilities to work collaboratively, and the students and their caregivers. He knew the district had adopted curriculum mapping as part of its overall strategic plan three years ago. He learned that the teachers in his school had not had positive experiences with the mapping process due to the tension and mistrust created by the yearly principal change and varied professional expectations.

Mr. Cayman was then hired as the official principal near the end of the school year. He asked three respected teachers to attend the national curriculum mapping conference with him during the summer: a veteran, a midcareer teacher, and one who had just finished her first year of teaching. During the conference, they gained insights into curriculum mapping that reshaped and expanded their understanding of the mapping concepts. They made connections to what the district had been doing and ways they could turn mapping into a positive initiative at their school. Together, they drafted an action plan for the coming school year that included creating a curriculum mapping council and planning the beginning-of-the-year faculty inservice.

When the teachers assembled at the faculty inservice meeting site, Mr. Cayman and the three teachers welcomed everyone and gave each person a wheeled backpack containing teacher supplies and an opening activity questionnaire. Mr. Cayman expressed how fortunate he felt to be working alongside the faculty as their principal. He gave a heartfelt summary of where they had been and where he and the three teachers envisioned they wanted to be educationally and emotionally. He informed them about the curriculum mapping conference. Then, each of the three teachers shared personal highlights and connections they made between curriculum mapping and the curriculum work focus for the coming school year.

The veteran teacher then spearheaded the day's opening activity. She asked everyone to retrieve the questionnaire from their backpacks. She asked them to take approximately five minutes to individually answer the following seven questions:

Who Are You?

1. What *events and/or trends* have had an impact on your generation?
2. What *music* has had an impact on your generation?
3. What *TV culture* has had an impact on your generation?
4. What *cultural memorabilia* has had an impact on your generation?
5. What *heroes* have had an impact on your generation?
6. What *describes* and *defines* your personal values?
7. How would you describe the *characteristics* of your work ethics?

Next, the teachers were asked to stand and form small groups of three or four people by finding other teachers who appeared to represent the same *you*. As they moved about and told one other what they had written, chuckles and laughter were heard as they discovered similarities in their like-generational answers. After a few minutes, the veteran teacher asked the teachers to now walk around the room and form new groups of three or four teachers whose members were from mixed generations. After a few moments of regrouping, the dynamics of the conversations were lively and engaged; but this time, the teachers were more focused on explanations rather than comparisons. The teachers began to express to one another how interesting the generational differences were because they really hadn't thought much about this before due to their meeting times being focused on student learning rather than one another's lives, including personal values and work ethics.

The next facilitator was the midcareer teacher who went to the conference. She got everyone's attention and used the comments she was hearing to segue into letting them know that the conference team had experienced this activity during a breakout session. She pointed out that during the session the presenter discussed the necessity to see how multi-generations who work together need to understand how each generation thinks, solves problems, and values work and personal life. She asked the teachers to gather around a screen near the front of the room. She gave a short PowerPoint presentation that contained several screen shots listing the similarities and differences between four generations related to the seven questions on the questionnaire: the Silent Generation (1922–1943), Baby Boomers (1944–1960), Generation Xers (1960–1980), and Millennials (1981–2000). As the faculty studied the information, one teacher mentioned that he was experiencing a *light bulb* moment. For the first time, he understood why they all had been handling much of what had been happening to them over the past few years so differently, internally and externally.

After the PowerPoint presentation and conversation were completed, the youngest teacher who attended the conference asked the teachers to move back to their tables and work as small groups to list some ah-ha moments they had by participating in the activity. After allowing some time for brainstorming, she listed their thoughts on chart paper to display around the room. She summarized the activity by expressing that their new generational awareness would help them be an interdependent faculty and

(Continued)

(Continued)

use their mixed-generational strengths to be the best they can be for each other and for the students.

For the remainder of the day, Mr. Cayman and the three teachers copresented segments of information to make curriculum mapping connections based on (1) what the district had been doing for the past three years, (2) what had been happening in their school during those three years, and (3) their school's expectations based on these past experiences and the drafted action plan. They also conducted a curriculum mapping basic training presentation to help everyone gain better insight into the intentions of mapping and building a common language, as this had not happened properly or adequately over the past few years. They ended with a call to create a curriculum mapping council. They were taken aback at the enthusiasm from the number of teachers who wanted to be a part of the council.

Mr. Cayman concluded the day by showing a short video presentation titled *A Peacock in the Land of Penguins: A Story About Courage in Creating a Land of Opportunity* (Gallagher & Schmidt, 2009), which featured a peacock who did not fit in with a colony of penguins. Eventually, the peacock left the colony and felt at home in a land with many types of birds who embraced and encouraged one another to think differently because they needed different perspectives to have the shared wisdom necessary to be the best they could be. The moral of the story was that *"the Land of Opportunity is not a place . . . It is a state of mind."* Mr. Cayman explained that his greatest desire for the school year was to explore all of their unique gifts and talents as professional learners and educators. He looked forward to working collegially to design curriculum and put it into practice with their students' best interests in mind.

When teachers value their principal as someone who desires to learn and share ideas, it becomes easier to reciprocate trust (Robbins & Alvy, 1995). Brewster and Railsback (2003) state,

> Building new relationships, whatever the circumstances, takes time; rebuilding relationships in which trust has been damaged can take far longer (Young, 1998). If we hope to make meaningful, lasting change within school communities, however, identifying increased educator trust as a priority and taking the time to develop it looks to be well worth the investment. "Without trust," as Blasé and Blasé (2001) write, "a school cannot improve and grow into the rich, nurturing microsociety needed by children and adults alike." (p.18)

Mr. Cayman was aware of what research has proven concerning teachers' willingness to be vulnerable with one another. He made certain that he too exhibited his willingness to be vulnerable as a learner to best support them in their curriculum design and instructional-practice processes. A principal must always be mindful that curriculum mapping is a systemic, second-order change model. A principal with a *let's get mapping implemented quickly and see results immediately* mentality can hurt the process rather than help. Teachers need time to not only construct initial understanding but also to collegially process their understanding.

Principals often wear a managerial hat. When curriculum mapping is implemented in a district or school, it is important that a principal does not confuse this role with being a leader. If a principal confuses these roles, there may be problems with implementing curriculum mapping's *process-driven* rather than *product-driven* mindset. A principal may need to rethink his or her managerial habits and requisites prior to implementing mapping, so there is not confusion once the initiative is in place.

Teachers in a district were being asked to learn how to write a month map using the established map-writing protocols and selected mapping system.

When a mapping trainer arrived at one of schools to provide teachers with additional support and feedback, the principal met her as she was setting up for the day. He told her that he was making sure the teachers were working on their maps and showed her a three-ring binder. He informed her that the binder contained a copy of all of the teachers' map months, which he has the teachers turn in a printed copy of at the beginning of each month.

The trainer inquired why he was having teachers turn in a paper document of the map months. The principal paused for a moment. "I need a copy for accountability purposes. When they turn them in, I check the maps to see if each teacher is following the protocols," he reflected. The trainer reminded the principal that curriculum mapping shifts thinking in two important ways. Teachers' accountability for providing curriculum evidence may now be handled differently than how it was in the past. The beauty of using an online mapping system is that no one has to turn in anything. If there is a date when teachers are expected to complete a task in preparation for a review or feedback—that is fine. Simply view the maps in the mapping system on or after that date. There is no need to print anything to keep in a binder. All maps are accessible by all teachers and administrators at any time.

She next mentioned that it is important that the teachers are provided feedback from other teachers rather than solely from an administrator. Accountability in mapping is teachers to teachers with administrative support. Curriculum mapping council members should be meeting regularly with their designated small groups as well as mixed groups to provide feedback to others. Council members want feedback on their maps as well. This creates or extends the collegial nature of mapping in a school's culture.

The trainer asked the principal if he was learning how to write administrative maps. He replied that he was attempting to write a professional development administrative map. She mentioned that he too should be receiving feedback from teachers on his map because the protocols for writing a professional development map are the same as a teacher's student-centered maps.

(Continued)

(Continued)

There should also be times when the teachers are engaged in teachers-to-teachers meetings, as they often begin asking one another thought-provoking, curriculum design questions that may not happen as openly if the meeting is perceived as an administrator-led, *let me tell you what you should be doing* forum.

The principal pondered what the trainer had pointed out. He admitted that it is hard to break old habits. "I will go green from now on and look at the maps online," he shared. "I will also have a follow-up meeting with the council members after your day here to rethink a plan for providing teacher-led feedback sessions. I truly see the value in mapping, and I want to make certain my teachers see and experience that value as well."

CURRICULUM RESPONSIBILITIES

Curriculum responsibilities can be overwhelming at times, not just for teachers, but for principals as well. Principals have to constantly maintain a balance between school-site-initiated and district-mandated curriculum accountabilities.

While there are times set aside for administrative meetings, principals often mention they need opportunities to share and discuss their personal needs for supporting their teachers as leaders while simultaneously trying to expand their own understanding involved in various initiatives.

Scheduling and meetings involving principals and other district administrators often leave no time to meet in person to reflect, ponder, and support one another in an open, honest, and transparent forum. If trust among a district's administrators is strong, creating a private online educational social network is an excellent way to establish an asynchronous thought-exchange forum. If trust is an issue, an alternative is to join an already established online networking forum. Online forums can be joined based on desired demographics, global connections, or specific initiatives, such as curriculum mapping or 21st-century learning.

While personal networking among principals is important, networking with district administrators to best address immediate concerns or problems that may surface as the district's curriculum mapping strategic plan and each school's action plan unfold is equally important.

District and School-Site Perspectives

Curriculum can be viewed through a wide-angle lens and a zoom lens. A principal needs to ensure that his or her teachers are consciously and consistently viewing curriculum from *both* perspectives. A principal who nurtures teachers to be curriculum design leaders within their own school as well as being involved in districtwide curriculum work will find implementation and reaching sustainability easier. If teachers have not taught in a variety of grade levels, they may not view curriculum through fully engaged wide-angle lenses. It is important for principals and teachers to gain insight and understanding into how teachers value learning and learning expectations in and among schools. Teachers' horizontal and vertical values may be influenced by variables such as

- multigenerational teachers' personal and professional experiences;
- previous or current experiences with curriculum design;
- previous or current experiences with authentic assessments that influence curriculum design;
- state or other standards' requisites that may or may not have been closely analyzed or open to questioning; and
- willingness or desire to think outside the box to upgrade or replace content, skill, or assessment expectations that reflect 21st-century learning and instructional practice.

Supporting Task Forces

Curriculum mapping asks teachers in and among schools to periodically participate in task forces rather than serve on committees. A task force is *the right people meeting for the right reasons at the right times* whether in one school or districtwide (Jacobs, 2008).

A principal needs to be supportive of both school-site-specific and districtwide task-force formations. If a principal does not support the necessity for his or her school to be adequately represented in a districtwide task force, the school, teachers, and—ultimately—the students may suffer in the short or long run.

A medium-sized district consisting of six elementary schools, two middle schools, and one high school informed each school's principal of the need to select teachers to serve on a Science Essential Maps Task Force to be involved and work collaboratively for one week at the beginning of the summer. The district science director sent an e-mail to each school's principal and curriculum mapping council members that included the task-force requisites. The task force would consist of herself, approximately 29 teachers, and a science liaison from an area educational-service center that would be supporting the task force's work.

As the summer break approached, one middle school principal and one elementary school principal had not turned in a selected teachers list. Even with reminder e-mails and phone calls, when the task force began their work, there was no representation from the elementary school and only one teacher from the middle school. The science director was not surprised by their behavior. In the past, these principals showed varying degrees of support for district initiatives. While she wanted to press the issue, she knew her efforts would be seen as an unnecessary confrontation and chose not to pursue the issue further.

The task force's week of collaborative work was extremely productive. Based on each school's Consensus Maps and previous learning facilitated by the area service-center liaison, the teachers worked to systemically design

(Continued)

(Continued)

big ideas and essential questions for selected units of study that would serve as their first attempt to revise and upgrade units of study to include technology integration and cornerstone assessments. The units were housed in the district's mapping system as Essential Maps. At the onset of the new school year, each school would be directed to choose to either copy and replace the units of study in their existing Consensus Maps or copy the revised or upgraded portions of the units into the Consensus Maps. The teachers at each school would then add supporting questions to the units and brainstorm instructional practices to support the new learning requisites. As the units are used, each teacher would reflect on the learning process and provide operational evidence in his or her Projected/Diary Map.

Toward the end of the week, a group of teachers was talking during a break time that included the attending elementary teachers and solo middle school teacher. They spoke to the science director and voiced their uneasiness about the upcoming implementation and accountability because there was no representation from one elementary school and only one teacher from one of the middle schools during this work week.

"We think what we have accomplished makes so much sense for our students. We have systemically thought through the development of the big ideas from the students' K–12 perspective, and the essential questions will cause them to think critically and transfer their learning," shared the solo middle school teacher. "I know this will go well in Raven Horn Middle School, but what about my school? What am I supposed to do? The Raven Horn teachers can work as a team to explain what we've done and collaborate with the other science teachers in their school to try it all out this coming year. But what about me? I am a team of one. I feel a burden that I don't think I should have to carry."

While the science director promised to work with him on making certain the learning expectations and accountability happened in his school, she knew that in reality the behavior pattern of his principal might make it difficult. She was thinking the same thing about the one elementary school with no task-force representation. It was frustrating to see the excitement and enthusiasm of the task force working diligently to ensure students have worthwhile learning experiences and knowing deep inside that the implementation would not be an equal effort in each school. She wished she had pressed the issue now that she had seen the passion the teachers had for the collegial work that had been accomplished. She knew she would need to meet with the assistant superintendent of curriculum to enlist his support and direction to resolve the lack of support concern aptly voiced by the teachers and to make certain that the units of study did in fact get implemented and supported properly by all of the principals.

Knowing that science was the first discipline to reach the Essential Map work, she wanted to make certain the implementation was positive. She decided that she would need to go to both of these schools' curriculum mapping council meetings to discuss proper implementation and how their survey feedback would help support the task force and future curriculum decisions.

As the narrative showcased, when a district forms discipline-specific or mixed-discipline task forces, principals need to support teachers directly or indirectly involved in the process as well as the results of the collaborative work. To display such support early on, it is recommended that principals attend any curriculum mapping work meetings to see the teachers in action. Even if a principal stays for only 15–30 minutes and asks some of the teachers to share about their involvement, his or her appearance builds, or continues to build, trust between a principal and his or her faculty as well as with teachers across the district.

Standards Accountability

Another duality a principal needs to deal with is the demands of standards-based learning and assessment-results accountability. With an increased importance in standards accountability, local, state, common core, national, or self-generated, the public competition of who's who among schools makes this a concern principals must wrestle with. When a school produces poor scores on one or more parts or demographics of a state or other mandated assessment, the first person held accountable is the principal. He or she is expected to immediately change students' scores for the better. This can cause a precarious situation for a school that is just beginning to implement curriculum mapping. The pressure to increase student scores straight away makes it difficult for teachers to have the necessary time and cognitive reserves to process, explore, and grapple with the procedures and mechanics involved in mapping.

Making a public-awareness statement early on that mapping does not and will not raise scores in an exponential manner in a matter of months is necessary. Mapping is a systemic process, which means gains in student success will take place, but most likely not in a significant external manner during the first year or two of full implementation. Many states have mediation requisites for a school or district that is underperforming. This may include reshaping a district's central office and the principals' authority, responsibilities, and roles. Some states mandate the use of curriculum mapping to expedite improving test scores that may lead to a misguided use of curriculum mapping.

Curriculum mapping is meant to be an ongoing process that leads to articulating, refining, replacing, and upgrading learning and instructional practice to improve and expand student learning (Jacobs, 1997, 2004, 2006, 2010). Curriculum mapping is not meant to be a quick fix; it is a replacement model for how all curriculum work is accomplished (Hale, 2008; Jacobs, 1997, 2004, 2006, 2010; Jacobs & Johnson, 2009; Udelhofen, 2005, 2008).

If a principal finds himself or herself in a situation where curriculum mapping is being treated as a quick fix to improve test scores, and a school site or districtwide emphasis is focused on *getting the maps done quickly*—which often translates into *no follow-up usage or ongoing review of the created maps*—mapping will be difficult to sustain. He or she needs to ask for an administrative meeting with all of the principals and the central-office curriculum administrators (assuming there is no curriculum mapping cadre in place) to address this concern, as it is not the intent of the curriculum mapping model or its tenets.

Hale (2008) outlines 10 curriculum mapping tenets:

1. Curriculum mapping is a *multifaceted, ongoing process* designed to improve student learning.

2. All curricular decisions are data and standards driven and in the students' best interest.

3. Curriculum maps represent both the planned and the operational learning.

4. Curriculum maps are created and accessed using 21st-century technology.

5. Teachers are leaders in *curriculum design and curricular decision-making processes.*

6. Administrators encourage and support teacher-leader environments.

7. Curriculum reviews are conducted on an *ongoing and regular basis.*

8. Collaborative inquiry and dialogue are based on curriculum maps and other data sources.

9. Action plans aid in *designing, revising, and refining maps.*

10. Curriculum mapping intra-organizations facilitate sustainability. (p. 4, emphasis added)

When synthesized, these tenets represent an ongoing collaborative teacher-leaders curriculum work environment. Tenet six calls on administrators to encourage and support the teachers as leaders, which includes the necessity for providing adequate time and meeting structures to allow teachers environments that are conducive to meeting and working horizontally and vertically to improve students' learning expectations and experiences. The curriculum mapping cabinet members, which include principals, need to start slow and create a vision, mission, and short- and long-range goals based on these tenets.

Raising standards-based test scores is only one facet of preparing 21st-century students. Challenging students and teachers to be critical thinkers who are prepared for a global social, political, and economic environment that is evolving exponentially is critical to curriculum design and instructional practices (Jacobs, 2010). While a principal needs to encourage and support teachers and students in the here and now, he or she must be cognizant of the needs of future students who may not be in his or her school building, the district, and at times, who have not yet been born.

Establishing a Curriculum Mapping Council

Designing, implementing, reviewing, and revising curriculum design and instructional practices are an ongoing collaborative process. Each school needs to balance the alignment of its curriculum goals with the district's goals as it strives to meet the needs of the students it immediately serves (Jacobs, 1997, 2004). Establishing each school's curriculum mapping council aids in the monitoring and support of ongoing curriculum work. Whether this team of teachers is literally referred to as a *council,* or if another term is used, is not important. What is important is clarifying the roles and responsibilities of the council members. Hale (2008) recommends,

> A school site's Curriculum Mapping Council consists of teachers, administrators, and technology support personnel who collectively represent all grade levels, disciplines, and support services. Curriculum Mapping Council membership is approximately represented in a 1:5 ratio—one Curriculum Mapping Council member to every five teachers. Council members become mentally and emotionally confident in all processes and procedures of curriculum mapping and the selected mapping system. Members participate in ongoing curriculum mapping professional learning opportunities to become familiar with the districtwide implementation plans in order to help collaboratively design annual school-site action plans. Curriculum Mapping Council members
>
> - Agree to at least a two-year service commitment (it is recommended that members rotate off and on in a staggered fashion so there is always a balance between fresh perspectives and seasoned participants);
> - Agree to actively participate in curriculum mapping professional learning opportunities (e.g., book or video study, conference attendance, district training, school-site-specific training);
> - Assist a designated team of five or six like or mixed-group faculty members in gaining personal and collective understanding, including both the districtwide and school-site requisites for designing various types of curriculum maps, recording maps in the mapping system, and using the created maps and the mapping system's search and report features to help with data collection when conducting curriculum reviews; and
> - Commit to meeting as a council in person each month to
>   - prepare or modify the school-site annual curriculum mapping action plans;
>   - discuss site-based teacher, grade level, or department progresses, challenges, and concerns, and if necessary, determine immediate actions or necessary modifications to the action plans based on the current pulse in relation to school-site and district mapping requisites;
>   - recommend immediate or future curriculum mapping or related professional development learning for the entire school, small groups, or individual teachers;
>   - plan for informal and formal celebrations of both the small steps and the giant leaps made regarding various aspects of the curriculum mapping processes and procedures; and
>   - assist school-site principal, other administrators, and fellow curriculum mapping cabinet members in any aspect of implementation or sustainability that calls for personal or collective support. (pp. 237–238)

The fourth bullet mentions meeting monthly. After mapping has been established, this requisite often changes to meeting once a grading period or semester because by this time there will be various task forces and teams working on curriculum that do not necessarily need input or direction from the council. Informing the curriculum mapping council members of what is taking place in an ongoing manner is important so that that the school at large stays informed.

While principals and other administrators may serve on the councils, they are seen as supporters of the teacher leadership and direction. A principal needs to encourage, engage, and support teachers involved in and beyond the curriculum mapping council by instilling and ensuring a schoolwide collaborative curriculum work environment. This environment may include such meeting forums as professional learning communities, critical friends, book studies, and periodic task forces that address a school's specific issues, problems, concerns, and bright spots.

Celebrations

It is important that the principal and curriculum mapping council periodically celebrate all of the hard work and dedication displayed by all the teachers in a school, including those who are willing to be trailblazers and initially serve on a curriculum mapping council. As Thomas J. Peters, coauthor of *In Search of Excellence* (quoted in Mason-Draffen, 2007), wisely noted, "Celebrate what you want to see more of" (p. 99).

Celebrations do not need to be costly events. Here are a few ideas principals have used to extend appreciation to their faculties without grand expenditures:

- Present cake and ice cream at a faculty meeting.
- Cook up a special breakfast before the start of a professional development day.
- Provide a chance to win door prizes (including a donated grand prize) such that everyone gets to enter and win at least one prize.
- Allow early release for teachers for one week (e.g., do not have to stay the mandated half-hour after school as contracts denote).
- Provide a special retreat site for the beginning-of-school-year professional development days, and treat everyone to catered meals.
- Present an awarded grant for placing an interactive whiteboard in every classroom.

New Teachers

The principal and curriculum mapping council members need to be cognizant of new teachers who may need a little or a lot of training and mentoring concerning curriculum mapping's processes and procedures. Most often, a designated council member mentors a specific new teacher for his or her first year in the school. The council member can provide help with the basic and advanced features of the selected mapping system, including how to access current and archived maps and how to begin the personal-mapping process; sharing the history of mapping in the district and the school; explaining the current district strategic plan and school's action plan, including expectations of a new teacher; and informing the teacher of any current curriculum work that he or she should be aware of or will be participating in that may directly or indirectly involve curriculum mapping.

Having archived and current curriculum accessible via maps for all teachers is an asset once curriculum mapping has been implemented and has reached a level of sustainability. Oftentimes, a teacher is not literally new to the district, but rather new to a particular school or grade level within a school. Having access to the district's systemic curriculum aids in minimizing disruptions to students' learning continuum when teachers retire or resign and new teachers join the faculty.

At the end of the school year, a private elementary school was losing half of its faculty to retirement or career changes. While new teacher candidates were being interviewed, some of the remaining faculty members made desired shifts in grade levels for the following school year. Because the faculty had been working on designing vertically aligned Consensus Maps for the past four years, each teacher who moved to a new grade level instantly had access to not only the grade level's collaborative maps but also to the teacher's personal Projected/Diary Maps as well.

During interviews, the prospective teachers were shown the Consensus Maps and asked if they were comfortable with the responsibilities associated with teaching the agreed-upon student learning for those grade levels. The teachers who were eventually hired commented on how much they appreciated not having to guess what the students had to know and be able to do. This information afforded them more time and energy for preparing their instructional practices for teaching their classes.

At the first faculty meeting of the school year, the senior faculty expressed how they now felt, more than ever, the value of the hours and days dedicated to designing their curriculum maps using their agreed-upon protocols. They also expressed that their selected curriculum mapping system was an essential tool, as it made their maps into a database that enhanced their work. While their school had been in existence for 15 years, they agreed it was the first time a major shift in faculty members took place with a smooth transition for teachers and, most importantly, their students.

NOT JUST MAKING MAPS—USING MAPS

A theme throughout this book has been that curriculum mapping asks teachers to be actively engaged in not only designing maps but also using the created maps to make ongoing decisions about what is in the students' best interests. To use the maps, it is prudent that all teachers and administrators know how to use the various search and report features in their selected mapping system. With awareness of its abilities and uses, a mapping system's features enhance curriculum conversations and decision making.

When curriculum mapping is initially implemented and the use of maps may feel foreign, it is important for the curriculum mapping cabinet and council members to learn about the mapping system's potential searching and reporting capabilities and brainstorm potential ways to use the maps in conjunction with these features and external data. Figure 5.2 includes a few examples of how curriculum maps may be used to explore questions raised within a single discipline, multiple disciplines, or one or more grade levels.

As teachers become familiar and comfortable with using the mapping system and making connections to external data, they will begin to brainstorm their own ways to use the maps to make data-based decisions. They will also begin to want to add information to the maps or mapping system once they realize its potential for creating evidence of their ongoing curriculum work.

Figure 5.2   Possible Uses for Curriculum Maps

Concern	Mapping System Feature
What courses contain a focus on Shakespearean literature?	• Keyword Search ○ Shakespeare* ○ Specific work (e.g., *Romeo and Juliet*) (Asterisk indicates a *truncation* search. Any word that begins with the letters preceding the asterisk will be in the results, such as *Shakespeare* and *Shakespearean*.)
What do students have to know (content) and be able to do (skills) related to the scientific process in our elementary school and middle school?	• Keyword Search ○ "scientific process" ○ hypothisi* ○ lab* (Quotation marks indicate a *phrase* search. This aids in the results not containing undesired isolate words.)
Are there any gaps, repetitions, or absences in learning expectations (content and skills) based on the K–12 media literacy standards?	• Compare Courses
Where do mathematics standards' indicators occur outside of mathematics courses in our high school?	• Standards Analysis
What types of assessments are being used for Grade 11 students regardless of course?	• Compare Courses • Assessment Type Frequency

A large high school's curriculum mapping action plan included implementing a cross-curricular literacy initiative in the fall of the new school year. The faculty had addressed the reality that literacy (i.e., reading, writing, speaking, listening, media) skill building should not be the sole responsibility of English teachers. The full faculty had worked collaboratively to determine the specific English/language arts standard indicators that would be included in the cross-curricular initiative during the spring semester of the previous school year. A literacy task force was then formed that would facilitate the initiative's implementation. They met the week before the new school year began to revisit the initiative's goals and solidify two implementation phases based on the faculty's agreed-upon action plan.

Phase one consisted of running a repeated two-part workshop during the first month of the school year. The English teachers agreed to share the responsibilities for facilitating the various sessions. The remainder of the faculty would be attending the workshop focused on learning or expanding understanding of the meaning and intent of the selected literacy-standard statements and suggested ways to integrate them into a course. During the second part of the workshop, participants would be provided time and support to begin the integration process when working on their individual maps.

During this process time, the participating teachers selected one Projected/Diary Map course with the goal of refining one existing skill expectation per month by embedding one or more of the literacy-standard indicators into the selected skill. The teachers were also encouraged to consider the need for revising the current aligned assessment or assessments associated with a revised skill.

For example, a skill statement for a mathematics teacher's trigonometry course originally read,

- Solve problems involving right triangles using the Pythagorean theorem

After revising, the skill statement read,

- Explain orally and in writing problems involving right triangles using the Pythagorean theorem

While the difference between the two skill statements may appear to be slight, the student-learning expectation now affected appropriate assessment choices based on the two integrated literacy-standard indicators this teacher selected to incorporate into the skill expectation:

Writing Standard

- *Revise writing to improve style, word choice, sentence variety, and subtlety of meaning after rethinking how questions of purpose, audience, and genre have been addressed.*

(Continued)

(Continued)

Speaking Standard

- *Speak using skills appropriate to formal-speech situations.*
  - *Use a variety of sentence structures to add interest to a presentation.*
  - *Pace the presentation according to audience and purpose.*
  - *Adjust stress, volume, and inflection to provide emphasis to ideas or to influence the audience.*

This teacher then chose to replace the current aligned assessment, which originally was paper-pencil problems, with

- Pythagorean Theorem Tutorial Online Video

He shared that he decided to take what he had learned in another recently attended workshop on integrating technology in the classroom. He felt that, because his students would be asked to focus on the audience aspects of the two selected indicators, an excellent idea is to have the students individually create an online tutorial. He shared during the workshop that he was going to have the students create their tutorials using a free online software program that allowed students to upload created videos to the Internet and be viewed by students worldwide. He would have his students choose to make the video for either a struggling student or one who may understand but wants a refresher. He mentioned that he felt if students could write a script with storyboard visuals to help others learn, they have to be able to solve problems as well as consider word choice and the learning needs of the intended audience.

At the end of each two-day workshop, that session's English teachers made note of when the teachers in attendance were planning on integrating the standard indicators in their classrooms to be available to provide continual support and have a follow-up meeting with each teacher to debrief implementation, discuss the results, and encourage each teacher for being willing to be a risk taker and trying a new approach to their discipline with a literacy viewpoint.

Before the winter break, the faculty met to celebrate and share in the successes of phase one's integration. A social studies teacher of 30 years expressed how his students' ability to make connections, text to text, text to self, text to world, and text to media with a variety of text had vastly improved. He shared that the strategies the English teachers explained and modeled in the workshop, plus their continued support in his implementation process, were greatly appreciated.

This high school began phase two in January. It centered on improving student achievement for targeted discipline focuses on the state assessment based on literacy-testing results that were cross-referenced with Consensus Maps and Projected/Diary Maps using the mapping system's search and report features.

Each department, with the aid of the literacy task force, created SMART (Specific, Measurable, Attainable, Realistic, Timely) goals during the fall semester. For example, a Grade-11 SMART goal for the English/Language Arts department was

95% of Grade 11's free/reduced meal program's female and male populations will achieve at least a 15% increase in reading proficiency and 20% increase in writing proficiency on the PSSA (Pennsylvania System of School Assessment) by June, 2009.

A Grade-10 SMART goal for the science department was

90% of Grade 10's male and female populations will achieve a 15% increase in reading comprehension of complex technical text by June, 2009, based on the Grade 9 and 10 Technical Reading Benchmark Assessment.

Each department chair stayed in close contact with the literacy task force to seek support, guidance, and encouragement when necessary to reach the department's SMART goal based on their supporting steps. The principal supported this new phase when teachers asked to revamp prep-period configurations to allow a better connection among department members for the winter and spring semesters.

Each department met once a month to focus on the SMART goal and their instruction and formative assessments. While the state testing results would not be available until summer, the departments answered questions via an online survey formulated by the literacy task force near the school year's end. The survey report was provided online and referred to during a faculty meeting. Teachers shared their personal-growth experiences based on collegially focusing on a specific goal. They noted that they would continue to create SMART goals not only with a connection to literacy but for focuses within their specific disciplines as well.

In the early spring, the literacy task force continued their personal and collegial learning by attended a training provided by the Pennsylvania Literacy Academy to enhance the faculty's literacy professional development. With the insights gained, they planned a faculty meeting to explore some of the ideas shared during the training. The facilitators of the meeting conducted a jigsaw using excerpts from two readings: *Creating a Culture of Literacy: A Guide for Middle and High School Principals* (Phillips, 2005) and *Active Literacy Across the Curriculum: Strategies for Reading, Writing, Speaking, and Listening* (Jacobs, 2006).

The jigsaw groups' discussions were lively. The facilitators asked for a volunteer from each group to share how the readings may influence their high school's next steps based on what had taken place during the school year. The literacy task force took notes and would be meeting to formulate a draft of the next school year's action plan, which would then be reviewed and eventually approved by the entire faculty. The principal closed the meeting

(Continued)

(Continued)

by showing appreciation for the entire faculty's commitment to improve student learning as well as acknowledging the task force and English/language arts department's efforts to make it a successful year for all. He also mentioned that, for the next school year, the establishment of a mandatory reading program for nonproficient readers would be a reality. Students entering the high school scoring basic or below basic on the state testing must take a mandatory reading class until they meet the established criteria. Two reading specialists had been hired to staff the reading program for 9th and 10th graders and one specialist for the Drop-In Center, a resource room where all students would be able to receive help before, during, and after school. Also, members of the National Honor Society would rotate volunteer time to provide free tutoring services to students who visit the Drop-In Center.

The impact of the two phases of implementation, plus the plans for the new year—that included student participation—forged a sense of community and a collective commitment among teachers, students, and administration concerning curriculum and instruction. The shared leadership, connections to multiple initiatives, and the implementation of a well-designed plan enabled the high school to increase the initial goal of improving student achievement in reading and writing. The literacy efforts were becoming a way of life that included the teachers finding value in using their collaborative and personal maps and the mapping process.

Because mapping systems are online, oftentimes teachers begin to link to, or embed, documents, images, websites, and other forms of retrievable data outside of the maps' searchable database to provide easy access rather than having to retrieve the desired information through another system or software service. Collaborative opportunities using the seven-step review process outlined in Chapter 2 can be incorporated in grade-level, department, or full-faculty meetings as well as task-force work. Using synthesized data compiled from information such as curriculum maps; testing results; surveys from teachers, students, parents, guardians, and work communities; and educational communities, a school site can make long- and short-term goals based on their curriculum focuses and instructional practices.

CONCLUSION

A principal's support for teachers involved in curriculum mapping is multifaceted. Support includes establishing, building, maintaining, and expanding trust; ensuring adequate time for teachers to be learners and curriculum leaders; and providing collegial structures both within a school and among schools.

As mentioned in the Preface, curriculum mapping is a model for developing, refining, and upgrading curriculum planning. Changing or replacing how curriculum work may have been accomplished in the past will evoke a variety of emotional responses from teachers. It is therefore wise for a principal to

- thoughtfully consider his or her behaviors and leadership style based on the traits and principles outlined in Appendix B, especially in relation to building or expanding trust between administration and faculty and among faculty;
- continually grow in personal understanding of single-discipline and interdisciplinary learning perspectives, technology-minded learning and assessment environments, and encouraging students to be global thinkers and participants (Jacobs, 2010);
- openly encourage and support teachers in their work to design, revise, replace, and upgrade the curriculum by recognizing the teachers as leaders and curriculum experts; and developing or sustaining school improvement by developing an environment where teachers function as professional learning communities that focus on clear goals and actions for improving student learning (DuFour & Eaker, 1998); and
- purposefully take small, calculated steps toward developing a school-site curriculum design and instructional practice mission and vision—based on the district's curriculum mapping vision and mission—that creates a synergy among grade levels and between departments as well as across school levels through the coleadership of the principal, the curriculum mapping council, and all teachers in each school site.

As mentioned previously, a principal's ongoing task is to synthesize the initiatives, requisites, and needs of multiple curriculum leaders, such as the superintendent of curriculum and instruction, districtwide curriculum directors, school-site coaches, grade-level representatives, and department chairs. A principal, along with members of the curriculum mapping cadre, cabinet, and council, need to be able to articulate connections between and among multiple initiatives, whether district or school-site intended.

Curriculum development engages the whole school, creates conversations around curriculum, and fosters ownership (Glatthorn & Jailall, 2009). When a principal meets the challenges of transformational leadership, curriculum knowledge, and the high-stakes accountability of student learning becoming teacher led, he or she will experience firsthand the benefits that curriculum mapping embraces.

REVIEW QUESTIONS

Whether you are a principal, central-office administrator, or teacher leader, attempt to answer the questions from a principal's perspective. Discuss your answers with a colleague or in a small group.

1. What level of understanding do you have of your district's and school's past, present, and desired future curriculum design and instructional practice work? How have you played a direct or indirect role in supporting this curriculum work?

2. How do you see yourself working alongside fellow administrators and teachers leaders involved in a districtwide curriculum mapping initiative to support your school's teachers as well as teachers throughout the district?

3. If curriculum mapping is considered the curriculum work hub, how do you perceive the current districtwide and school-site initiatives fitting into the curriculum mapping initiative? Share a specific example of how you can see curriculum mapping and curriculum maps connecting to another initiative. How can you see the curriculum mapping process connecting to classroom, school, or district data to aid in data-analysis reviews of student achievement?

4. How do you plan to provide sufficient, quality time for your teachers to meet to adequately learn the processes and procedures involved in curriculum mapping and developing maps? What creative ideas do you have for creating ongoing meeting structures (in your school and among schools in the district) based on the district's current or revised strategic plan and your school's curriculum mapping action plan once they have been created?

5. How do you see professional development changing (e.g., time, location, differentiation) based on the implementation of curriculum mapping and using the maps as a part of data-informed decision making?

6. Who are the teachers in your school that you are considering as members of the curriculum mapping cabinet? Which teachers would you ask to join in the teacher-leadership process when establishing your school's curriculum mapping council? Make a list of the teachers for the two levels of mapping leadership teams, including each teacher's strengths as well as why you consider these teachers to collectively be a good choice. Be ready to share the names and your reasoning for each teacher and each team's professional and personal dynamics.

6

What Do Professional Development Administrative Maps Look Like?

Leadership and learning are indispensable to each other.

—John F. Kennedy

There are many administrators who want to learn how to write administrative maps. To do so, an administrator or teacher leader must first decide what kind of administrative map he or she wants to record. The first kind is a *professional development* map. This map is written with the same map-element protocols as a curriculum map because the focus is on what learners must know (content) and be able to do (skills). Professional development learners are most often teachers, staff members, or administrators.

The second kind of administrative map is a *professional roles* map. It focuses on an administrator's work environment rather than on learners' knowing and doing. Because of this, three elements in this kind of a map transform from *content*, *skills*, and *assessments* to *responsibility*, *actions*, and *evidence*. Chapter 7 is dedicated to protocols and providing examples for writing a professional roles map.

PROFESSIONAL DEVELOPMENT MAPS: QUALITY MAP WRITING

When a curriculum mapping implementation begins, administrators often see the potential for personally participating in the map-writing process. If not provided with a clear understanding of the two kinds of administrative maps, *each with a different purpose,* administrators have a tendency to mix the two kinds in one map without realizing it. This can be a disservice to teachers who are in the beginning or intermediate stages of learning how to write quality maps based on curriculum design protocols.

Skill Statements Versus Action Statements

The map element that most often becomes mixed is *skills.* Hale (2008) defines *skill* as "what students must do in relation to the knowing (content). Skills are cognitive *ability,* physical *action,* or a combination of both. . . . A skill represents ability or action competency, not an activity leading toward competency" (p. 51). Teachers as curriculum map designers are asked to write cognitive-skill statements using a specific protocol: *measurable verb-target-descriptor.* Likewise, a professional development map's skill statements need to be written with the same protocol because the map's skills represent what the learner must cognitively do. This is not the case for a professional roles map as the verb-based statement represents a literal action *by the person recording the map,* not a second-party learner. That is why the professional roles map's field is titled *actions* rather than *skills.*

A literal action statement may at first appear to be a skill statement, as both begin with a verb. The question in a map reader's mind must always be, "Who is responsible for the verb's action?" Take a moment to study the following statements gleaned from professional development maps that were recorded in the skills field.

- Identify visually and orally standards symbols within the mapping system
- Categorize in writing educator concerns related to 3 staff support structures using intensity degree from greatest to least
- Compare and contrast in writing BRI data with other classroom assessment data
- Create electronically a teacher website page with at least 2 links within the site
- Present workshop titled *Using PowerPoint to Create Talking Books*
- Provide background about and access to newly purchased social studies books
- Review bus routes for the year with Business Office
- Spruce up building and grounds

While all eight statements begin with a verb, the first four bullets are truly skill statements in that a *second-party learner* is responsible for the statements' cognitive action or ability. This is not the case for the four remaining bullets. These statements inform the reader of the *map writer's actions.* Therefore, having two *distinct* kinds of administrative maps alleviates the potential for mixed messages concerning skills for learners versus actions of a map writer or writers.

As shared previously, when administrators choose to write professional development maps, they use the same wording, format, and intra-alignment protocols as teachers designing curriculum maps. For in-depth information regarding design protocols for each map element's wording, format, and intra-alignment, it is recommended you read Chapter 4 of *A Guide to Curriculum Mapping: Planning, Implementing, and Sustaining the Process* (Hale, 2008). For a quick reference writing guide, use the protocols and examples in Figure 6.1.

Unit Names

Appendix A focuses on teachers collaboratively developing systemic unit names. Oftentimes, administrators choose to develop their own set of systemic unit names, so their maps can serve as a database for archived and current-year administrative information. Figure 6.2 represents a Midwest school district's administrative topic/theme unit names and a few examples from administrators' maps.

Whether or not a district's administrators choose to develop systemic unit names, if a unit name repeats more than once in a given academic year (which may include summer months for administrators), the first time it is used, the unit is given a Roman numeral. The next time or times the unit name is used, the unit name is given the next sequential Roman numeral. A revisited unit name may not necessarily be included in each month. If a unit name appears *only once* in an administrative map, it *does not* need a Roman numeral, as there is no need to indicate it is being revisited in the same academic year.

Housing Administrative Maps: Mapping System Considerations

Experience has led to not only differentiating between the two kinds of administrative maps but also *where* the maps are housed within a mapping system. Because professional development maps are learner oriented, they use the same content, skills, and assessment element titles and therefore can be housed in the same locations (district or school sites) as student-centered curriculum maps. The administrators simply need to create appropriate *course names* (e.g., Assistant Principal; Math Curriculum Coordinator; Technology Coordinator) within the appropriate school or district location in the mapping system and begin the map-writing process.

Because professional roles maps are writer oriented and have different element fields (responsibility, actions, evidence), administrators need to have a new location (e.g., school) created in the mapping system. This may need to be done by the mapping system company at the company office or may be accomplished locally by someone with administrative rights, depending on the selected mapping system.

Figure 6.1   Professional Development Map Elements: Wording, Format, and Intra-Alignment Protocols

	Unit Name	Content	Skills	Assessments (Evaluations)	Activities/ Strategies	Resources	Standards
Wording	• Theme/Topic • Theme/Topic: Descriptor • Unit Name Signifier: Theme/Topic	• Noun/ Noun Phrase: Descriptor	• Measurable verb-target-descriptor *Do not begin skill statement with the words:* Demonstrate Understand Learn Know Show Use *(they are not considered measureable for preciseness of learning)*	• Assessment written as defined-noun phrase • Evaluation written in parentheses (Evaluation: descriptor representing evaluative method or methods/tool or tools) • If an assessment is formative or informal (rather than summative or formal), include FOR prior to Assessment Name (e.g., A1-A2. FOR Book Study Meetings)	• Short summary statement • May choose to attach comprehensive information aligned to summary statement	• If there is no dedicated resources element field, the term *Resources* starts with a capital letter and is in italics	Professional development content/skills learning may or may not have alignable standards. If there are professional standards, and they have been loaded or added into the mapping system, how and where the standards are embedded within the map varies depending on the mapping system used.

100

	Unit Name	Content	Skills	Assessments (Evaluations)	Activities/Strategies	Resources	Standards
Format	• All capital letters • Boldfaced (if system capable)	• Each word begins with a capital letter	• Statement begins with capital letter • No period needed at end of statement	• Each word begins with a capital letter • Evaluation information, if included, is recorded in parentheses directly after assessment • May choose to attach assessment and/or evaluation information • Indicate formative assessment by using capital letters FOR prior to assessment name	• Summary begins with capital letter • May or may not be more than one sentence	• If there is no dedicated field for resources,* listed directly beneath appropriate Content • Each listing begins with double dash *If dedicated field, include appropriate intra-alignment coding prior to listing resources	
Intra-Alignment	• Not applicable	• Begin visual intra-alignment using alphabet letters	• Aligned to content using letters • Aligned to assessments using letter/number coding	• Aligned to content and skills using letter/number coding	• Aligned to content and skills using letter/number coding	• Not applicable unless separate field; then aligned to content or content and skills	

(Continued)

Figure 6.1 (Continued)

Examples	Unit Name	Content	Skills	Assessments (Evaluations)	Activities/ Strategies	Resources	Standards
	CURRICULUM MAPPING I	A. Map Types: Projected/ Diary, Consensus, Essential	A1. Identify orally purpose for 4 types of curriculum maps A2. Compare and contrast visually and orally map elements utilized in 4 types of maps	A1-A2. FOR Map Identification Quiz (Evaluation: Facilitator Ob/ Teacher Feedback)	A1. Working in small teams, teachers participate in a Map Treasure Hunt as a learning opener	A. --Essential to Consensus to Projected/Diary Map Handout	
	SAFETY: INFECTIOUS DISEASES	A. Bloodborne Pathogens: Prevention	A1. Define in writing 3 pathogens: Hepatitis B (HBV), Hepatitis C, Human Immunodeficiency Virus (HIV) A2. Sequence in writing 4-step universal precautions: flood exposed area with water, clean with soap/disinfectant, report incident, seek medical attention	A1-A2. 10 MC Test	A1-A2. Watch DVD, stopping periodically to emphasize learning points	A. --Bloodborne Pathogens DVD --OSHA BBP Guidelines Handout	

Unit Name	Content	Skills	Assessments (Evaluations)	Activities/ Strategies	Resources	Standards
TECHNOLOGY INTEGRATION I	Web 2.0 Tool: Wiki	A1. Create a wiki page consisting of text only	A1-A2. FOR Wiki Page Creation (Evaluation: Facilitator Ob/ Learner Feedback)	A1-A3. Participate in a Wiki Webinar	A. --Media Lab --Interactive Whiteboard Handout	
		A2. Embed images into wiki page	A1-A2. District Website Wiki Link Creation			
		A3. Contribute content (text/image) to an already-created wiki page	(Evaluation: Peer Ob/Teacher E-mail Feedback)			
			A3. FOR Contribution Exercise (Evaluation: Facilitator Ob/Teacher Feedback)			

Note: If a school or district is using essential/supporting questions, and administrators want to include them in a professional development map, where the questions are included in the map will depend on how the elements' fields are set up within the mapping system.

Figure 6.2   Example of Systemic Administrative Unit Names

Topic/Theme Unit Name	Topic/Theme Unit Name: Descriptor
LEADERSHIP	LEADERSHIP: PROFESSIONAL DEVELOPMENT LEADERSHIP: DATA ANALYSIS
COMMUNICATION	COMMUNICATION: STUDENTS COMMUNICATION: ONLINE NEWSLETTER
COLLABORATIVE PROCESSES	COLLABORATIVE PROCESSES: PTO COLLABORATIVE PROCESSES: BUILDING EXPANSION
INSTRUCTION	INSTRUCTION: MATHEMATICS CURRICULUM INSTRUCTION: FIELD TRIPS I
CULTURE/CLIMATE	CULTURE/CLIMATE: STUDENT RECOGNITION CULTURE/CLIMATE: EXTRACURRICULAR
MANAGEMENT	MANAGEMENT: SCHOOL SAFETY DRILLS II MANAGEMENT: SPELLING BEE

For example, some of the sample professional role maps included in the next chapter are from a district wherein the administrators chose to call the professional roles maps location within their mapping system in a "school" titled *NAFC Maps.* As with professional development maps, administrators will need to create appropriate course names for a newly created location. Depending on how the learning organization's mapping system functions, administrators will be able to access and record both kinds of administrative maps even though each kind of map is located in a different area within the mapping system.

Collaborative Versus Personal Documentation

Just as some planned-learning curriculum maps are written collaboratively (Essential Maps, Consensus Maps), professional development maps can be developed collegially and housed as such within the mapping system. Then, individual administrators copy the collaborative map into their personal Projected/Diary Map accounts and personalize the information within the map based on what really happened.

If an administrator is solely responsible for professional development trainings, workshops, or meetings, the administrator would design a Projected/Diary Map to provide documentation of his or her personally planned learning and the experienced operational learning.

PROFESSIONAL DEVELOPMENT MAP MONTH SAMPLES

Web-based maps are *live* and *interactive.* The sample administrative map months in Chapters 6 and 7 are static and cannot convey the full scope of an interconnected map-database experienced when viewing maps within a online mapping system. As shared in the Preface, in the unit samples, underlined text indicates a *live* link to a Uniform Resource Locator (URL) embedded into the map. If you were online, when the underlined text is clicked, you would be instantly directed to the embedded website.

Each sample map month's units are displayed in tables. As each commercial mapping system has a unique configuration for housing the collective units per month, a table generically conveys the map element information without needing to be concerned with the specifics for a particular mapping system. For example, some mapping systems house the units by specific months while others house them by weeks within the months to aid in displaying a unit or units that involve overlapping months (e.g., September [Week 3]–October [Week 5] indicates a three-week unit that bridges September and October).

The following sample map months include a variety of professional development focuses. You may find it beneficial to compare these *learner-oriented* map samples with the professional roles *action-oriented* map samples beginning on page 126.

CONCLUSION

Administrative mapping is advantageous for three reasons. One, it provides the opportunity for administrators to walk in the same shoes as teachers during the intensive learning curve when introduced to writing curriculum maps based on a set of protocols and curriculum design expectations. Two, it provides administrators with the ability to communicate via current and archived maps within a mapping system. For example, a new administrator appreciates having access to the previous administrator's maps just as a new teacher appreciates having access to a previous teacher's map. Third, it allows administrators to use maps as a data-collection venue to make informed decisions. Oftentimes, administrators will collaboratively choose to individually map a particular focus so they can create a yearly database of information. Administrators who choose to personally design professional development administrative maps often comment that the writing process provides them with a deeper understanding of the cognitive processes asked of teachers who are asked to design curriculum maps.

Figure 6.3   Professional Development Map Month: High School Principal

Month: October (Week 5)–October (Week 8)

Unit: INSTRUCTION: NON-TENURED TEACHERS

Content	Skills	Assessment	Activities	Resources
A. Assessments: Test Writing Strategies	A1. Convert in writing general/specific learning targets into Level 1 questions (rote/recall/comprehension)/Level 2 questions (application/evaluation)/Level 3 questions (analysis/inferences) A2. Clarify orally and in writing item characteristics for created selected response and criterion reference items for selected general/specific learning targets A3. Create in writing series of test items based on selected response/criterion reference item-building criteria and 3-item-arrangement criteria (group together items measuring same learning outcome; when possible, items arranged so all same-type items are grouped together; items arranged in order of increasing difficulty) A4. Critique orally and in writing created formative/summative exams based on creation criteria	A1-A4. Teacher-created Tests/Quizzes Biweekly Critiques (Evaluation: Mentor-Teacher Review/ Rubrics) A2, A4. FOR Principal/Master Teacher Discussions (Evaluation: Peer Review/Teacher Feedback)	A1-A4. Chapter-discussion sessions including chapter exercises A3. Test of Franzipanics exercise	A. Selected chapters* from --*Classroom Assessment: What Teachers Need to Know*, James Popham --*Classroom Assessment for Student Learning*, Richard Stiggins --*Classroom Assessment and Grading That Work*, Robert Marzano *Chapter selection varies due to a teacher's needs

Content	Skills	Assessment	Activities	Resources
B. Observations: Instructional Strategies	B1. Identify visually, orally, and in writing at least 2 strategies used by master teachers during observed lesson B2. Evaluate visually, orally, and in writing students' engagement/interaction when identified instructional strategies are involved in observed lesson B3. Plan in writing and implement lesson plans using selected identifiable instructional strategies	B1-B2. 2 Master Teachers Lesson Observations (Evaluation: Master Teacher-Teacher Dialogue/Personal Notes/Checklist [provide copy to Assistant Principal] B3. Master Teacher Observation (Evaluation: Master Teacher-Teacher Dialogue/Master Teacher Notes/Checklist [provide copy to Assistant Principal])	B1. Review of recommended instructional strategies: --Identifying similarities and differences --Summarizing and note taking --Reinforcing effort and providing recognition --Homework and practice --Nonlinguistic representations --Cooperative learning --Setting objectives/ providing feedback --Generating and testing hypotheses --Questions, cues, and advance organizers	B. --Master Calendar Substitutes --*Classroom Instruction That Works*, Robert Marzano, Debra Pickering, Jane Pollock

Figure 6.4 Professional Development Map Month: Middle School Principal

Note: This map is written by a principal who chose to record a student-oriented professional development map.

Month: August

Unit: CULTURE/CLIMATE: BE A BETTER BULLPUP

Content	Skills	Assessment	Activities	Resources
A. 6th-Grade Orientation: Academic Success at Hazelwood	A1. Identify orally and in writing effective strategies for note taking, remembering, studying, taking tests A2. Monitor in writing successful use of personal strategies in various disciplines	A1–A2. Individual Student Counseling Survey (Evaluation: Counselors/ Student Feedback/Action Plan) A2. FOR 6th-Grade Academy Student Logbook (Evaluation: Counselor Ob/Student Feedback)	A1–A2. Small-group discussions with upper class students to brainstorm ideas for effective studying in school and at home	A. --Counselors --How To Study --HMS WebNews
B. Dress Code: Acceptable Clothing/ Accessories	B1. Identify visually and orally acceptable dress for outerwear, T-shirts, shirts, pants, dresses, footwear, jewelry, purses, book bags/backpacks B2. Sequence orally first warning to expulsion criteria and due-process procedures	B1–B2. Principal, Upper Class Students, 6th-Grade Students 20-Minute Discussion Groups (Evaluation: Peer Commentaries/Rubric)	B1. Discussion Questions: --What if students were allowed to wear anything to school? --Are dress codes necessary? B1. Example/Non-example PowerPoint presentation created and presented by upper class students	B–D. --Student Handbook B. --Am I Dressed Appropriately? PowerPoint

Content	Skills	Assessment	Activities	Resources
C. School Layout: Buildings, Campus	C1. Identify visually and in writing 17 locations (bus stop/6th, 7th, 8th grade wings/fine arts wing/main office/nurse's office/counselor offices/media center/gymnasium/ swimming pool/auditorium/ cafeteria/football field/baseball field/track/visitors parking) using bird's-eye-view map	C1. FOR School Map Label Locations Exercise (Evaluation: Upper Classman/Student Feedback)		C. --School/Grounds Map
D. Activities: After School at Hazelwood	D1. Identify orally 16 available activities: *Cocurricular Sports* --Football --Baseball --Basketball --Volleyball --Swimming --Track --Cross-Country --Cheerleading *Cocurricular Arts* --Jazz Band --Orchestra --Choir --Dance --Drama --Video Productions --Visual Arts --Yearbook D2. Identify orally academic regulations and behavior rules associated with activities of interest	D1-D2. FOR Principal-Counselors-Students 15-Minute Discussion Groups D1. Online and Media Center Student Sign-Ups	D1-D2. Presentations by upper class students sharing insights into offered activities during opening assembly	D. --Athletic Director --Activity Sponsors

Figure 6.5   Professional Development Map Month: Elementary School Principal

Month: September

Unit: COLLABORATIVE PROCESSES I

Content	Skills	Assessment	Activities	Resources
A. Continuous School Improvement: Vision, Mission Belief Statements	A1. Evaluate orally and in writing text for current school belief statements A2. Revise in writing Vision/Mission statements text where necessary based on embedding 21st-century thinking and learning using consensus model	A1-A2. Online Vision/Mission Statements Publication A1-A2. FOR *Do We Need Statement Revisions?* Discussion (Evaluation: Large-Group Consensus)	A1. Pose question: *Do our current statements represent the school that we are today and want to be tomorrow?* Analyze text inferences that could be made based on this question and each statement's text by working in small groups and writing thoughts/findings on chart paper.	A. --Facilitators: Nancy Schmidt, Margo Muriel, Tom Arnold --School Website: <u>Our Belief Page</u> --LCD Projector

Unit: CULTURE/CLIMATE: STUDENT BEHAVIOR I

Content	Skills	Assessment	Activities	Resources
A. Conflict Resolution: Schoolwide Bullying Program	A1. Classify orally and in writing 9 types of bullying (social exclusion or isolation; physical bullying; bullying through lies and false rumors; having money or other things taken or damaged; threats or being forced to do	A1-A3. FOR Antibullying Kickoff Assembly A1-A3. 20 (MC/FinB) Quiz A1-A2. FOR 20 Matching Bullying Classification Exercise	A1-A3. Small-group discussions during teacher training	A. --Olweus Bullying Prevention Program Teacher Guide --Olweus Antibullying Posters

Content	Skills	Assessment	Activities	Resources
	things; racial bullying; sexual bullying; cyberbullying [cell phone or Internet]) A2. Classify orally and in writing each type of bullying as direct form or indirect form using real-world examples A3. Distinguish orally and in writing bullying from aggression: bullying involves (a) negative behaviors intentionally targeted at a specific individual; (b) repetitive nature versus one-time incident; (c) power imbalance between students			--Olweus School Kick-Off Event Supplies

Unit: CURRICULUM MAPPING I

Content	Skills	Assessment	Activities	Resources
A. Mapping Software: Login, Add/Edit Features	A1. Locate online website using software URL A2. Log in and personalize user name and password	A1-A3,A5. FOR Projected/Diary Map Creation (Evaluation: CM Council Member Ob/Teacher Feedback)	A4. Participate in Search and Find Treasure Hunt to locate and learn use of each icon in add/edit window	A. --Software User Guide

(Continued)

Figure 6.5 (Continued)

Content	Skills	Assessment	Activities	Resources
	A3. Create new map by selecting appropriate course, year, month A4. Identify orally 11 icons (save, save as, bold, italics, underline, cut, copy, paste, attach standards, attach documents, attach websites) in add/edit window A5. Save and close created map	A4. FOR Icon Application Exercise (Evaluation: CM Council Member Ob/Teacher Feedback)		
B. Map Design: Unit Name, Content, Skills	B1. Explain orally systemic reason for map design format/protocols when writing unit name (CAPITAL LETTERS), content (Key Noun/Noun Phrase: Descriptor, skill (Measurable verb-target-descriptor) B2. Create and save digitally practice Projected Map month unit using appropriate systemic unit name, content listings, skill statements	B1. FOR Large-Group Discussion (Evaluation: CM Council Member Ob/Teacher Feedback) B2. Online Projected Map Month (Evaluation: CM Council Member Ob/Rubric)	B1. Map-writing practice sessions in Technology Lab	B. --Quality Map Writing Reminder Sheets --Example/Non-Example Handout --Technology Lab

Figure 6.6   Professional Development Map Month: Curriculum Mapping Coordinator

Month: February

Unit: CURRICULUM MAPPING CADRE I				
Essential Questions	*Content*	*Skills*	*Assessment*	*Resources*
EQ: How does accurate knowledge influence critical change? SQ: How can curriculum mapping promote a systemic-learning continuum for our students? SQ: How may past and present cultures in each school site and districtwide influence curriculum mapping's implementation and sustainability?	A. 5 Components To Ensure Systemic Change: Vision, Skills, Incentives, Resources, Action Plan B. Curriculum Mapping: Emotional Factors	A1. Evaluate orally and in writing 5 components in relationship to systemic change and district culture A2. Analyze orally and in writing relationship among change components in relationship to 4 present and future needs: curriculum design, instructional practice, learning structures, collegial work cultures B1. Predict in writing potential challenges for curriculum mapping in general and in relationship to current curriculum focused and related initiatives B2. Ascertain orally and in writing potential conflicts with current and future needs related to teachers' ability to meet frequently horizontally and vertically B3. Ascertain orally and in writing trust of district at large, administrators to teachers, teachers to teachers regarding curriculum design and curriculum practice	A1-A2. 5-Category Comparative Matrix Analysis (Evaluation: Cadre Commentaries/ Feedback) A2. FOR Small-/Large-Group Discussions/ Summary Notes B1-B3. Potential Curriculum Mapping Implementation Concerns/Questions Online Document B2-B3. FOR Potential Concerns/Challenges Discussion	A-D. --Skype sessions with CM consultant/trainer A. --Curriculum Mapping Implementation Critical Components Matrix --Second-Order Change Handout B-D. --Excerpts from *A Guide to Curriculum Mapping*, Hale B. --Excerpts from *Navigating Comprehensive Change*, Chenoweth & Everhart --Google Docs Emotional Factors

(Continued)

Figure 6.6 (Continued)

Essential Questions	Content	Skills	Assessment	Resources
	C. Curriculum Mapping Cabinet/Councils: Establishment Criteria	C1. Identify in writing roles and responsibilities requisites for teacher leadership positions: district level, school site level C2. Determine in writing critical components, topics for teacher leadership curriculum mapping training	C1. Job Descriptions/Requirements Online Document C1. CM Cabinet/Councils Potential Membership List C2. FOR Summer Curriculum Mapping Cabinet Workshop Action Plan C2. June CM Workshop Brochure Draft	C. --Google Docs Criteria Thoughts
	D. Map Elements: Unit Name, Content, Skills, Assessments/Evaluations, Resources, Activities/Strategies, Standards	D1. Define orally curriculum design (learn) versus curriculum practice (teach/instruction) D2. Classify orally and in writing 7 elements as curriculum design or curriculum practice D3. Define visually, orally, and in writing quality map: map reader does not need map writer or writers present to correctly interpret map data D4. Analyze and distinguish orally and in writing map elements reflecting quality versus moving toward quality D5. Summarize orally and in writing rationale for establishing quality districtwide element wording, format, intra-alignment norms D6. Analyze orally and in writing need for continuing use of outside consultation/training	D1–D5. FOR Quality Curriculum Map Elements Concerns/Questions Responses D1. FOR Large-Group Definitions D3–D5. FOR Is This A Quality Map? Exercise (Evaluation: Administrative Ob/Rubric) D3–D6. Consultation Position Online Summary (Evaluation: Peer Review/Feedback) D6. FOR Plus/Delta T-Chart	D. --Sample Curriculum Maps --Writing Quality Maps With Design in Mind PowerPoint

Figure 6.7   Professional Development Map Month: Special Education Director

Month: August

Unit: INDIVIDUAL EDUCATION PLAN (IEP) IMPLEMENTATION		
Content	Skills	Assessment
A. IEP Special Services: Classroom Modifications, Testing, Accommodations	A1. Articulate orally and in writing IEP student's special education services based on 4 criteria (general/special education teachers recommendations, services appropriate for targeted needs, review of prior implementation plan, student's progress within plan framework) using state/district documentation procedures A2. Record in writing general education alternatives IEP student receives based on cognitive, physical, and environmental needs using anecdotal evidence A3. Recommend, implement, and monitor IEP prescribed modifications for instructional environments A4. Articulate in writing accommodations for IEP student's classroom, district, and state testing environments based on instructional accommodations and IEP testing allowances pursuant to state laws in tandem with Individuals with Disabilities Education Act (IDEA), Elementary and Secondary Education Act (ESEA), Americans with Disabilities Act (ADA)	A1-A2, B1-B2. School Quarterly Presentations (to School Administration, including Board of Education) A1. Committee for Special Education Annual Meeting (Evaluation: SpEd-GenEd Teachers/Parent Conferencing) A1. FOR Periodic Reviews (Evaluation: SpEd-GenEd Teacher Conferencing) A2. IEP Online Documentations A3. FOR Classroom Observation Monitoring (Evaluation: SpEd-GenEd Teachers Conferencing) A4. IEP/504 Plan (Teacher/Staff) Testing Accommodations

(Continued)

Figure 6.7 (Continued)

Unit: REGULATION COMPLIANCE		
Content	*Skills*	*Assessment*
A. Legal Rights: Due Process	A1. Record and send referral evidence to district's appropriate special education committee or special education director using necessary/legal documentation (possible IEP student's path to receiving official special education services) within 60-day window according to state procedures A2. Provide/assist general education teachers in learning procedures involved in a student's special education referral process from beginning stages to placement in special education program A3. Explain orally and in writing parental rights as the rights relate to their children potentially and already receiving special education services A4. Ensure through periodic review that necessary/legal forms are completed properly for each potential IEP student A5. Ensure orally and in writing the system of due process, including special education mediation and impartial hearings, are in compliance A6. Monitor changes in state/federal procedures related to IDEA, ESEA, ADA, and local laws enacted that affect current special education program requisites	A1. IEP Referral Submission Form (Special Education Director, Board of Education, or State or Federal Reporting Agency) A2. FOR One-on-One/Small-Group Discussions A4-A5. Periodic Conversations/Documentation Inspections A6. FOR E-mail, Newsletter, State/Federal Report Readings

Figure 6.8   Professional Development Map Month: Technology Integration Director

Month: January

Unit: COLLABORATION III				
Content	Skills	Assessment	Activities	Standards
A. Social Networking: Wikis Resources --*Wikis in Plain English* Common Craft Video --Interactive Whiteboard	A1. Identify visually and digitally 6 features of a wiki environment (create, save, edit, embed media, discussion tab, create new page) A2. Construct a wiki including at least 4 elements using text and images	A1-A2. Collaborative Wiki Website Creation (Evaluation: Peer Review/ Class-Created Rubric)	A1. Discuss orally basic operations (edit, save) of using a wiki	A. NETS-T 1.d NETS-T 2.c NETS-T 3.b
B. Group Editing: Google Docs Resources --Interactive Whiteboard	B1. Identify visually and digitally 7 Google Docs features (create [file types], save, edit, share, revision history, folders) B2. Upload previously created document into dashboard; save B3. Invite members to view only/view-edit saved document B4. Edit document by adding information/deleting information B5. Trace revision history of changes to edited document	B1-B3. Google Docs Person Invitation Exercise B4-B5. Collaboratively Edited Document (Evaluation: Peer Review/ Colored Text Contributor Differentiation Printout)	B1. Investigate Google Docs online through facilitator demonstration B2. Each teacher creates personal Google account (if s/he does not already have an account)	B. NETS-T 1.b NETS-T 1.d NETS-T 3.b

(Continued)

117

Figure 6.8 (Continued)

Unit: DIGITAL CITIZENSHIP IV				
Content	Skills	Assessment	Activities	Standards
A. Digital Resources: Ethical Use Resources --*A Fair(y) Use Tale* YouTube Video	A1. Defend orally and in writing the necessity for copyright protection using real-world examples A2. Define in writing creative commons licensing and apply to real-world examples A3. Create in writing digital citations for protected works	A1-A3. *Considering Copyright* Media with Citations Creation/Presentation (Evaluation: Peer Review/Rubric) A1. FOR Copyright Protection 2-Team Debate (Evaluation: Facilitator Ob/Learner Feedback)		A. NETS-T 1.c NETS-T 3.d NETS-T 4.a NETS-T 4.c
B. Digital Resources: Validity Resources --Validity Articles from Professional Digital/ Technology Magazines/Periodicals	B1. Identify orally and in writing 3 critical factors (origin, purpose, author) for validating a digital resource B2. Evaluate orally and in writing digital resources to determine validity based on 3 critical factors using online searches of primary/ secondary sources	B1-B2. 5 Resources Validity Checklist/Draw Conclusions Group Presentation (Evaluation: Peer Review/Group Feedback)	B1. Article Jigsaw Activity B1. Discuss/list additional factors that may be helpful in determining a resource's validity	B. NETS-T 1.b. NETS-T 1.d NETS-T 3.d

REVIEW QUESTIONS

An insightful way of understanding what teachers cognitively experience when learning the protocols and processes of designing curriculum is to attempt to personally write a professional development administrative map. Hopefully, reading this chapter has whetted your appetite to give it a try.

As there are two kinds of administrative maps, you may first want to read Chapter 7 and then discuss your responses to the statements and questions in both chapters with a partner or in a small group.

1. I can see the potential for writing administrative maps because _____ (fill in the blank). To do so, I think we need to talk more about _____ (fill in the blank).

2. Given that there are two kinds of administrative maps, I am trying to figure out if we should begin with all of us writing one kind of administrative map, so we can help each other with the map-writing learning-curve process. Or, should we divide up and have some of us attempt to write a professional development administrative map and others try to write professional roles administrative maps, so we can learn from one another's experiences?

3. If we decide to write either type of administrative map, should we first come to agreement on systemic unit names? If yes, why? If no, why not?

4. Who do we need to talk to about creating a new location within our mapping system so we can have a different template (responsibility, actions, evidence) for writing professional roles maps?

5. Do we need someone to help us input the course names (e.g., Elementary Principal; Science Curriculum Director) for either kind of administrative map, or can we do this on our own within our mapping system?

7

What Do Professional Roles Administrative Maps Look Like?

By working faithfully eight hours a day, you may eventually get to be a boss and work twelve hours a day.

—Robert Frost

An administrator's official job description usually does not include the innumerable hats worn daily, let alone monthly or yearly. From the motivating to the monotonous, the responsibilities of an administrator are vital to a school or district functioning smoothly and successfully. Administrators, especially ones new to a position, often dream of having accessible records that convey the important responsibilities and actions taken by those who previously held that job title. In the past, this dream was rarely a reality; with curriculum mapping, it is becoming routine.

WRITING PROFESSIONAL ROLES ADMINISTRATIVE MAPS

As mentioned previously, while a professional development administrative map focuses on learners' expectations, a professional roles administrative map focuses on the map writer. This kind of map represents an administrator's personal record of his or her *responsibilities, actions,* and *evidence.* This administrative map is most often recorded by an individual as a Projected/Diary Map. There may be situations where two or more administrators are responsible for a particular event or program, such as managing a districtwide summer school program. If this is the case, the administrators may prefer to first work collegially to develop an Essential Map and/or a Consensus Map that include the agreed-upon responsibilities, actions, and—if applicable—planned evidence. The administrators who are then responsible for executing the event or program in a particular year, which may change annually, will personally copy the Essential Map or Consensus Map into their own accounts and document the operation of the current year's event or program in a Projected/Diary Map.

Self-Centered Versus Learner Centered

The term *self-centered* does not indicate egotism or self-absorption. It simply denotes the primary purpose of a professional roles administrative map. Many administrators who choose to write this kind of map want to create a personal occupational history for themselves and for those who follow in their footsteps. A secondary benefit often emerges when administrators begin to read one another's professional roles maps within a school or across the district. They often discover they have varying perceptions of roles and responsibilities and oftentimes discover some responsibility overlaps or responsibilities that appear to be redundant. This leads to collegial dialogue and agreement related to the in-question responsibilities, as well as provides clarity for what the administrators would like to see included in their administrative roles maps.

A large high school's administrative team, consisting of a principal, four assistant principals, and four program directors, decided to map their roles. During their yearly administrative retreat, they set aside time to draft their individual Projected Maps in the districtwide mapping system. On the last day of the retreat, they read each other's maps using the seven-step review process.

The principal facilitated the large-group comparison review. The administrators discovered some maps appeared to have overlaps and gaps in their responsibilities. One such overlap was the coordination of the school, district, state, and college-placement testing procedures and processes. It was collegially decided that for the coming school year each grade level's assistant principal would be responsible for coordinating the testing for the students.

Another discovered overlap involved the parking lots. One administrator was in charge of student parking and another was in charge of busing. These two responsibilities caused these two administrators to have to speak to one another before making any major or minor decisions. The administrative team decided to combine the two responsibilities into one and had one administrator be responsible for both. The collegial discussions continued and led to clarity and slight shifts in responsibilities, including such areas as the school's safety plan, fire drills, and master scheduling.

(Continued)

(Continued)

A large gap, or as some thought, an absence, was the lack of a record of instructional leadership responsibilities. Clarifying each grade level's assistant principal's specific responsibilities immediately freed up more time that could be allocated for instructional leadership. The principal asked the assistant principals to work with teachers to utilize their students' various testing results and plan appropriate professional learning community (PLC) focuses that could be included in the administrative roles maps. A comment was made that in the future it would be worthwhile to generate PLC professional development administrative maps. As the school year progressed the administrative team met periodically to revisit their Projected/Diary Maps. They commented on how the mapping process was aiding them in being more efficient as a team and better serving students and teachers' needs.

One major change was made in the summer after the first school year of mapping the administrative roles. When the administrators met and reviewed the year, they decided for the next school year, the role of the assistant principals would be modified so that an assistant principal would loop with a grade level for four years. In other words, the administrator assigned to the incoming ninth-grade students would be responsible for their academic and social well-being from their freshman to senior year. The theory was that this pattern would allow for a more personalized education for students, including a deeper mentorship from the guidance counselors who were taking on the same loop rotation, and a stronger social connection between administration, students, and the surrounding community.

At an administrative retreat a few years later, a comment was made that their commitment to mapping the administrative roles proved beneficial far beyond what they originally envisioned. A new assistant principal shared that he was thrilled to have access to what had been happening administratively and could start with a clear direction and expectation of his personal roles and responsibilities.

Map-Writing Protocols

When compared to the professional development administrative maps protocols (Figure 6.1, pages 100–103), the professional roles protocols are less complex (Figure 7.1). This is because this kind of administrative map expresses one's personal responsibilities and actions rather than others' cognitive learning expectations.

Chapter 6 mentions that the element headings for an administrative roles map are different from a curriculum map or professional development administrative map. Therefore, it is recommended that the administrative roles maps be housed in a separate location within a district's selected mapping system. Most mapping systems can create a pseudo school and title the school *Administrative Maps.* The map template would replace the *content, skills,* and *assessments* element names with *responsibilities, actions,* and *evidence.*

Administrators may choose to collaboratively develop administrative roles systemic unit names to aid in housing like information and conducting searches within the district's curriculum mapping system. To gain clarity in the

Figure 7.1 Professional Roles Map Elements: Wording, Format, and Intra-Alignment Protocols

	Unit Name	Responsibility	Actions	Evidence	Resources
Wording	• Theme/Topic • Theme/Topic: Descriptor	• Noun/Noun Phrase: Descriptor	• Verb-descriptor	• Succinct statement or summary	• If there is no dedicated resources element field, the term *Resources* starts with a capital letter and is in italics
Format	• All capital letters • Boldfaced (if system capable)	• Each word begins with a capital letter	• Statement begins with capital letter • No period needed at end of statement	• Statement or summary begins with capital letter or each word starts with capital letter • No period needed at end of summary or statement • May choose to attach evidence documents	• If there is no dedicated resources field,* listed directly beneath appropriate Content under the term *Resources* • Each listing begins with double dash *If dedicated field, include appropriate intra-alignment coding prior to listing resources
Intra-Alignment	• Not applicable	• Begin visual intra-alignment using alphabet letters	• Aligned to responsibilities using letters • Aligned to evidences using letter/number coding	• Aligned to responsibilities and evidences using letter/number coding	• Not applicable unless separate field; then aligned to responsibilities or responsibilities/evidences.
Examples	**EVALUATIONS I**	A. Teachers: Non-Tenured	A1. Conduct initial meeting with teacher to read/discuss Professional Competency Domains A2. Aid teacher in identifying targeted focus area, personal plan, professional development/ mentor needs, timeline A3. Conduct 5 unannounced walk-throughs	A1-A2. Teacher Meeting A1-A2. Individual Teacher Self-Improvement Plan Packet A3. Walk Through Checklist/Comment Sheet A4-A6. Teacher Self-Improvement Evaluation Form	A. --Professional Competency Domains Website --Teacher Evaluation Form #184

(Continued)

Figure 7.1 (Continued)

124

Unit Name	Responsibility	Actions	Evidence	Resources
		A4. Observe 2 announced lessons A5. Write formal evaluation and meet with teacher to provide feedback and discussion opportunity A6. Send formal evaluation copy to district/file copy/give copy for teacher		
FUNDRAISING: ANNUAL BOOK FAIR	A. Book Fair: Scholastic Resources --Scholastic Book-Fair Posters	A1. Confirm planned fair dates with district office A2. Ask for parent/community volunteers to man stations/sale tables A3. Schedule times for children/adults to shop A4. Announce (flyer, school website) book-fair dates/hours A5. Prepare return materials and schedule pick-up A6. Purchase leveled pleasure reading materials through profit	A1. Post dates on master calendar and website A2. Volunteer list A3-A4, B1. Flyer sent out week previous; Website announcement up beginning of month A5. Scholastic pick-up call A6. Purchase Order	
	B. Guest Author and Guest Illustrator: Regis Margate, Henry Herne	B1. Plan assembly highlighting author and illustrator to kick off book-fair week B2. Schedule class rotation times to meet with author and illustrator B3. Arrange hotel and airport pick-up of author and illustrator	B1. Assembly and book signing setup area B2. Classroom rotation schedule B3. E-mail/phone call correspondences B3. Volunteer cell phone confirmation of pick-ups/drop-offs	

reasoning and process for developing systemic names, read the information included in Appendix A.

PROFESSIONAL ROLES MAP MONTH SAMPLES

As mentioned previously, each sample map month is visually displayed in a table format because each web-based commercial mapping system has a slightly different configuration.

The following sample map months include a variety of professional role focuses. You may find it worthwhile to compare these *writer action-oriented* samples with the professional development *learner-oriented* map samples starting on page 106 in Chapter 6.

CONCLUSION

To appreciate what teachers go through involving the cognitive learning processes for designing quality curriculum maps, many administrators choose to learn how to design and write professional development administrative maps. Writing professional roles administrative maps is easier because the protocols are not as involved and rigorous. Some administrators choose to begin with writing professional roles maps and later learn the processes for designing professional development maps.

REVIEW QUESTIONS

You may have already read Chapter 6. If you have not yet done so, you may want to before responding to the review questions in both chapters and discussing your responses to the questions with a partner or in a small group.

1. How may recording professional role maps aid you and your fellow administrators in creating a current and archived history of your job responsibilities?

2. What specific responsibilities can you see as being beneficial for administrators to document throughout the district or in your particular school or office through the use of administrative roles Projected/Diary Maps?

3. How do you foresee using your selected mapping system's search and report features to aid administrators in collegial conversations regarding the information in professional roles administrative maps?

Figure 7.2 Professional Roles Map Month: High School Assistant Principal

Month: August

Unit: SCHEDULING

Responsibility	Actions	Evidence	Resources
A. Registration: Grades 9-12	A1. Update and change class schedules based on 4-year plans and student needs A1. Participate in early registration process in August during predetermined dates and times	A1. Attend/participate in assigned registration days prior to school beginning	A. --Prep Headquarters --Student Transcripts --STI

Unit: COLLEGE AND CAREER COUNSELING I

Responsibility	Actions	Evidence	Resources
A. Senior Night Informational Meeting: Presentation Preparations	A1. Prioritize college application and scholarship goals for the year A2. Identify areas of focus for senior year A3. Evaluate current credit requirements for graduation A4. Create PowerPoint for parents/guardians and students attending Senior Night Out A5. Answer questions and provide follow-up information as needed based on parent/guardian, student requests	A1-A5, C1-C3. Explain college application process at Senior Night Out/Refer students and parents/guardians to Prep Headquarters for specific instructions A1-A3. PowerPoint presentation A1-A5. Oral presentation in auditorium A5. Follow-up phone calls and e-mails/meeting with specific students	A. --PowerPoint Presentation --Personal Experience Sharing
B. Senior Credits Checks/Evaluation: Graduation Requirements For Senior Student	B1. Review all senior transcripts prior to meeting with students B2. Compare necessary to earned credits on credit check sheet for each student B3. Determine diploma type for each student B4. Define career cluster for each student B5. Sequence necessary steps for makeup credits for graduation for necessary students	B1-B5. Meet individually with each student to discuss credits, career/college plans, and graduation plan B2-B3. Prepare Excel spreadsheet report for principal B2. Complete Credit Checklist for each student B4. Complete Career Cluster Enrollment Form B5. Complete Make-up Profiles	B. --Transcript --4-Year Career Plan --Prep Headquarters --STI

Unit: COLLEGE AND CAREER COUNSELING I

Responsibility	Actions	Evidence	Resources
C. College Applications: Student Preparation Based on Counselor Recommendations	C1. Determine each student's application is complete by reading/reviewing C2. Determine what information counselor needs to make recommendations and sign application C3. Transfer completed application with envelope to school secretary responsible for attaching official transcript C4. Organize mailing by school secretary of completed college applications	C1-C2. Submit completed college application with pink Transcript Request Form C1-C2. Turn applications into counselor for completion and obtain counselor recommendation and signature C3-C4. Applications mailed and pink Transcript Request Form filed with the date application/transcript is mailed	C. --STI Transcripts --Blue Cards (Permanent Record)

Figure 7.3 Professional Roles Map Month: Elementary School Principal

Month: November (Week 12)–November (Week 13)

Unit: COMMUNICATION: PARENTS/STUDENTS

Responsibility	Actions	Evidence
A. Artists in Residence Program: Frisch Marionettes Variety Show	A1. Schedule assembly for the last day before winter break, reserve gymnasium for show A2. Contact PTO with the cost of the assembly A3. Arrange meeting time with puppet troupe to set up in gymnasium and discuss setup needs with custodians A4. Create and send home flyers/invitations to parents/guardians A5. Attend show with all classes including a lively, upbeat show featuring songs, dance, and hilarious routines, and meeting puppeteers after show to discuss art with students	A1. Master school calendar update on school website A2. E-mail and phone call exchange with Mrs. Lily, PTO President A3. E-mails to/from troupe coordinator A4. Flyers (and school website reminder on home page) A5. Frisch Marionettes Variety Assembly

Month: November (Week 13)–December (Week 15)

Unit: COLLABORATIVE PROCESSES: PARENT-TEACHER ORGANIZATION

Responsibility	Actions	Evidence
A. Salvation Army: Christmas Adopt-a-Family Program	A1. Identify and screen needy families from our community to select 5 neediest A2. Type list of identified families' children's sizes and toy choices using codes for confidentiality A3. Collect clothing items, shoes, games/toys for identified families A4. Coordinate delivery dates/times with PTO members and Salvation Army A5. Deliver gifts/canned food to identified families	A1. PTA meeting A2. Family Wish Lists A3. Family Fun Drive (2 weeks) A4-A5. Delivery day (went to all 5 homes/apartments to deliver) A5. Thank you notes from families
B. American Legion/Salvation Army: Canned Food Drive	B1. Collect canned foods, paper supplies, and other nonperishable items for families in our community for Christmas B2. Ask students in all grades to write/draw holiday cards to add to collected items being delivered B3. Compile collected items/cards in boxes B4. Contact American Legion food drive coordinator for pick-up (Salvation Army canned food for identified families)	B1. Canned food drive bins in hallway near main office B2. Holiday cards (Grades K-5) B3-B4. Collection pick-up

Month: December (Week 14)–December (Week 14)

Unit: CULTURE/CLIMATE: EXTRA-CURRICULAR

Responsibility	Actions	Evidence
A. Before/After School Clubs: Floor Hockey, Jump Rope Team Resources --YMCA	A1. Discuss needs for/challenges of providing activities both before and after school A2. Contact local YMCA to recruit leaders and volunteers to begin clubs in the new year when school is back in session A3. Review created plan, each club's attendance policies, meeting schedules, intramural events A4. Create flyer to inform and invite students to join	A1.-A2. Initial YMCA/school meeting A3. Follow-up YMCA/school meeting A4. Hard copy and online flyer

Month: December (Week 14)–December (Week 14)

Unit: MANAGEMENT: SAFETY

Responsibility	Actions	Evidence
A. Drills: Fire, Earthquake Resources --Fire Safety Procedures Posters --Earthquake Safety Procedures Posters	A1. Ask custodians to check classroom and common area postings for exiting directions for fire drill A2. Ask teachers to remind students of exiting path from classroom/area for fire drill A3. Ask teachers to practice earthquake drill sequence steps (duck, cover, roll) with students A4. Report official fire and earthquake drills to central office	A1. Classroom and common areas visual check A2. Unannounced fire drill A3. Unannounced earthquake drill A4. Drills Form E-mail/Attachment

Figure 7.4 Professional Roles Map Month: High School Special Education Department Chair

Month: September

Unit: BEGINNING OF SCHOOL YEAR

Responsibility	Actions	Evidence
A. Organization: IEPs, Paperwork, Protocols	A1. Manually collect all records/files from junior high schools	A1. Get all files to psychologist's secretary
	A2. Create in writing beginning of year agenda for department meeting	A2. Distribute and review agenda at department meeting
	A3. Develop IEP mentor lists through department meeting	A3. Review mentor lists for finalization and give to psychologist's secretary
	A4. Compose Fall Mentor Timeline	A4. Distribute and review timeline at initial department meeting
	A5. Initiate accommodations notifications with SpEd teachers:	A5. Review accommodations sheets submitted by mentor teachers
	--SpEd teachers review each student's accommodations	A6. Meet with counselor, mentor teacher, psychologist to analyze schedule, determine, and implement necessary changes; consult with parents/guardians
	--Make copy of accommodation for each of the student's RegEd teachers	A7. Meet with new teachers and review training information
	--Attach mentor cover sheet to each accommodation	A8. Meet with counselor, administrator, and/or psychologist, as situations arise, to find solutions to issues
	--File each accommodation in file folder for each RegEd teacher	A9. Meet with secondary SpEd director and review information
	--When all accommodations are collected, e-mail RegEd teachers to come and pick up their file folder of student accommodations sheets (teachers must sign for their folder)	A10–A11. Distribute list in hard copy form (teacher mailboxes) and through department e-mail
	A6. Adjust student schedules according to IEP services pages (addendum to IEP as necessary)	A12. Verify materials received against inventory sheet
	A7. Organize initial IEP training for new teachers	A13. Mark paperwork errors as necessary, and return to mentor teachers for corrections
	A8. Solve any teacher/class coverage issues as they arise through discussion with counselor, administrator, psychologist	A14. Meet with teachers and review information
	A9. Classify numbers of SpEd students by category (resource, self-contained, itinerant)	
	A10. Generate teacher contact list for department	
	A11. Generate emergency phone contact tree for department	
	A12. Confirm, intake, and inventory materials and supplies from capital and warehouse orders	
	A13. Evaluate completed IEP addendum paperwork (based on A6)	
	A14. Explain SpEd department procedures, IEPs, teaching/classes, school policies, as well as other pertinent information as appropriate, necessary, and/or requested to continuing and new teachers	

Unit: SPECIAL NEEDS TESTING

Responsibility	Actions	Evidence
A. AIMS Testing: Accommodations	A1. Generate list of students who will not take AIMS test A2. Generate list of students needing special print (e.g., large print, Braille) A3. Generate list of students needing oral/aural (e.g., test read to student), physical (e.g., fine motor movement assistance) and/or environment (e.g., quiet space) accommodations	A1-A3. Give accommodation lists to administrative assistant in charge of coordinating AIMS testing

Unit: COMPLIANCE MEETINGS

Responsibility	Actions	Evidence
A. IEP/ Compliance: Attendance	A1. Facilitate IEP meetings A2. Participate and contribute to HIT, SIC, IEP, Department Head, Special Education Department Head, Special Education department, and other related meetings	A1. Lead meetings and work through issues as they arise. A2. Contribute to meetings as appropriate to help reach meeting objectives

Figure 7.5 Professional Roles Map Month: Elementary Mathematics Coach

Month: April

Unit: COACHING TEACHERS VIII		
Responsibility	*Actions*	*Evidence*	*Resources*

Responsibility	Actions	Evidence	Resources
A. Individual: New to Faculty Teachers	A1. Meet with teacher to review series of math lessons for mathematical concepts, structure/sequence, materials A2. Discuss 5 strategies to engage students: hands-on, gender-friendly, learning styles, connect prior knowledge, accountable talk A3. Model preselected lesson for teacher; debrief for use of 5 strategies A4. Observe teacher presenting preselected lesson; provide coaching feedback	A1–A4. Mrs. Swayze Meetings (Grade 5 Area-Perimeter Lesson/Rounding Lesson) A1–A4. Mr. Lee Meetings (Grade 1 Number Sets Lesson/3-D Shapes Lesson)	A. --Coaching Observation Form --Coaching Feedback Form
B. Collaborative: Teacher Share-Out Meetings	B1. Facilitate grade-level group meetings focusing on successes/areas of concern, strategies B2. Promote sharing of materials, ideas, methods, approaches for specific content/skills learning B3. Set up times for teacher-requested peer-teaching observations B4. Teach class for teacher observing peer-teacher lesson B5. Plan for next month's critical content/skills learning using month-at-a-glance conversations	B1–B5. 40-Minute Bimonthly Meetings (meet during common performing arts time)	B. --Share-Out Planning Form --Peer Observation Form
C. Data Analysis: Daily Formatives, End-of-Unit Assessments	C1. Analyze data results to diagnose immediate interventions (individual, flex groups, power days) C2. Select activities to focus on students' targeted content/skills (games, online programs, materials)	C1. Weekly Grade-Level Excel Results C2. Teacher-Requested Activity Preparations	

132

Unit: MATH PROFESSIONAL LEARNING COMMUNITY VI

Responsibility	Actions	Evidence	Resources
A. Collaborative Dialogue: Article Focus	A1. Read articles based on pregenerated questions A2. Share articles' thoughts using meeting protocols (new protocol: getting in the last word)	A1–A2. Schoolwide Math Coaches PLC Meeting	A. --*Using Calculators in Elementary Math Teaching* Article --*Educators Battle Over Calculator Use: Both Sides Claim Casualties* Article --*The Use of Calculators Gets at the Heart of Good Teaching* Article
B. Guest Speaker: Lucy West	B1. Attend 3-day math coaching workshop, including keynote presentations, panel discussions, video observations, strategies discussions, accountable talk B2. Develop districtwide Top 5 critical questions to use when coaching teachers	B1. District Office Meeting Hall B2. Top 5 Critical Questions Reminder Sheet	B. --*Content-Focused Coaching* Handbook --Lucy West

Unit: PARENT INVOLVEMENT VIII

Responsibility	Actions	Evidence	Resources
A. Math Literacy: Newsletter	A1. Write K–5 articles (general math concepts, not grade-level specific) A2. Create newsletter including articles, artifacts, photos, school/district math-learning opportunities A3. Provide copy clerk with newsletter-master to copy and deliver to each class	A1–A3. *Mad About Math!* September Newsletter	A. --*Mad About Math!* September Newsletter

(Continued)

Figure 7.5 (Continued)

Unit: PARENT INVOLVEMENT VIII

Responsibility	Actions	Evidence	Resources
B. Parent Workshops: K-2/3-5 Math Mornings	B1. Send survey home to K-2/3-5 parents/care givers to select desired focuses based on student-learning needs B2. Develop a K-2 and 3-5 2-hour workshop based on survey data B3. Prepare to present workshop (gather materials, copy handouts, reference materials, shop for food/snacks) B4. Present K-2 and 3-5 workshops on different days (9-11 AM)	B1. Survey Return Slip B2-B3. Preparation B4. Grades K-2 Fractions Math Morning (10/14) B4. Grades 3-5 Translations Math Morning (10/27)	B. --Geoboards/Rubber Bands --Attributes Blocks --Grid Paper

Unit: TUTORING PROGRAM

Responsibility	Actions	Evidence	Resources
A. Student-Needs Identification: Criteria, Contact	A1. Review high-stakes testing results (failing, borderline 400-425), teacher recommendations to determine students needing services per grade level A2. Contact parents/caregivers to inform of potential services and how services will benefit child A3. Secure 2 buses for transportation after services	A1. 4 Collaborative Math Coaches/Teachers Criteria Meetings A2. E-mail Exchange (hard copy when necessary) A2. Returned Permission Slips A3. T-20/A Transportation Request	A. --Phone Call Contacts, when necessary
B. Tutoring Team: Teacher Applications, Training	B1. Contact via e-mail/hard copy faculty interested in 2-days-a-week after-school tutoring (Tuesday/Thursday with stipends) B2. Train teachers on 5 aspects of tutoring materials (teacher manual, lesson plans, mandatory strategy = equation, work, show thinking, sentence to sum up)	B1. Teacher-Tutor List B2. 2-hour After-School Training	B. --*Mathematics Navigator Program* --*Tutoring* PowerPoint

Figure 7.6   Professional Roles Map Month: Middle School Librarian/Media Specialist

Month: March

Unit: CONTENT AREA COLLABORATION		
Responsibility	*Actions*	*Evidence*	*Resources*
A. Grade 6 Literature IRP: Nonfiction Suggestions	A1. Develop/update list of titles A2. Consult 6th grade literature teachers regarding the updated lists before finalizing A3. Make necessary revisions based on results from consultation A4. Post finalized pdf version of suggested nonfiction reading list on the library Book Lists website A5. Post pdf version of IRP assignment/requirement from classroom teachers on the library Book Lists website A6. Contact cooperating public librarian regarding Quarter 2 IRP lists and requirements A7. Modify last year's Dewey bookmark for distribution to students A8. Assist students in finding nonfiction IRP books	A1-A4. Post accurate IRP suggestion lists on library website A5. Post IRP assignments/ requirements on library website A6. Acknowledgment e-mail from public librarian A7. Distribute Dewey bookmarks to students (deweybkmkv2.png) A8. Students select IRP books	A-B. --NoveList K-8 Plus A. --Last year's list --Junior Library Guild selections --Books from professional library --Last year's Dewey bookmark
B. Grade 7 Literature IRP: Mixed Genres Suggestions (Based on Lexile Number)	B1. Present how to search for books based on Lexile numbers and keyword in InfoCentre B2. Present how to search for books based on Lexile and keyword in NoveList K-8 Plus B3. Present how to identify if a book is available in the school collection or not in NoveList K-8 Plus B4. Assist students in finding books in a specific genre within a given Lexile range	B1-B3. Conduct presentation on techniques for identifying IRP books B4. Students select books for IRP that meet required criteria	B. --NoveList K-8 Plus --InfoCentre online catalog

135

Figure 7.6 (Continued)

Responsibility	Actions	Evidence	Resources
C. Grade-8 English IRP: Award Winners Suggestions	C1. Identify newest award-winning titles C2. Add new award winners to the reading lists in InfoCentre C3. Add award information to MARC record in InfoCentre C4. Update library website with links to various book award websites (e.g., Newbery, Edgar Awards) C5. Develop bookmark with approved book awards for distribution to students C6. Inform and direct students to what resources are available from school to identify/select an award-winning book for IRP	C1-C3. Place award winners on display in search areas C4. Book awards website update C5. Create bookmark (awardbkmk.doc) and display C6. Conduct student presentations	
D. EPIC Program: Cell Processes	D1. Locate books on cell processes containing quality illustrations/diagrams and simplified information D2. Prepare selected books for in-classroom use	D1. Select books D2. Check out books to teacher and place on delivery cart	
E. Grade-8 Geography: Mr. Philips' Class-African Countries	E1. Select books/materials on African countries from our collection based on Mr. Philips' guidelines E2. Update selected titles and descriptions to Country Research Pathfinder website	E1. Identify books/materials and place on delivery cart E2. Pathfinder website update	

Unit: PEER COLLABORATION

Responsibility	Actions	Evidence	Resources
A. Product Demonstrations: LME Media/Learning Specialists	A1. Present MARC Wizard demonstration for LME media and learning specialists to show how Lexile information can be added to InfoCentre records A2. Present NoveList K-8 demonstration for LME media and learning specialists to show how students and staff can search for books based on Lexile, availability within school, and book content/topic	A1-A2. Meet with LME media and learning specialists to show them the products and how they are used with Lexile information	

Unit: COLLECTIONS DEVELOPMENT

Responsibility	Actions	Evidence	Resources
A. Acquisitions: New Books	A1. Order additional books for collection according to collection needs A2. Receive books via mail system A3. Acquire and/or process MARC records through MARC Wizard A4. Import MARC records into InfoCentre A5. Add additional cataloging information where needed A6. Prepare books for circulation (acquisition information written inside back cover, spine and barcode labels, book protectors) A7. Display new books A8. Announce arrival of new books with PowerPoint slides on building announcement system A9. Add new books to existing lists where appropriate	A1-A6. New books available and findable in InfoCentre A7-A8. Students and staff aware of new books A9. Lists reflect updated collection	

Unit: LEADERSHIP/RESOURCE COMMUNICATION

Responsibility	Actions	Evidence	Resources
A. District Meetings: TLC	A1. Prepare IMC for district TLC meeting (host) A2. Attend district TLC meeting as building rep A3. Report back to building-level TLC results from district meeting	A1. Meeting site preparation A2-A3. Attend meeting, take notes, and report back to building TLC	
B. Relationship Building: Teacher, Parent-Guardian/Home, Student	B1. Develop handout with information on home and school access to IMC resources B2. Distribute handout at school to teachers and students B3. Inform parents-guardians/home of IMC resources available through school and home access	B1. Prepare handout B2. Handout made available to students and staff in building B3. E-mail handout to office manager to add to parent newsletter	

Figure 7.7 Professional Roles Map Month: Assistant Superintendent of Curriculum and Instruction

Month: May

Unit: COMMUNICATION: COMMUNITY

Responsibility	Actions	Evidence
A. Community Relations: Liaison	A1. Attend YMCA board meeting A2. Participate in new restaurant ribbon-cutting ceremony A3. Participate in Read Across America activities at various elementary schools A4. Encourage and solicit participation from the community for Read Across America activities	A1-A4. Outlook Calendar A1. Board meeting minutes A2-A3. Press photos A4. Volunteer list (per school)

Unit: COLLABORATIVE PROCESSES: PROBLEM SOLVING

Responsibility	Actions	Evidence
A. NAHS Lunch Schedule: Transition to 7-Period Day	A1. Attend high school administrative meeting with Barger, Jensen, Briscoe, Amerson A2. Brainstorm and research possible solutions to adjusted lunch schedule	A1-A2. Outcome pending A2. Collaborative solutions suggestions document

Unit: LEADERSHIP: CONTINUOUS SCHOOL IMPROVEMENT

Responsibility	Actions	Evidence
A. Secondary Buildings: School-Improvement Plans	A1. Review independently each school's improvement plan, and supply feedback on template form A2. Review plans and written feedback with curriculum team A3. Schedule and hold meetings with secondary administrators to provide verbal feedback and suggestions for final submission of school-improvement plans	A1-A2. Written feedback template form A3. Final submission of School Improvement Plans
B. Weekly Curriculum Team Meetings: Sharing of Information	B1. Meet with Director of Elementary Education, Director of Secondary Education, Coordinator of Student Data, Director of Student Support Services, and Director of Technology B2. Share current issues going on in various buildings and levels B3. Share current student-achievement data based upon AYP, PL221, ISTEP B4. Share and discuss information on current best practices and schedule attendance at workshops, conferences, and professional development as needed (current initiatives include Wireless Generation, RTI, Curriculum Mapping) B5. Receive updates on current initiatives (Curriculum Mapping, Read 180, RTI)	B1-B5. Weekly Meetings B3. Current state and local data B4. Attend RTI Conference B5. Attend Wireless Generation Webinars
C. Professional Development Center (PDC): Submission Proposal Preparations	C1. Work collaboratively with selected central-office directors, school administrators, and teachers (PDC team) to brainstorm effective use of meeting spaces/presentation needs for professional development activities (formerly JVCC center) C2. Enlist input from Building and Grounds Staff on building-material selections C3. Develop rationale for requesting 32-computer wireless lab to maximize staff-training opportunities C4. Create purchase orders for tables and chairs (classroom style and rounds), podiums, whiteboards, LCD projectors, computers, front-desk/entrance-area furniture based on cost comparisons C5. Generate and submit final PDC proposal	C1-C5. BOE PDC Proposal submitted for approval C1. 2-part initial PDC team meetings with follow-up e-mail communications and phone calls C2. Central office meeting C3. PDC Team Proposal Draft (Evaluated by central-office administrators)

Appendix A

What Are Considerations for Developing Systemic Unit Names?

One for all, and all for one.

—Alexandre Dumas, *The Three Musketeers*

Based on the famous line from *The Three Musketeers*, the all for *one* in curriculum mapping represents all teachers focusing on a student's K–12 learning journey, which often includes 40 to 65 teachers per student (Jacobs, 2006). Therefore, thinking systemically about collaborative curriculum design is an important facet of curriculum mapping. Jacobs (2006) notes,

> Curriculum mapping does not guarantee that all of these teachers will become intimately acquainted with Johnny's needs or his experience. What it can do is provide a real data base allowing any of his teachers to find what he has experienced and is experiencing currently, and it can communicate with more precision with any of the flotilla of teachers through technology. (pp. 114–115)

Schools and districts that consider themselves advanced in collaborative curriculum work may reach a new pinnacle when considering a need for organization-wide *design* agreement. Curriculum mapping asks teachers to not think in isolation (e.g., one grade level or one course) or in semi-isolation (e.g., one school). Instead, teachers are asked to consider the entire student landscape (e.g., feeder pattern or feeder patterns of the entire district). Therefore, considerations for planning how to strategically organize and record students' learning continuum within curriculum maps, regardless of current school site or current teacher or teachers, is an important step in the systemic mapping process.

Likewise, Jacobs's words *through technology* speak of the 21st-century need to use an online mapping system (Hale, 2008; Jacobs, 1997, 2003, 2004, 2006; Jacobs & Johnson, 2009). Almost all curriculum mapping systems require a teacher or teachers to begin the map-writing process by recording a unit name before entering any map elements (e.g., essential questions/big ideas, content, skills). When teachers independently create unit names without considering students' vertical learning journeys and housing those learning expectations in a mapping system, it makes it difficult to find gaps, redundancies, or absences when conducting reviews. Inconsistent names may also prevent a mapping system's search and report features from functioning to full capacity.

DEVELOPING SYSTEMIC UNIT NAMES

Developing systemic unit names aids in aligning curriculum in all types of maps: Essential Maps, Consensus Maps, and Projected/Diary Maps. Systemic unit names provide map writers and readers with *preliminary insight* into learning expectations contained within units of study. As shared in Chapter 1, unit names serve as pseudo-electronic binders (units of study) that sit on shelves (months) within courses (bookcases) housed in a mapping system (library).

A Process-Based Experience

The process for developing systemic unit names has recommended procedures and protocols that are detailed further in this appendix. The following snapshot captures the teacher-leadership engagement involved in the systemic unit-name development process.

In a large school district, the full social studies departments at the middle school and high school were joined by teachers representing kindergarten through Grade 5 from the four elementary schools to participate in a full-day meeting. The facilitators consisted of three teachers: one, a member of the curriculum mapping cabinet; and the other two, members of curriculum mapping councils. The district had begun their curriculum mapping initiative approximately one year before, and K–12 unit name task forces had already met and developed unit names for all disciplines.

For social studies, the districtwide unit name task force chose to develop concept-based signifier unit names because teachers had been expressing a desire to replace portions of the current curriculum by revisiting and revising the district's topic-based units of study. The teachers felt that by adding conceptual lenses to the curriculum, student learning would be enhanced regarding what students may currently view as a series of unrelated facts and topics. The goals for the social studies professional development day were to (1) review and reflect on the unit name task force's developed unit name signifiers and corresponding big ideas; (2) list the current topic-based unit of studies in each grade level related to state standards, which teachers had worked on horizontally for the past three years; and (3) evaluate current units of study in relationship to using conceptual lenses as learning filters for vertically reoccurring topic-based units of study.

After reviewing the unit name signifiers and big ideas, the teachers took a stretch break. They returned to find large pieces of chart paper labeled by grade level or course. The teachers proceeded to list their current units of study on the chart paper. They hung the lists sequentially from kindergarten

(Continued)

(Continued)

through 12th grade and conducted a gallery walk. One teacher commented, "No wonder the kids say 'we did that before.' Based on the names of some units of study, it looks like they may be correct."

Next, two facilitators took colored markers and circled like units of study appearing on various charts. The teachers were able to quickly see that seven different unit topics appeared to reoccur vertically in various grade levels. One in particular was *Ancient Egypt*. This unit appeared on the Grade 6, Grade 8, and Grade 10 charts. While the students' claims of experiencing the same learning may merit credibility, the facilitators cautioned that no one should jump to the conclusion that these units are redundant. The facilitators asked the teachers representing the three grade levels to jot down on the charts a quick summary of the content, skills, and summative assessments emphasized in each *Ancient Egypt* unit. While these teachers recorded this information, the remaining teachers read through the state standard document for these grade levels' learning related to ancient Egypt.

The teachers began to notice there appeared to be some overlapping redundancy. The upper-grade teachers mentioned they have to include the learning because students do not remember much because there are several years between the units of study. A facilitator pointed out that this type of concern is one of the reasons for the day's vertical meeting. She said it is important to begin to ask design questions such as, "Why is it that a majority of students forget? What is it critical that they remember?" She added that this dilemma is addressed in an excerpt from Dr. Heidi Hayes Jacobs's (1997) book, *Mapping the Big Picture*. Jacobs highlights a teacher's thoughts while contemplating what sixth graders should focus on during a U.S. Constitution unit study: "What are the *most important concepts* that my students should investigate about the Constitution in four weeks? What should they *remember* and *reflect on* a year from now?" (p. 26, emphasis added).

Another facilitator posed a question to the three grade levels' teachers: "What should our students remember and reflect on *conceptually* when once again encountering ancient Egypt?" All the teachers joined in the discussion as the three teachers openly dialogued and explored this question. They considered the concept-based unit name signifiers in relationship to the current topical content and skills involved in each unit of study. They also discussed (1) students' maturation at each of the grade levels; (2) each grade level or course's aligned discipline and cross-discipline standard statements; and (3) desired outcomes, including performance and/or product assessments that may not currently be in the units of study to encourage application of conceptual lenses during prior and recent learning.

The teachers had an ah-ha moment when they realized the topic-based units of study could involve more than one unit name signifier for a particular unit of study. After considering standards expectations for the topic of ancient Egypt as well as the content and skills emphasized, they decided the appropriate unit names would be

- (Grade 6) **HUMAN/PHYSICAL GEOGRAPHY: ANCIENT EGYPT** due to the strong emphasis on the role of the Nile and its effect on culture and lifestyle.

- (Grade 8) **POWER AND GREED: ANCIENT EGYPT** due to the strong emphasis on various dynasties' pharaohs, queens, and significant leaders in Upper and Lower Egypt.
- (Grade 10) **INNOVATIONS: ANCIENT EGYPT** due to an emphasis not only on the development of utilitarian tools and royal extravagance but also on connections between how innovations of this time period still influence present-day living.

The end of the day came quicker than the teachers expected. They commented on how meeting as a vertical team made such a difference in discussing what is important for their students to be learning. They asked the facilitators when it would be possible to meet in this configuration again because there was much to still discuss and contemplate.

Unit Name Types

Throughout this appendix, the generic term *unit name* will be used to represent *three* types of unit names that vary slightly concerning wording, format, and purpose (see Figure A.1).

Two unit name types explicitly express a *specific* discipline's theme or topic. The third type, *unit name signifier,* does not explicitly express a specific discipline when reading only the signifier recorded to the *left* of a colon. This is because a signifier is used to represent a conceptual focus (e.g., big ideas or enduring understandings) that can potentially be transferred and applicable within a specific discipline, cross-disciplines, or multiple disciplines. For example, if teachers determine that an enduring understanding associated with the unit name signifier **EXPLORATION** is *people's desire to investigate unknown or unfamiliar areas causes them to think differently and act bravely,* various disciplines could use the signifier's conceptual lens for *discipline-specific* topics or themes:

- **EXPLORATION: U.S. WESTWARD MOVEMENT**
- **EXPLORATION: 21ST CENTURY SCIENTIFIC DISCOVERIES**
- **EXPLORATION: MODERN DANCE**

The transferable conceptual lens remains the same in each example above. Only when reading the theme or topic focus to the *right* of the colon does a specific discipline become apparent. These three examples are not meant to convey that unit name signifiers must be developed and used intentionally for cross-curricular or interdisciplinary learning. When desiring to use a concept-based type of unit name, many learning organizations choose to utilize unit name signifiers specifically for single-discipline use.

The procedure for developing cohesive unit names for a particular discipline is not a simple process. Education is a social science. Each discipline has its own uniqueness, including past and current cultures and beliefs. For example, one K–12 unit name task force may choose to use a *single* unit name type while another task force may choose to use a *combination* of unit name types. Coming to agreement on

Figure A.1   Three Types of Unit Names

Topic/Theme Unit Name	Topic/Theme Unit Name: Broad or Narrow Descriptor	Concept-Based Unit Name Signifier: Theme/Topic
• A broad theme or topic category of learning used in a grade level or course, or series of grade levels or courses. • This type of unit name may represent a learning focus that is (a) a stand-alone unit not revisited horizontally during an academic year or (b) revisited again during an academic year.	• A unit name focus may be recorded first using a broad theme or topic-based unit name and then followed by a colon and a relational descriptor used in a grade level or course, or series of grade levels or courses. • This type of unit name may represent a learning focus that is (a) a stand-alone unit not revisited horizontally during an academic year or (b) revisited again during an academic year.	• A generalized concept (conceptual lens) of learning used in a grade level and, most importantly, a series of grade levels or courses. • A unit name signifier term or phrase represents generated big ideas or enduring understandings. • A unit name signifier encourages horizontal and vertical conceptual continuity that asks students to revisit big ideas or enduring understandings via various themes and topics. This enables students to make transferable connections between generalizations and specific themes or topics. • The unit name signifier is recorded to the *left* of the colon. A specific theme or topic focus is recorded to the *right* of the colon.
Examples	*Examples*	*Examples*
MICROSOFT WORD (Business Technology) **FRIENDLY LETTER** (English/Language Arts) **BIOMES** (Science) **NUMBER SENSE IV** (Mathematics) **ELEMENTS OF MUSIC II** (Music) **U.S. WESTWARD MOVEMENT** (Social Studies)	**ARTWORLDS: ASIAN** (Visual Arts) **COMPREHENSION: INFORMATIONAL TEXT I** (Reading/ELA) **FARM MACHINERY: TRACTORS** (Agriculture) **TEAM SPORTS: FOOTBALL** (Physical Education) **CULINARY TOOLS: CUTLERY II** (Culinary Arts) **U.S. WESTWARD MOVEMENT: SETTLEMENTS** (Social Studies)	**ECONOMICS: FOREIGN TRADE** *The unit name signifier's generalizations may be appropriate in Social Studies or Mathematics learning.* **COMMUNITIES: FRIENDSHIPS II** *The unit name signifier's generalizations may be appropriate for Social Studies or Foreign Language learning.* **INNOVATIONS: DNA TESTING** *The unit name signifier's generalizations may be appropriate for Science, Social Studies, Technology, or Industrial Arts learning.* **EXPLORATION: U.S. WESTWARD MOVEMENT** *The unit name signifier's generalizations may be appropriate in Social Studies or Science learning.* *Note: The italic commentaries are not meant to convey mandatory use in specific disciplines. They simply support the notion that a unit name signifier is designed to represent concepts that can be generalized and therefore transferable.*

• It is recommended that unit names are written in *all capital letters* and *boldfaced* (if possible) when recorded in a curriculum mapping system to visually set them apart from the remaining map elements.

• A unit name focus that is revisited *more than once horizontally* in an academic year may be followed by a Roman numeral to indicate the repeated focus's content and skills have been modified (changed or expanded).

how curriculum will be systemically interpreted, managed, and recorded in a mapping system expresses well curriculum mapping's interdependency.

It is highly recommended that unit names be considered and developed by discipline-specific K–12 (or appropriate grade level or course spans within your learning organization) task forces early on in the mapping implementation phases before teachers get in the habit of independently naming units of study when they officially begin mapping the curriculum. Administrators and teacher leaders involved in the prologue (e.g., curriculum mapping cadre, cabinet, and/or councils) often choose to create temporary unit names during their initial map-writing learning phase until unit name task forces can be formed and official systemic unit names are developed. As long as teachers know systemic unit names are still to be determined, they are usually satisfied with using temporary ones in the interim.

Thinking Design, Not Practice

Developing systemic unit names is a part of curriculum *design*. Teachers are most often comfortable with, and usually have had greater training in, curriculum *practice*. Because of this, unit name task-force members, which often include teachers beyond the informed curriculum mapping cabinet and council members, will need to be trained in the rationale and purposes for developing systemic unit names when designing horizontally and—most importantly—vertically aligned curriculum.

Each discipline's unit name task force's how-to procedures will vary. For example, some disciplines have *process skill* standard strands (e.g., Problem Solving, Reasoning and Logic, Questioning), and others do not. If a task force is meeting that has such standard strands, unit name-design considerations will need to be explored, such as,

- Should a process skill standard strand have (1) its own unit name wherein learning expectations are recorded as explicit content and skills (e.g., **SCIENTIFIC PROCESS; REASONING AND PROOF**) or (2) be embedded within nonprocess skill-oriented units of study content and skills learning (e.g., **METEOROLOGY; SHAKESPEAREAN TRAGEDIES**)?
- If process skill standard strands' learning expectations are embedded into nonprocess skill-oriented units' content and skills, what considerations are necessary for formative and summative assessments designed to dually measure the process skill/nonprocess skill learning expectations?

What may be *right* for one discipline may not be for another. Likewise, what works best for one learning organization may not be what works best for another organization. It is important to be aware that there are a variety of design models used nationally and internationally. A learning organization may choose to use a design model attributed to a person or persons' particular requisites while another may choose to create its own unique design. Regardless, there is no guarantee that a recognized or personally designed model has addressed a need for *systemic* unit names representing commonality among and between units of study housed in a mapping system.

Collegial agreement may or may not come easy depending on each discipline's task force's experience with collaborative, systemic curriculum design prior to curriculum mapping. Some disciplines will be more challenging than others. For example, many find it easier to agree upon systemic unit names for mathematics than for English/Language Arts.

Designing interdisciplinary unit names involves different considerations than designing single-discipline unit names. Twenty-first-century thinking (Jacobs, 2010) embraces project-based interdisciplinary units of study. As each unit may include a wide variety of disciplines, the incorporation of concept-based unit name signifiers as a precursory lens to the critical concepts may prove beneficial to teachers as map readers and curriculum reviewers.

Summary

For curriculum mapping to reach sustainability, an emphasis must be placed on the necessity for designing a *systemic structure*. One common mapping implementation oversight is to try to hurry the cognitive processes involved in designing collegial systemic curriculum. Oftentimes, teachers who have been asked to participate in a newly formed unit name task force inquire, "Can't we just use some other district's unit names?" The answer is simple: *Another district is not our district*. Ownership of the *collaborative process* is as paramount in curriculum mapping as in any systemic-change environment (Fullan, 2001).

When just beginning this component of curriculum mapping, those facilitating a unit name task force may be unsure and uneasy leading the meeting or meetings due to a lack of confidence or assurance concerning what the agreed-upon unit names will end up looking like at the onset of the task force meeting. *This is normal and to be expected.* Allowing all members of a unit name task force, which includes the facilitators, to move through the stages of disequilibrium to reach equilibrium is an important part of the process.

Equilibrium is an active, metacognitive process that leads to self-regulation, a fundamental factor in the development of understanding, and is necessary for all learners, including adults (Duckworth, 1964). Therefore, it is wise for administrators and teacher leaders to be proactive facilitators and gain preliminary insights and suggestions via this book, by talking in person or online to mapping consultants or trainers experienced in these processes, or by networking with a district or districts that have had prior experience with mapping and developing systemic unit names. With or without others' guidance, it is important to go forward and do as Aristotle so aptly stated: "One must learn by doing the thing, for though you think you know it, you have no certainty until you try" (DesiQuotes.com, n.d.).

STANDARDS DOCUMENTATION AND UNIT NAMES

Potential facilitators of unit name task forces need to be aware of the *variations* and *nuances* related to standards documents. Most public or private organizations or institutions generate standards documents via a specialized, highly qualified group of experts developing a discipline's standard statements. For example, the

Arizona State Department of Education has various disciplines within the K–12 Arizona Academic Content Standards documentation. Because a different committee designed each discipline's documents, there is a variance to each discipline's document *structure.* A document's structure may affect how to best house student learning within units of study and unit names within a mapping system.

Standards Documents

A discipline's standards committee will choose a way to subdivide student learning expectations into strands. Each strand contains a specific focus. While the term *strands* may not be literally used in your standards' subdivisions, it is an implied term meaning "a narrowing down of a larger entity." To illustrate this point, scan the strand structure for three Arizona Academic Content Standards disciplines prior to the onset of Common Core State Standards terminology (Figure A.2).

The narrowing strands are usually straightforward. The structure becomes *more diversified* when the committee narrows the learning *within* a discipline's strands. For example, Arizona's academic standards term for this next narrowed-down level is *concepts.* Take a few moments to study a few of Arizona's concept variations (Figure A.3).

Notice the visual art strands have four *consistent* concepts for *each* of the three strands. Concept one is the only exception wherein each strand has a

Figure A.2   Arizona Academic Content Standards Strand Structure in Three Disciplines

Mathematics
Strand 1—Number and Operations
Strand 2—Data Analysis, Probability, and Discrete Mathematics
Strand 3—Patterns, Algebra, and Functions
Strand 4—Geometry and Measurement
Strand 5—Structure and Logic

Science
Strand 1—Inquiry Process
Strand 2—History and Nature of Science
Strand 3—Science in Personal and Social Perspectives
Strand 4—Life Science
Strand 5—Physical Science
Strand 6—Earth and Space Science

Visual Arts
Strand 1—Create
Strand 2—Relate
Strand 3—Evaluate

Figure A.3 Comparisons of Arizona Academic Standards: Strands Versus Concepts

Visual Art

Strand 1—Create

Concept 1: Creative Process
Concept 2: Materials, Tools, Techniques
Concept 3: Elements and Principles
Concept 4: Meanings and Purposes
Concept 5: Quality

Strand 2—Relate

Concept 1: Artworlds
Concept 2: Materials, Tools, Techniques
Concept 3: Elements and Principles
Concept 4: Meanings and Purposes
Concept 5: Quality

Strand 3—Evaluate

Concept 1: Art Issues and Values
Concept 2: Materials, Tools, Techniques
Concept 3: Elements and Principles
Concept 4: Meanings and Purposes
Concept 5: Quality

Science

Strand 4—Life Science

Concept 1 (K–4): Characteristics of Organisms
Concept 1 (5–8): Structure and Function in Living Systems
Concept 1 (HS): The Cell

Concept 2 (K–4): Life Cycles
Concept 2 (5–8): Reproduction and Heredity
Concept 2 (HS): Molecular Basis of Heredity

Concept 3 (K–4): Organisms and Environments
Concept 3 (5–8): Populations of Organisms in an Ecosystem
Concept 3 (HS): Interdependence of Organisms

Concept 4 (K–8): Diversity, Adaptation, and Behavior
Concept 4 (HS): Biological Evolution

Concept 5 (HS): Matter, Energy, and Organization in Living Systems (Including Human Systems)

Mathematics

Strand 3—Patterns, Algebra, and Functions

Concept 1: Patterns
Concept 2: Functions and Relationships
Concept 3: Algebraic Representations
Concept 4: Analysis of Change

Strand 4—Geometry and Measurement

Concept 1: Geometric Properties
Concept 2: Transformation of Shapes
Concept 3: Coordinate Geometry
Concept 4: Measurement—Units of Measure/Geometric Objects

Strand 5—Structure and Logic

Concept 1: Algorithms and Algorithmic Thinking
Concept 2: Logic, Reasoning, Arguments, and Mathematical Proof

unique focus: Strand 1—Creative Process; Strand 2—Artworlds; Strand 3—Art Issues and Values. Developing unit names may therefore be easier for visual arts than for science.

For science, each strand has a *different* set of concepts that *vary* at *different* grade-level spans. This design structure is used for all six science strands. Due to the great variety in the six strands' concepts, a K–12 science unit name task force may want to consider the various types of unit names when discussing potential systemic unit names based on the great variety. In mathematics, there are *different* concepts per strand that remain *consistent* K–12. This consistency makes this discipline relatively easy and straightforward for coming to agreement on how to structure and develop agreed-upon systemic unit names for generalized courses. There may need to be further discussion in upper grades concerning appropriate unit names for specialized courses.

Sometimes, a discipline's standards document's narrowed-down structure may be *minimal* and therefore does not provide clear direction for how to best structure unit names. For example, Arizona's foreign language strands are *Communication, Culture, Connections, Comparisons,* and *Communities.* Within each strand, there are *no* concepts. Instead, there are *grade-level ranges* of expectation: *Readiness* (Kindergarten), *Foundations* (Grades 1–3), *Essentials* (Grades 4–8), *Proficiency* (Grades 9–12), and *Distinction* (Honors). Within each range, there are very few standard statements, and the ones included are rather ambiguous and can be interpreted in many ways.

Because of this, a K–12 foreign language unit name task force may choose to generate unit names based on unit name signifiers using the state's strand terminology. If this is the choice, the task force would then generate big ideas or enduring understandings for each signifier. Next, they would begin to explore potential themes or topics that may appear to the right side of the colon that are unique or shared among the discipline's grade-level ranges. For example,

- **CONNECTIONS: FOLK TALES** *Readiness*
- **CONNECTIONS: INFORMATIONAL TEXT** *Foundations*
- **CONNECTIONS: PODCAST** *Essentials*
- **CONNECTIONS: CROSS-SUBJECT REPORT** *Proficiency*
- **CONNECTIONS: CONTENT STUDY** *Distinction*

Another important consideration is that state standards are often reviewed, revised, or reversioned. Therefore, it is important to note that the developed systemic unit names should be designed first and foremost based on the essence of the current standards. Then, when minor or major changes are made to the standards documents in the near or far future, the teacher-designed curriculum (i.e., Essential Maps, Consensus Maps, Projected/Diary Maps) do not need to be scrapped and started over; instead, they simply need to be reviewed and revised accordingly.

Generalized Versus Specialized Courses

In most K–12 disciplines, as students enter late middle school and high school they begin to experience specialized courses such as calculus, chemistry, or advanced drawing. Therefore, a K–12 unit name task force must be aware that general courses' unit names may not work for specialized courses. Specialized courses may need unit names specific to a course or series of courses. Likewise, developed unit names for general courses may not be appropriate for all the generalized courses. For example, if a task force determines that **PHONO-LOGICAL AWARENESS** will be a unit name, it will most likely be used for units of study kindergarten through third grade. Fourth grade and beyond would not normally have use for this unit name unless there is a unique situation.

Summary

The information in this section expressed thoughts concerning possible strand variations in standards documents. Each discipline's unit name task force will need to explore and consider the three unit name types and determine which one or ones would best aid in representing and recording the curriculum. It is important to note that any agreed-upon list of unit names developed by a task force should be considered a *work in progress*. Once the collaborative work begins and maps are being designed, unit names often need slight modifications or additions. There should be follow-up communication between unit name task force members and all teachers regarding necessary changes. Often, members who are a part of a discipline or combined disciplines' unit name task force are also members of a collaborative curriculum map design team and can provide input and suggestions when concerns or desired changes are voiced. It is likely that the developed unit names will naturally evolve as teachers participate in the ongoing process of designing units of study.

UNIT NAME DEVELOPMENT CONSIDERATIONS

Considerations in this section are meant to inform, not dictate. They are based on numerous experiences with a variety of learning organizations. Some of the information in the step-by-step section is complex. You may want to read through it a few times for cognitive processing as well as discuss the various steps with others involved in leadership roles pertaining specifically to curriculum mapping or curriculum work.

Unit Name Task Force

When designing unit names for a specific discipline or combination of disciplines, a unit name task force needs to represent all grade levels (and courses) in the learning organization. A unit name task force's ability to work collegially will depend on variables including cultural and educational beliefs about student-learning expectations. Other factors that may influence the curriculum design unit name process consist of

- familiarity with a discipline's horizontal *and* vertical standards structure;
- preexisting scope and sequences wherein teachers have placed standard statements *verbatim* into quarter, semester, or month blocks but have *not* focused on designing systemic units of study where standard statements have been

o broken apart (unpacked), causing teachers to come to agreement on the standard statements' explicit *and* implicit learning expectations; and

o broken apart (unpacked) standard statements have been translated into agreed-upon content and skill statements within units housed in a mapping system;

- preexisting units of study that teachers have designed and implemented individually, by grade level or department, schoolwide, or districtwide that are purely based on standards interpretation, *not* duplications of current or past textbooks;

- teachers' capabilities and experiences in working together collegially with curriculum *design* in mind;

- *ample* time set aside to design curriculum (e.g., frequent full or half days versus trying to find a half hour here and there; preferably not taking teachers away from their classroom teaching time); and

- previous, present, and future *professional development* and *support* for making personal and collaborative sense of curriculum work and how that influences

   o cognitive connections related to (1) curriculum mapping, (2) data-based decision making, and (3) learning/teaching professional development;

   o understanding and integration of 21st-century skills and learning related to replacing, growing, and reversioning curriculum design and instructional practice;

   o learning procedures and processes involved in designing collaborative curriculum map or maps (e.g., developing unit names; prioritizing standard statements; breaking apart standard statements; reviewing maps); and

   o generating comfort levels individually and collaboratively for using the selected mapping system in relationship to housing, copying, and retrieving curriculum maps.

Step-by-Step Thoughts

When developing unit names, the following steps are recommended to aid in ensuring a systemic focus when a single-discipline unit name task force meets. Please be aware that if a cross- or multidiscipline unit name task force is formed, many of the same steps and processes are involved.

1. For each discipline's task force, make certain there is teacher representation from *each* grade level and *each* school site:

   a. If the learning organization is small (*one* teacher *per* grade level or series of grade levels or courses), all teachers responsible for teaching a particular discipline will be a part of the task force.

   b. If the learning organization is medium-sized (*one* elementary school, *one* middle school, and *one* high school with *two or more* teachers per grade level, K–8, and the high school's departments divide the courses by expertise), the unit name task force should have *at least* one teacher from each grade level, K–8, and one teacher per course offered at the high school.

   c. If the learning organization is large (*multiple* elementary schools, *one or two* middle schools, and *one or two* high schools), it is recommended that the task force consist of teachers from every school wherein *with careful planning* teachers represent all grade levels and courses. For example, a formed science unit name task force may consist of

○ a kindergarten teacher from Elementary School A representing Grades K–3;

○ a first-grade teacher from Elementary School B representing Grades K–3;

○ a second-grade teacher from Elementary School B who has also taught in the primary grades in Elementary Schools A and D representing Grades K–3;

○ a third-grade teacher from Elementary School C representing Grades 3–5;

○ a fourth-grade teacher from Elementary School D who has also taught in the intermediate grades in Elementary Schools C and E representing Grades 3–5;

○ a fifth-grade teacher from Elementary School E representing Grades 3–5;

○ three science teachers from one middle school and three science teachers from the other middle school;

○ and four science teachers from the one high school to round out the 16-member team.

d. The exception to the Step 1 recommendation of each school/each grade level literally being present is when the learning organization is of grand scale, wherein multiple elementary schools, middle schools, and high schools create *two or more* vertical feeder patterns. While there needs to be representation for every grade level and course offered, in this case, a unit name task force often has 20 to 25 members consisting of one or more discipline-specific administrators (e.g., districtwide math curriculum director; feeder-pattern math coordinator) and teacher leaders (e.g., math-literacy coaches at each school site) who are joined by a selected number of classroom-teacher representatives.

e. For specialized disciplines, such as art, music, physical education, foreign language, family and consumer science, or industrial arts, the total number of teachers responsible for a discipline's grade levels and courses most likely will not exceed 10 to 20 people regardless of the organization's size (except for grand-sized organizations). Therefore, all the discipline's teachers are a part of the unit name task force.

f. It is recommended that special education teachers be included in the process of developing unit names. Each special education teacher can personally decide which discipline or disciplines (as well as grade level or levels) he or she wants to represent.

g. It is highly recommended that a list of *alternative* teachers be generated so that if a specific grade level's or course's unit name task-force member has an emergency or other reason for not being able to attend the task-force meeting or meetings, the horizontal and vertical representation is not weakened due to a gap in grade level or levels, course or courses.

h. It is important that a unit name task force includes curriculum mapping cabinet members and, if established, curriculum mapping council members. These teacher leaders play a significant role because they (1) can provide insight into the big picture of curriculum mapping due to more learning experience, (2) have been exposed to the logic and reasoning for developing systemic unit names, and (3) have an expertise in the discipline area or areas they represent on a unit name task force. These teachers often cofacilitate the meetings. They may facilitate independently from or in conjunction with district or school-site curriculum specialists (see i).

i. District or school-site discipline specialists, such as curriculum directors, coordinators, coaches, department chairs, or consultants, should be a part of a unit name task force as supporters or facilitators of the teacher-led process.

2. To prepare for the unit name task-force meeting or meetings, the facilitators need to have preliminary discussions focused on

a. Determining ahead of time what *unit name type or types* the task-force members may be considering. Discussion concerning explanation of similarities and differences of each type and design ramifications for using particular types will also need to be planned. For example, if the task force will be asked to develop unit name signifiers, the task-force members will need to be trained on the necessity to not only develop the unit name signifier *terms* or *phrases* but the development of big ideas or enduring understandings that *represent* the meanings behind each term or phrase. Facilitators may need to build their own background knowledge and understanding of conceptual-based learning. Erickson (2002, 2007) addresses the purposes for conceptual lenses and generalizations. Wiggins and McTighe (1998) and McTighe and Wiggins (2004) ask teachers to design units of study wherein students experience multiple perspectives framed around big ideas and enduring understandings.

b. Planning the first phase of the initial meeting day, which focuses on the necessary *background knowledge* for the task-force members *because* they may or may not all be well versed in the terminology related to curriculum mapping; the systemic nature of curriculum mapping; a mapping system's relational database; or how units of study are created and housed within the mapping system.

c. Planning for phase two of the initial meeting day, which includes exploration and dialogue pertaining to unit name type or types being considered. This may take a short or long time depending on the type or types of unit names involved, selected discipline, participants' comfort level with the task expectations, and time spent on background knowledge.

d. Proactively planning for *what ifs*, including variables such as

o the task-force members not cognitively grasping the systemic purpose of mapping or the to-be-developed unit names;

o the process and procedural steps for developing the unit names; or

o the task-force members not working well together.

Due to any of these or other unplanned-for variables, there may need to be a second meeting to develop unit names. Therefore, it is wise to plan a follow-up day, just in case.

e. Plan for unit name task-force meeting behavior protocols to be established at the onset of the first meeting. Having explicit expectations will better enable the task force to reach the meeting tasks and goals. Protocols may already be in place at a particular school or schools that can be used as is or modified for the task-force meetings.

3. The ultimate goal of the task force is to develop a list of collaboratively agreed-upon, initial systemic unit names. The reason for using the term *initial* is that, as mentioned previously, the list may be modified or expanded once teachers become actively engaged in using the unit names during the curriculum design process.

The unit name task-force members need to be informed up front that there will be challenging moments during the meeting time. Even when task-force members have a strong knowledge base and understanding of a discipline or disciplines, each member's personal educational, intellectual, and emotional factors can affect the processes and procedures.

DESIGN THOUGHTS FOR UNIT NAME TYPES

There are design implications depending on the unit name type or types chosen. As an administrator or teacher leader who may be a unit name task-force facilitator, it is important to be aware of the potential nuances.

Topic/Theme Unit Name *Versus* Topic/Theme Unit Name: Descriptor

When comparing the first two unit name types in Figure A.1, it may appear that there is not a strong difference between the two types as there is simply the addition of a descriptor in the second type. However, when contemplating how to best house and record the content and skills *within* units of study, there is a definite difference between the two types. Compare and contrast the content and skills expectations in the *unit* of study in Figure A.4 versus the *units* of study in Figure A.5.

The two-figure comparison visually represents the design ramifications related to using topic *descriptors* in a unit name. Content and skills housed in theme/topic unit names can be broader or more diverse than content and skills

Figure A.4 Topic/Theme Unit Name

Unit: MEASUREMENT III	
Content	*Skills*
A. Time: ½ Hour, ¼ Hour	A1. Identify in writing time on analog/digital faces A2. Solve 1-step word problems using numerals and colon to represent solutions
B. Money: Mixed Coin/Bill Sets up to $10.00	B1. Add and record in writing total amounts displayed by sets of coins and bills (penny, nickel, dime, quarter, half dollar, 1-dollar bill, 5-dollar bill) using dollar symbol ($), decimal point (.), cent symbol (¢) B2. Solve 2-step computation (addition/subtraction) word problems
C. Standard Length: Inch, Foot, Yard	C1. Measure manipulatively and in writing lengths to nearest ½ inch using real-world objects and illustration representations C2. Estimate in writing real-world and illustrated lengths without tools C3. Record in writing lengths using numerals/words, numerals/symbols (', ")
D. Temperature: Fahrenheit, Celsius	D1. Record in writing temperature using degree symbol (°) by reading thermometer scale D2. Convert in writing metric to standard/standard to metric using conversion formula and calculator

housed in a theme/topic name with a narrowed descriptor topic focus or focuses. Neither of these two unit name types is a clear-cut right or wrong choice when designing curriculum.

When a discipline's unit name task force chooses to use theme/topic unit names, it is not uncommon for the initial list of potential unit names to be 8 to 10 *broad category* terms or phrases. Sometimes, a task force may then be asked to decide on descriptors. This does not usually work well because it can stifle the teachers' sense of design creativity when the task force is disbanded and teacher teams begin to actually design curriculum maps for a particular grade level or course. Considerations for what descriptors may be is a natural point of the discussion process when determining the theme/topic names. When theme/topic unit names are combined with descriptors, there are endless unit name possibilities. While the choice of the actual descriptors can be part of the task force's role, it is recommended that it be ultimately left up to the teachers when actually designing the units of study. If there is an issue or concern with

Figure A.5   Topic/Theme Unit Name: Broad/Narrow Descriptor Unit Names

Unit: MEASUREMENT TIME	
Content	*Skills*
A. Time: ½ Hour, ¼ Hour	A1. Identify in writing time on analog/digital faces A2. Solve 1-step word problems using numerals and colon to represent solutions

Unit: MEASUREMENT MONEY	
Content	*Skills*
A. Money: Mixed Coin/Bill Sets up to $10.00	A1. Add and record in writing total amounts displayed by sets of coins and bills (penny, nickel, dime, quarter, half dollar, 1-dollar bill, 5-dollar bill) using dollar symbol ($), decimal point (.), cent symbol (¢) A2. Solve 2-step computation (addition/subtraction) word problems

Unit: MEASUREMENT LENGTH	
Content	*Skills*
A. Standard Length: Inch, Foot, Yard	A1. Measure manipulatively and in writing lengths to nearest ½ inch using real-world objects and illustration representations A2. Estimate in writing real-world and illustrated lengths without tools A3. Record in writing lengths using numerals/words, numerals/symbols (', ")

Unit: MEASUREMENT TEMPERATURE	
Content	*Skills*
A. Temperature: Fahrenheit, Celsius	A1. Record in writing temperature using degree symbol (°) by reading thermometer scale A2. Convert in writing metric to standard/ standard to metric using conversion formula and calculator

any descriptor's wording, it will naturally become a point of conversation when the teachers begin conducting vertical reviews.

The following scenario highlights a mathematics unit name task force that decided to develop topic/theme unit names and discussed possibilities for topic/theme unit names and descriptors.

K–12 Mathematics Unit Name Task Force

A district arranged for unit name task forces in four disciplines (mathematics, science, social studies, and English/Language Arts) to meet sometime during the first two weeks after the academic school year ended.

The district consists of seven elementary schools, three middle schools, and two high schools. For the K–12 mathematics task force, there was teacher representation from all schools and grade levels as well as multiple schools' mathematics coaches. The total number of task-force members was 30 teachers, including 5 teachers from the curriculum mapping cabinet. The task force met as a full team for one day; for the specialized mathematics courses (late middle school and high school), the appropriate teachers met for a second half-day meeting.

Prior to the first day's meeting, the five cabinet members, mathematics coaches, and assistant superintendent of curriculum met to discuss the potential use of all three unit name types. They met via online meetings and conference calls with four districts that had developed unit names to gain various process perspectives. From talking with the districts, the preplanning members decided that for mathematics the first two types of unit names would be the best for organizing the curriculum within the district's mapping system.

At the onset of the first day's meeting, the facilitators took turns presenting background knowledge. They shared that the task force's goal was to come to agreement on systemic theme or topic unit names (and if possible, consider potential descriptors) for the general mathematics courses offered K–8. For the specialized courses, such as Algebra I, Algebra II, Trigonometry, and Calculus, the middle school and high school members would be meeting to develop unit names specific to each course or series of courses on a second day.

Part One

The facilitators began the in-depth conversation concerning the state standards mathematics strands: Problem Solving; Reasoning and Proof; Communications; Connections; Representation; Number Sense and Operations; Algebra; Geometry; Measurement; Statistics and Probability. While it did not take long for the task-force members to come to agreement that unit names could easily be based on the standard strands topic or theme-based terminology, the collegial dialogue deepened when they

(Continued)

(Continued)

began to discuss the first five strands representing thinking-skill processes. A facilitator posed three questions:

1. Should these five strands become stand-alone topic/theme unit names (e.g., **REPRESENTATION**)?

2. Or, should the standard statements *within* each thinking-skill process strand be embedded as content and skill statements within the remaining five strands' units of study? For example, in a **GEOMETRY** unit of study, content and skill statements would include embedded thinking-skill process learning expectations within the content or skill statements. The skill statement *Represent manipulatively and in writing arrays* that includes the target *manipulatively* embeds the *Representation* thinking-skill process strand, which asks students to *use physical models*.

3. Or, should there be a combination of the two? For example, at the beginning of the year, **REASONING AND PROOF** could be its own unit of study, so students explicitly learn content and skills related to this standard and then for the remainder of the year the thinking-skill process standard statements are embedded in the topic strands' units of study?

After rich dialogue and discussion, the task force agreed that elementary school courses should include at least two explicit thinking-skill process units of study—one at the beginning of each academic year and the other sometime during the academic year. For the middle school and high school courses, the thinking-skill process strands would be embedded into the topic-based strands unless a team of teachers designing a particular course's curriculum decided to include a specific thinking-skill unit of study.

After a stretch break, the facilitators explained the design ramifications when using broad or narrow descriptors in conjunction with the drafted theme or topic unit names. They wrote on chart paper:

- **NUMBER SENSE I**
- **NUMBER SENSE II**

- **NUMBER SENSE: ADDITION**
- **NUMBER SENSE: MIXED COMPUTATION**
- **NUMBER SENSE: PLACE VALUE**
- **NUMBER SENSE: FRACTIONS**

The facilitators asked the teachers to brainstorm some potential content that could be found within units of study with these unit names. The task-force members quickly caught on to the point being made. The teachers felt that they did not want to dictate what the descriptors would be if a teacher team chose to use them in a particular grade level or course. What they did do was brainstorm potential content learning that could be housed in the agreed-upon topic/theme unit names and compared them vertically. A facilitator recorded the teachers' suggestions in a T-chart graphic organizer in an electronic document. The day passed quickly and ended with the topic/theme-based K–8 unit names in place. The task-force members commented on how much they enjoyed the day as it was the first time they had ever met with teachers from a K–12 grade range and found it engaging and enriching.

Part Two

During the next meeting day, the middle school and high school task-force members returned to develop unit names for the specialized courses. Because they had the experience of the previous day, they immediately started to work on the task. By noon, the teachers had generated the specialized courses unit names and ended their time together.

Part Three

The task-force facilitators e-mailed the finalized K–12 unit names to the assistant superintendent of curriculum who in turn posted the documents on the district website's curriculum mapping page, so everyone had access to the initial unit names.

Using Initials for Topic/Theme Unit Name: Descriptor

A discipline's unit name task force may choose to modify the second type of unit name (Topic/Theme Unit Name: Descriptor) by abbreviating the broader topic/theme terminology using initials. Figure A.6 represents three of the offered disciplines in a private K–12 Catholic school that chose to develop abbreviation initials to represent the broader topic/theme unit name prior to the colon and descriptor. The teachers in this school had begun their curriculum mapping implementation with writing Projected/Diary Maps without first working collaboratively on systemically considering how they would systemically house the units of study in their selected mapping system. Because of this, there was no horizontal or vertical continuity or consistency regarding the school's collective units of study. Since they had already been developing units, rather than starting with brainstorming prospective theme/topic unit names, they chose to review the current topic-based unit names to look for explicit or implicit similarities.

During one discipline's task-force meetings, a teacher inquired, "What if two or more disciplines use the same initial? Wouldn't that mean undesired units would be retrieved when searching vertically?" A fellow teacher commented that the search feature in their mapping system has a filter for subject areas and can be narrowed down to search in only their discipline when running a search report.

While there were moments of frustration during the decision-making process, the collaborative, systemic work that took place to determine the appropriate theme/topic-based unit names to be recorded prior to the unit's topic focuses already in their maps brought the teachers together professionally with fresh eyes for their students' learning continuum. Many teachers shared that, while they had been mapping simply because they were told to, the unit

Figure A.6   Initial Abbreviations for Topic/Theme Name: Descriptor Unit Names

Broader Topic/Theme	Examples
Science **E** = Earth **P** = Physical **L** = Life **S-P** = Scientific Process	**E: TECTONIC PLATES** **L: MENDELIAN INHERITANCE** **E/L: BIOMES** The initial signifies the main focus of the unit. This is not to say that other focuses are not included. If more than one focus is strongly represented in a unit, use the signifying initials in order from greatest emphasis to the least, separated by a slash.
Social Studies **W** = World **A** = American **T** = Texas *(plus one of the following)* **G** = Geography **H** = History **C** = Culture **E** = Economics	**WH: GREEK CIVILIZATION** **TG: NATURAL RESOURCES** **AE/AH: TAXATION** The two initials signify the main focus of the unit. This is not to say that other focuses are not included. If more than one focus is strongly represented in a unit, use the signifying initials in order from greatest emphasis to the least, separated by a slash or slashes.
Religion **H** = Hebrew **G** = Greek **C** = Christian *(plus)* **S** = Scripture **C** = Catholic or Church **B** = Biblical *(plus)* **H** = History **S** = Sacraments **T** = Tradition **M** = Morality **J** = Justice **WR** = World Religions	**HS: PSALMS** **BH: PATH OF THE PATRIARCHS** **S: SACRAMENT OF INITIATION** **M: CHOOSING LIFE** **CH/J: SERVING POOR/VULNERABLE** The one or two initials signify the main focus of the unit. This is not to say that other focuses are not included. If more than one focus is strongly represented in a unit, use the signifying initials in order from greatest emphasis to the least, separated by a slash.

naming process provided them a venue for personally seeing and experiencing why they needed to be mapping.

Concept-Based Unit Name Signifiers: Topics/Themes

A unit name signifier represents the agreed-upon *generalized concept* or *concepts* of learning that may be revisited horizontally, but most importantly, vertically. The signifier word or short phrase *represents* the big ideas or enduring understandings associated with the concept-based word or phrase. A unit name signifier's *transferable* big ideas or enduring understandings asks students to revisit a signifier's generalization or generalizations over a series of academic years to aid in making connections to specific themes or topics. The unit name signifier is located to the *left* of the colon, and the specific theme or topic to the *right* side of the colon (as shown in Figure A.7).

Figure A.7   Concept-Based Unit Name Signifier: Theme or Topic Focus Samples

- **GOVERNMENTS: 1776**
- **CYCLES: SEASONS**
- **STRUCTURES: PYRAMID DESIGN**
- **EVOLUTION: VOLCANOES**
- **GLOBAL CONNECTIONS: HOLIDAYS**
- **ETHICS: INTERNET PIRACY**
- **PERFORMANCES: SPRING DANCE RECITAL**

Unit name task forces that develop unit name signifiers may or may not use words or phrases *explicitly* included in a discipline's standards document. The signifier needs to represent a *generalization*. Erickson (2007) defines a *generalization* as "two or more concepts stated in a relationship . . . that can be tested against, and supported by, the facts" (p. 31). Generalizations aid students in *synthesizing* their learning by causing them to transfer concepts from prior learning experiences to new knowledge experiences through application of logic, thought, and reasoning. A unit name signifier's *conceptual lens* becomes a filter through which to explore the current theme or topic and the associated content and skills.

For example, a K–12 science unit name task force agreed that a K–12 concept-based unit name signifier will be **SYSTEMS**. One of the generalizations (big ideas/enduring understandings) they developed for this signifier was *the interaction or interdependency of the parts of a whole affect the whole*. They determined, based on the theme or topic learning encountered over the years, that students will revisit this conceptual lens when studying specific themes or topics that needed to be addressed based on state standards:

- **SYSTEMS: SOLAR** (*Grade 2*)
- **SYSTEMS: BIOMES** (*Grade 4*)
- **SYSTEMS: CELLS** (*Grade 7*)

While they agreed that each unit of study needs to include specific science topics and related facts, the concept-based generalizations will affect the selected content, skills, and assessments within each unit of study to be certain that students have the opportunity to generalize and transfer the big ideas to new learning over time.

Jacobs (2010) suggests the use of conceptual science ideas expressed by Felipe Fernández-Armesto in *Ideas That Changed the World* (2003) as a way to frame students' science learning:

- Here Comes the Sun: The IDEA of a Sun-Centered Universe
- No Dice: The IDEA of an Orderly Universe
- Invisible Powers: The IDEA of Harnessing Natural Energy
- Tooth and Claw: The IDEA of Natural Selection
- Calculating Machine: The IDEA of Artificial Intelligence
- Time's Arrow: The IDEA of Linear Progression (p. 45)

If teachers study these ideas and choose to use them as the basis for the enduring understandings or big ideas, the unit name signifiers may be the initials of the key words in each idea. For example, Sun-Centered Universe may become SCU, Harnessing Natural Energy may be HNE, and Artificial Intelligence may become AI. Single or multiple conceptual lenses would then precede the theme or topic focus:

- **SCU/HNE: OUR COMMUNITY AND THE WORLD**
- **AI: FUTURISM, HERE AND NOW**

Unit name signifiers are meant to *stay consistent* in and across grade levels and courses. The topic or theme may change *horizontally* during an academic year as well as *vertically* through two or more academic years. While unit name signifiers and corresponding big ideas or enduring understandings are meant to be used K–12 (or whatever span is appropriate for your learning organization), be aware of three realities:

1. Teachers may find the need to expand the unit name signifiers as they begin the actual process of designing units of study. If this happens, it is important that teachers also (1) develop corresponding big ideas or enduring understandings for the new signifier; and (2) inform a member or members of the unit name task force, so the new signifier and its big ideas or enduring understanding can be added to the discipline's official unit name signifier list.

2. A particular grade level or course may not find it necessary or appropriate to use one or more of the unit name signifiers developed for a discipline.

3. Specialized courses outside of general studies may need to develop specialized unit name signifiers unique to the course or courses being designed.

Because unit name signifiers are meant to represent transferable understandings, signifiers are often used in multiple disciplines. For example, the big idea associated with the signifier mentioned previously, *systems,* does not need to be confined to science. Social studies and mathematics are two disciplines that come to mind wherein *the interaction or interdependency of the parts of a whole affects the whole.* This does not mean that a learning organization must plan to develop unit name signifiers with the ability for use in various disciplines. It simply expresses the transferability potential.

A discipline choosing to develop unit name signifiers may soon discover that when teachers begin to develop units of study and focus on the specific themes or topics, the learning expectations may connect multiple standard strands. This often leads to collegial dialogue focusing on the question:

- What conceptual lens or lenses do we want our students to view the current or future learning through based on the relationship between the desired facts, topics, themes, and concepts *not only during their academic years,* but for a lifetime of personal and professional application?

Twenty-first-century thinking embraces project-based interdisciplinary units of study (Jacobs, 2010). If a school or district uses interdisciplinary units exclusively or occasionally when designing curriculum, it is worthwhile to consider representative unit name signifiers that express the key concepts that embrace a school or districts' enduring understandings horizontally and vertically.

Depending on the specific discipline or multiple disciplines in focus, a developed list of unit name signifiers may consist of approximately 6 to 10 terms or phrases that have corresponding big ideas or enduring understandings. When the teacher teams begin to design the units of study, the unit name signifiers can be combined with various themes or topics throughout the grade levels and courses, where the potential for unit name signifier: topic/theme unit names is numerous. One final note: determining big ideas or enduring understandings associated with concept-based signifiers can be applied to broad topics or themes (e.g., probability/statistics) as well.

Roman Numerals

Hale (2008) mentions using Roman numerals after unit names to indicate that a specific unit name is being revisited *horizontally in an academic year.* For example,

GEOMETRY I *(Sept)*   **GEOMETRY II** *(Oct)*   **GEOMETRY III** *(Dec)*

A revisited unit name may *not* necessarily be included in *each* month of the academic school year. For example, see the italic months above.

When a unit name is used again *within* an academic year, the unit name is assigned the next sequential Roman numeral. While the particular unit name or unit of study may be revisited in an academic year, the content and skills-learning expectations within the unit of study *varies* or *increases* in expectation. In other words, the content and skills in a new unit of study are *not* identical to a previous like-named unit of study, as shown in Figure A.8.

Figure A.8   Comparisons of Like-Named Units of Study

Month		Content	Skills
Sept.	**GEOMETRY I**	A. 2-Dimensional Shapes: Circle, Square, Triangle	A1. Identify in writing examples of real-world and illustrated shapes using name and descriptive terms: center, point, arc, side, angle A2. Illustrate and label in writing each shape
Oct.	**GEOMETRY II**	A. 2-Dimensional/ 3-Dimensional Shapes: Circle/Sphere, Square/ Cube, Triangle/Pyramid	A1. Identify in writing examples of real-world and illustrated shapes using name and descriptive terms: center, point, arc, side, face, base, edge, angle A2. Illustrate and label in writing each shape
		B. Symmetry: Line of Symmetry	B1. Identify in writing symmetry line using polygons B2. Draw symmetry line using polygons
Dec.	**GEOMETRY III**	A. Transformation of Shapes: Flip, Rotate	A1. Flip figures across line of reflection in coordinate plane A2. Rotate figures 180 degrees with fixed point as center of rotation

Using Roman numerals to signify revisited unit names can be applied to *any type* of unit name:

- **MUSIC THEORY I**
  (Topic/Theme Unit Name)

- **PROBABILITY/STATISTICS: TRIALS/RESULTS I**
  (Topic/Theme Unit Name: Broad/Narrow Descriptor)

- **ECONOMICS: NORTH AMERICAN TRADE III**
  (Concept-Based Unit Name Signifier: Topic/Theme)

Roman numerals are most often used for *topic/theme* unit names as this type of unit name is the most generic. When used with *topic/theme: broad/ narrow descriptor* or *concept-based unit name signifier: theme/topic* unit names, the Roman numeral indicates that the *narrowed-down* learning to the *right* of the colon is being revisited.

Remember that Roman numerals are only used to represent revisited units of study *horizontally* in one academic year. They are *not* used vertically in a series of two or more academic years. For example, if a third-grade reading map includes **VOCABULARY DEVELOPMENT I** through **VOCABULARY DEVELOPMENT VII**, a fourth-grade reading map would *not* start using the unit name **VOCABULARY DEVELOPMENT VIII**. The first time this unit name is included in the fourth-grade reading map, assuming the unit of study will appear *more than once* in the academic year, it would read **VOCABULARY DEVELOPMENT I**. If a unit name appears *only once* in a curriculum map, it *does not* need a Roman numeral because there is no need to indicate it is being revisited in the same academic year.

The Issue of *When*

When designing collaborative maps, whether Essential Maps or Consensus Maps, teachers oftentimes express concern about the autonomy of *when* the agreed-upon unit of study must occur during an academic year. To address this concern, it must first be recognized that all mapping systems maps are recorded based on months (and in some systems, weeks). Therefore, a question such as this may be posed: "If we record a unit of study in September (Essential Map or Consensus Map), do I (in a Projected/Diary Map) have to guarantee that the learning will take place in the same month or weeks it is recorded in the collaborative map?"

A simple yes or no answer cannot be stated. It is a bit more complex than that. The answer may be yes for one learning organization and no for another, or yes for one discipline and no for another. The design decision must always depend on what is in the best interests of the students receiving the learning (Jacobs, 1997, 2004, 2006). It is recommended that the decision of when units of study take place are made as needed rather than trying to determine the correct response before it is necessary.

If teachers decide they want to create flexibility for when, *how is this visually represented in a collaborative map?* Based on numerous schools' and districts' experiences, the most successful method is through the use of asterisks *after* the appropriate unit names within *collaborative* maps:

- No Asterisk: The unit of study must take place *in the month (or weeks)* it currently lives in.
- One Asterisk: The unit of study may take place any time *during the academic year.* Where it currently lives in the collaborative map serves as a *placeholder* or *possible recommendation.*
- Two Asterisks: The unit of study may take place any time *within the quarter or semester* it lives in.

When working with administrators and teacher leaders learning about the use of asterisks, they asked, "What if we want to send the message that the learning can happen at any time as long as it is *before* the state testing window, which for us is in April?" They were asked to brainstorm possible ideas. They came up with the idea of using three asterisks after the appropriate unit names.

Figure A.9 provides a few examples and explanations of asterisked unit names.

Figure A.9   Examples of Using Asterisks in Conjunction With Unit Names

Unit Names	Explanation of When Learning May Take Place
HEALTH AWARENESS: SAY NO TO DRUGS (Oct)	This unit of study must take place in October. The teachers who designed the collaborative map agreed on this due to October officially being National Drug Awareness Month.
MEASUREMENT I* (Sept) **MEASUREMENT II*** (Nov) **MEASUREMENT III*** (Jan)	These units of study, which are currently housed in the first month of three grading periods, can be learned during any month in the academic year. For example, a teacher may choose to have students learn **MEASUREMENT I** in September, October, or early December.
ELEMENTS OF MUSIC: TIMBRE I** (Aug) **ELEMENTS OF MUSIC: TIMBRE II**** (Sept)	These units of study can be learned at any time during the quarter or semester based on the agreed-upon timeframe limit. One teacher may chose to have students learn the unit of study housed in August in August, and another teacher may choose to have students learn this unit of study in October.
U.S. CONSTITUTION*** (Sept)	This unit of study may be learned at any time during the academic year as long as it takes place before the state testing window, which is in early April in this district.

Please note that the only curriculum maps that may contain asterisks are Essential Maps and Consensus Maps. The asterisks *are removed* when a collaborative map is copied into a Projected/Diary Map. Note: The removal of asterisks may also occur when copying an Essential Map into a Consensus Map if a school's teacher team agrees to do so and assigns a unit of study to a specific month, week, or weeks.

CONCLUSION

Regardless of the types of maps being designed, early development of unit names is worthwhile. To enhance the likelihood of reaching sustainability, disciplines' systemic unit names should be developed early on. It often frustrates teachers that when they are asked to write maps and are not provided clear direction on what to title units of study when recording them in a mapping system. When told later there are now specific systemic unit names to be used, teachers' response may be, "Why weren't we given these names before we started mapping?"

Based on numerous unit name task-force experiences, here are three concluding thoughts:

1. When teachers serve on multiple unit name task forces, as elementary teachers often do, they comment on how different the cognitive process, dialogue, and unit name outcomes are per task force. This speaks loudly to the uniqueness of the process. Always remember that the process is as important as the by-products (agreed-upon unit names) generated from these systemic-focused meetings.

2. From one district to another, there cannot be a pat answer as to what unit name type or types is right for any discipline. What matters is what is right for a particular discipline and how the teachers systemically choose to make sense of organizing the curriculum within a mapping system to enhance the ability for horizontal and vertical articulation.

3. You can never fully grasp all that is involved in this process until you attempt it. Numerous administrators and teacher leaders have commented that, while they were leery going into the process (even though they cognitively understood the purpose and desired outcome), it was in the *let's just do it* trenches that they began to experience the immediate and long-term value in asking teachers to go outside their comfort zones and begin to truly think with an aspen grove mentality, as mentioned in Chapter 1.

REVIEW QUESTIONS

Based on your learning organization's past or present teacher-led systemic design decision-making experiences, discuss your responses with a partner or in a small group.

1. Has our learning organization ever looked at student learning expectations from a true K–12 continuum perspective? If yes, have we ever looked into the collaborative agreement on unit names based on what this appendix asks of teachers as leaders and decision makers? If no, what needs to take place to move us in this design direction?

2. How has reading this appendix made me think differently about curriculum mapping being a systemic-change model? As curriculum mapping is not a *quick fix* initiative, how do I/we need to think or rethink the necessity for developing unit names for all of our disciplines?

3. Considering where we are currently in our curriculum mapping initiative, what planning do we need to do to begin to develop discipline-specific unit name task forces? Who will be in charge of the overall process? Who will facilitate each discipline's task-force work?

4. Looking at our approved calendar for this school year, and potentially the next school year, when will we be able to plan for K–12 unit name task forces to meet, as it takes approximately one day (and sometimes two) per discipline? During school days with substitutes? After school with stipends? Professional development days? In the summer with stipends?

Appendix B

OFFICER FOUNDATIONS OF THE UNITED STATES MARINE CORPS: LEADERSHIP TRAITS

> *Leadership traits are tools Marines use to judge leadership ability. It is a metric that helps identify our strengths and weaknesses and improve ourselves as leaders.*

Bearing—Bearing is looking, acting, and speaking like a leader whether or not these manifestations indicate your true feelings. Some signs of these traits are clear and plain speech, an erect gait, and impeccable personal appearance.

Courage—Knowing and standing for what is right, even in the face of popular disfavor, is often the leader's responsibility.

Decisiveness—Decisiveness guides a person to accumulate all available facts in a circumstance, weigh the facts, choose and announce an alternative which seems best. Often a decision made promptly is better than a potentially exact one made at the expense of more time. Decisiveness is a bias for action.

Dependability—Dependability permits a senior to assign a task to a junior with the understanding that it will be accomplished with minimum supervision. The understanding includes the assumption that the initiative will be taken on small matters not covered by instructions.

Endurance—Endurance—withstanding pain during a conditioning hike, physical training event, etc.—is an example of improving stamina, which is crucial in the development of leadership. Leaders are responsible for leading their units in physical endeavors and for motivating them as well.

Enthusiasm—Displaying interest in a task and optimism that the task can be successfully completed greatly enhances the likelihood that the task will be successfully finished.

Initiative—Since officers and noncommissioned officers (NCOs) often work without close supervision, emphasis is placed on being a self-starter.

Integrity—A Marine's word is his or her bond. Nothing less than complete honesty in all of your dealings with subordinates, peers, superiors, and others.

Judgment—Sound judgment is important because leaders must be able to quickly decide upon a correct course of action in order to gain the respect of their subordinates. Poor judgment often costs lives and time.

Justice—Displaying fairness and impartiality is critical in order to gain the trust and respect of people, particularly when exercising the responsibility as a leader.

Knowledge—Learning about current developments in military and naval science and world affairs is important for your growth and development.

Loyalty—The motto of our Corps is *Semper Fidelis!* You owe unswerving loyalty up and down the chain of command, to seniors, subordinates, and peers.

Tact—Consistently treating peers, seniors, subordinates and others with respect and courtesy is a sign of maturity. This deference must be extended in all conditions regardless of your true feelings.

Unselfishness—Looking out for the needs of your subordinates before your own is the essence of leadership. Do not confuse this with putting these matters ahead of the accomplishment of the mission.

OFFICER FOUNDATIONS OF THE UNITED STATES MARINE CORPS: LEADERSHIP PRINCIPLES

Leadership principles are ideas that help build on leadership traits by giving guidance on how to apply those traits when dealing with Marines and each unit.

Be technically and tactically proficient. Before you can lead you must be able to do the job; the first principle is to know your job. As a Marine you must demonstrate your ability to accomplish the mission and be capable of answering questions and demonstrating competence in your military occupational specialty (MOS). Respect is the reward of the Marine who shows competence. Tactical and technical competence can be learned from books and from on-the-job training.

Know yourself and seek self-improvement. This principle of leadership is developed through the use of leadership traits. Evaluate yourself using the leadership traits to determine your strengths and weaknesses. Having an accurate and clear understanding of yourself and a comprehension of group behavior helps you determine the best way to deal with any given situation.

Know your Marines and look out for their welfare. One of the most important principles is you should know your Marines and how they react to different situations. This knowledge can save lives. A Marine who is nervous or lacks self-confidence should never be put in a situation where an important, instant decision must be made. Knowledge of your Marines' personalities will enable you, as the leader, to decide how to best handle each Marine and determine when close supervision is needed.

Keep your Marines informed. Marines are inquisitive by nature. To promote efficiency and morale you should inform your Marines of all happenings and give reasons why things are to be done. The purpose of giving out information is to be sure that your Marines have enough information to do their job intelligently and to inspire their initiative, enthusiasm, loyalty, and convictions.

Set the example. As Marines progress through the ranks by promotion, all too often they take the attitude of "do as I say, not as I do." Nothing turns Marines off faster! As a Marine leader, your duty

(Continued)

(Continued)

is to set the standards for your Marines by personal example. The Marines in your unit all watch your appearance, attitude, physical fitness, and personal example. If your personal standards are high then you can rightfully demand the same of your Marines. If your personal standards are not high you are setting a double standard for your Marines and will rapidly lose their respect and confidence. Remember, your Marines reflect your image. Leadership is taught by example.

Ensure the task is understood, supervised, and accomplished. This principle is necessary in the exercise of command. Before you can expect your Marines to perform, they must know first what is expected of them. You must communicate your instructions in a clear, concise manner. Talk at a level that your Marines are sure to understand but not at a level so low that would insult their intelligence.

Before your Marines start a task, allow them a chance to ask questions or seek advice. Supervision is essential; without it, you cannot know if the assigned task is being properly accomplished. Subordinates view too much supervision as harassment; it effectively decreases their initiative. Allow subordinates to use their own techniques and then periodically check their progress.

Train your Marines as a team. Every waking hour Marines should be trained and schooled, challenged and tested, and corrected and encouraged with perfection and teamwork as a goal. This is the basis for what makes Marines fight in combat; it is the foundation for bravery, for advancing under fire. Teamwork is the key to successful operations. Teamwork is essential from the smallest unit to the entire Marine Corps. As a Marine officer, you must insist on teamwork from your Marines. Train, play, and operate as a team.

Make sound and timely decisions. The leader must be able to rapidly estimate a situation and make a sound decision based on that estimation. Hesitation or reluctance to make a decision leads subordinates to lose confidence in your abilities as a leader. Loss of confidence in turn creates confusion and hesitation within the unit. Once you make a decision and discover it is the wrong one, do not hesitate to revise your decision. Marines respect the leader who corrects mistakes immediately instead of trying to bluff through a poor decision.

Develop a sense of responsibility in your subordinates. Another way to show your Marines that you are interested in their welfare is to give them the opportunity for professional development. Assigning tasks and delegating the authority to accomplish tasks promotes mutual confidence and respect between the leader and subordinates. If you fail to delegate authority, you indicate your lack of trust and confidence in your subordinates and their abilities.

Employ your unit in accordance with its capabilities. Successful completion of a task depends upon how well you know your unit's capabilities. If the task assigned is one that your unit has not been trained to do, failure is very likely to result. Failure lowers your unit's morale and self-esteem. You would not send a motor transport operator to operate a TOW missile, nor would you send three Marines to do the job of ten. Seek out challenging tasks for your unit, but be sure your unit is prepared for and has the ability to successfully complete the mission.

Source: United States Marine Corps. (2009). *Officership Foundations.* The Basic School, Marine Corps Training Command. Camp Barrett, VA: Author. This is a work of the U.S. Government and is not subject to copyright protection in the U.S. However, foreign copyrights may apply.

References

Alvermann, D. E., & Phelps, S. F. (1998). *Content reading and literacy: Succeeding in today's diverse classroom.* Boston: Allyn & Bacon.

Bacon, K. (2009). Director quotes. *Brainyquote.com.* Retrieved March 21, 2010, from http://www.brainyquote.com/quotes/keywords/director_2.html

Bass, B. M. (1985). *Leadership and performance beyond expectations.* New York: Free Press.

Blasé, J., & Blasé, J. (1998). *Handbook of instructional leadership: How really good principals promote teaching and learning.* Thousand Oaks, CA: Corwin.

Blasé, J., & Blasé, J. R. (2001). *Empowering teachers: What successful principals do* (2nd ed.). Thousand Oaks, CA: Corwin.

Brewster, C., & Railsback, J. (2003). *Building trusting relationships for school improvement: Implications for principals and teachers.* Retrieved March 21, 2010, from http://educationnorthwest.org/webfm_send/463

Burns, J. M. (1978). *Leadership.* New York: Harper and Row.

Chenoweth, T. G., & Everhart, R. B. (2002). *Navigating comprehensive school change: A guide for the perplexed.* Larchmont, NY: Eye On Education.

Darling-Hammond, L. & Richardson, N. (2009). Teacher learning: What matters? *Educational Leadership, 66*(5),46–53.

Davies, B. (2005). *The essentials of school leadership,* Thousand Oaks, CA: Corwin.

DesiQuotes.Com. (n.d.). Aristotle quotes. *DesiQuotes.Com.* Retrieved April 16, 2010, from http://www.desiquotes.com/author/aristotle/

Donaldson, G. A. (2009). The lessons are in the leading. *Educational Leadership, 66*(5), 14–18.

Duckworth, E. (1964). Piaget rediscovered. *Journal of Research in Science Teaching, 2*(3), 172–175.

DuFour, R., & Eaker, R. (1998). *Professional learning communities at work: Best practices for enhancing student achievement.* Alexandria, VA: Association for Supervision and Curriculum Development.

DuFour, R. (2005, July). *Culture shifts: Becoming a professional learning community.* Keynote presentation given at the Professional Learning Communities Summer Institute, Salt Lake City, UT.

Eldredge N., & Wynne, P. (2000). *Life in the balance: Humanity and the biodiversity crisis.* Princeton, NJ: Princeton University Press.

Erickson, L. H. (2002). *Concept-based curriculum and instruction: Teaching beyond the facts.* Thousand Oaks, CA: Corwin.

Erickson, L. H. (2007). *Concept-based curriculum and instruction for the thinking classroom.* Thousand Oaks, CA: Corwin.

Fernández-Armesto, F. (2003). *Ideas that changed the world.* London: Dorling Kindersley Publishers Ltd.

Fullan, M. (2001). *Leading in a culture of change.* San Francisco: Jossey-Bass.

Gallagher, B. J., & Schmidt, W. H. (2009). *A peacock in the land of penguins: A story about courage in creating a land of opportunity*. Retrieved July 23, 2009, from http://www.perrythepeacock.com/

Glanz, J. (2006a). *What every principal should know about collaborative leadership*. Thousand Oaks, CA: Corwin.

Glanz, J. (2006b). *What every principal should know about cultural leadership*. Thousand Oaks, CA: Corwin.

Glanz, J. (2006c). *What every principal should know about ethical and spiritual leadership*. Thousand Oaks, CA: Corwin.

Glanz, J. (2006d). *What every principal should know about instructional leadership*. Thousand Oaks, CA: Corwin.

Glanz, J. (2006e). *What every principal should know about operational leadership*. Thousand Oaks, CA: Corwin.

Glanz, J. (2006f). *What every principal should know about school-community Leadership*. Thousand Oaks, CA: Corwin.

Glanz, J. (2006g). *What every principal should know about strategic leadership*. Thousand Oaks, CA: Corwin.

Glatthorn, A. A., & Jailall, J. M. (2009). *The principal as curriculum leader: Shaping what is taught and tested*. Thousand Oaks, CA: Corwin.

Hale, J. A. (2008). *A guide to curriculum mapping: Planning, implementing, and sustaining the process*. Thousand Oaks, CA: Corwin.

Hoerr, T. R. (2005). *The art of school leadership*. Alexandria, VA: Association for Supervision and Curriculum Development.

Hord, S. M. (1997). *Professional learning communities: What are they and why are they important?* Retrieved March 21, 2010, from http://www.sedl.org/change/issues/issues61/supportive_leadership.html

Jacobs, H. H. (1997). *Mapping the big picture: Integrating curriculum and assessment K–12*. Alexandria, VA: Association for Supervision and Curriculum Development.

Jacobs, H. H. (2003). Connecting curriculum mapping and technology. *Curriculum Technology Quarterly, 12*(3), 1–8.

Jacobs, H. H. (2004). *Getting results with curriculum mapping*. Alexandria, VA: Association for Supervision and Curriculum Development.

Jacobs, H. H. (2006). *Active literacy across the curriculum: Strategies for reading, writing, speaking, and listening*. Larchmont, NY: Eye On Education.

Jacobs, H. H. (2008, January). *Curriculum mapping: A big picture view*. Keynote presentation given at the Regional Curriculum Mapping Conference, Glendale, AZ.

Jacobs, H. H. (2010). *Curriculum 21: Essential education for a changing world*. Alexandria, VA: Association for Supervision and Curriculum Development.

Jacobs, H. H., & Johnson, A. J. (2009). *The curriculum mapping planner: Templates, tools, and resources for effective professional development*. Alexandria, VA: Association for Supervision and Curriculum Development.

Johnson, A., & Johnson, J. L. (2004). Long-term journey that transformed a district. In H. H. Jacobs (Ed.), *Getting results with curriculum mapping* (pp. 36–51). Alexandria, VA: Association for Supervision and Curriculum Development.

Kallick, B. (2006, July). *Mapping and systemic change*. Keynote presentation given at the Twelfth National Curriculum Mapping Institute, Santa Fe, NM.

Kallick, B., & Colosimo, J. (2009). *Using curriculum mapping and assessment data to improve learning*. Thousand Oaks, CA: Corwin.

Kowalski, T. (2006). *The school superintendent: Theory, practice, and cases* (2nd ed.). Thousand Oaks, CA: Sage.

Lao Tzu. (1999–2010). Lao Tzu quotes. *Thinkexist.com.* Retrieved March 21, 2010, from http://thinkexist.com/quotation/a_leader_is_best_when_people_barely_know_he/214091.html

Leon, A. (2005, August). Communication skills. *Alexis on technology.* Retrieved April 14, 2010, from http://aot.alexisleon.com/2005/08/17/communication-skills.html

Marzano, R. J. (2003). *What works in schools: Translating research into action.* Alexandria, VA: Association for Supervision and Curriculum Development.

Marzano, R. J., Waters, T., & McNulty, B. A. (2005). *School leadership that works: From research to results.* Alexandria, VA: Association for Supervision and Curriculum Development.

Mason-Draffen, C. (2007). *151 quick ideas to deal with difficult people.* Franklin Lakes, NJ: Career Press.

Maxwell, J. C. (1999–2010). John C. Maxwell quotes. *Thinkexist.com.* Retrieved March 21, 2010, from http://thinkexist.com/quotation/a-leader-is-one-who-knows-the-way-goes-the-way/535658.html

McTighe, J., & Wiggins, G. (2004). *Understanding by design professional development workbook.* Alexandria, VA: Association for Supervision and Curriculum Development.

Parker, A. (2009). Alan Parker quotes. *Brainyquote.com.* Retrieved March 21, 2010, from http://www.brainyquote.com/quotes/authors/a/alan_parker.html

Phillips, M. (2005). Creating a culture of literacy: A guide for middle and high school principals. Reston, VA: National Association of Secondary School Principals.

Ramsey, R. D. (2003). *School leadership from A to Z: Practical lessons from successful schools and businesses.* Thousand Oaks, CA: Corwin.

Reeves, D. B. (2005, April 7). *Transforming research into action.* Keynote presentation given at the Standards and Assessment Conference, Denver, CO.

Reeves, D. B. (2009). *Leading changes in your school: How to conquer myths, build commitment, and get results.* Alexandria, VA: Association for Supervision and Curriculum Development.

Robbins, P., & Alvy, H. B. (1995). *The principal's companion: Strategies and hints to make the job easier.* Thousand Oaks, CA: Corwin.

Senge, P., Cambron-McCabe, N., Lucas, T., Smith, B., & Kleiner, A. (2000). *Schools that learn: A fifth discipline fieldbook for educators, parents, and everyone who cares about education.* New York: Doubleday.

Skerritt, T. (2009). Director quotes. *Brainyquote.com.* Retrieved March 21, 2010, from http://www.brainyquote.com/quotes/keywords/director_13.html

ThinkExist.com. (1999–2010). *Albert Einstein quotes.* Retrieved April 14, 2010, from http://thinkexist.com/quotation/teaching_should_be_such_that_what_is_offered_is/15567.html

Tribuzzi, J. (2009, July). *Active literacy: Mapping reading, writing, speaking and listening in the curriculum.* Pre-academy presentation given at the Fifteenth National Curriculum Institute, Park City, UT.

Truesdale, V., Thompson, C., & Lucas, M. (2004). Use of curriculum mapping to build a learning community. In H. H. Jacobs (Ed.), *Getting results with curriculum mapping* (pp. 10–24). Alexandria, VA: Association of Supervision and Curriculum Development.

Tyson, T. (2010). Making learning irresistible: Extending the journey of Mabry Middle School. In H. H. Jacobs (Ed.), *Curriculum 21: Essential education for a changing world* (pp. 115–132). Alexandria, VA: Association for Supervision and Curriculum Development.

Udelhofen, S. (2005). *Keys to curriculum mapping: Strategies and tools to make it work.* Thousand Oaks, CA: Corwin.

Udelhofen, S. (2008). *Keys to curriculum mapping: A multimedia kit for professional development.* Thousand Oaks, CA: Corwin.

United States Marine Corps. (2009). *Officership foundations.* The Basic School, Marine Corps Training Command. Camp Barrett, VA: Author.

Wee, D. (2007). *Are your people better off when they leave than when they got there?* Retrieved March 21, 2010, from http://www.leader-values.com/Content/detail.asp?ContentDetailID=1294

Wiggins, G., & McTighe, J. (1998). *Understanding by design.* Alexandria, VA: Association for Supervision and Curriculum Development.

Wiles, J. (2009). *Leading curriculum development.* Thousand Oaks, CA: Corwin.

Young, M. D. (1998). *Importance of trust in increasing parental involvement and student achievement in Mexican American communities.* Paper presented at the annual meeting of the American Educational Research Association, April, 1998. San Diego, CA: ERIC Document Reproduction Service No. ED423587.

Index

CORWIN
A SAGE Company

The Corwin logo—a raven striding across an open book—represents the union of courage and learning. Corwin is committed to improving education for all learners by publishing books and other professional development resources for those serving the field of PreK–12 education. By providing practical, hands-on materials, Corwin continues to carry out the promise of its motto: **"Helping Educators Do Their Work Better."**